OTHERS IN MIND

Why are we so prone to guilt and embarrassment? Why do we care so much about how others see us, about our reputation? What are the origins of such afflictions? It is because we are members of a species that evolved the unique propensity to reflect upon themselves as the object of thoughts, an object of thoughts that is potentially evaluated by others. But, Philippe Rochat's argument goes, this propensity comes from a basic fear: the fear of rejection, of being socially "banned" and ostracized. *Others in Mind* is about self-consciousness, how it originates and how it shapes our lives. Self-consciousness is arguably the most important and revealing of all psychological problems.

Philippe Rochat is a professor in the Department of Psychology at Emory University in Atlanta. Born and raised in Geneva, Switzerland, he earned a Ph.D. at the University of Geneva, where he was trained in psychology by Jean Piaget and his close collaborators. The author of *The Infant's World* (2001), Rochat is currently researching the emergence of a moral sense during the preschool years in children all over the world growing up in highly contrasted cultural environments and socioeconomic circumstances.

Others in Mind

SOCIAL ORIGINS OF SELF-CONSCIOUSNESS

Philippe Rochat

Emory University

CAMBRIDGE
UNIVERSITY PRESS

CAMBRIDGE UNIVERSITY PRESS
Cambridge, New York, Melbourne, Madrid, Cape Town, Singapore,
São Paulo, Delhi, Dubai, Tokyo

Cambridge University Press
32 Avenue of the Americas, New York, NY 10013-2473, USA

www.cambridge.org
Information on this title: www.cambridge.org/9780521729659

© Philipe Rochat 2009

First published 2009
Reprinted 2010

Printed in the United States of America

A catalog record for this publication is available from the British Library.

Library of Congress Cataloging in Publication Data

Rochat, Philippe, 1950–
    Others in mind : social origins of self-consciousness / Philippe Rochat.
        p. cm.
    Includes bibliographical references.
    ISBN 978-0-521-50635-9 (hardback) – ISBN 978-0-521-72965-9 (pbk.)
    1. Self-consciousness (Sensitivity) 2. Self-knowledge, Theory of. 3. Self – Social aspects.
    I. Title.
    BF575.S4R63   2009
    155.2–dc22   2008019650

ISBN 978-0-521-50635-9 Hardback
ISBN 978-0-521-72965-9 Paperback

CONTENTS

v

FOREWORD

JERÔME BRUNER

This is an astonishing book, astonishing both in its range and in what it seeks to make clear. Its central concern is with the nature and origins of selfhood, a distinctively human phenomenon. Its rather contrarian view is that Selfhood emerges as a product of inevitable uncertainties about our acceptance by the larger group or, more broadly, as a product of our doubts about how Others see us. Self, in a word, is then a joint project, *Cogitamus, ergo sum*, rather than the simplex Cartesian *Cogito, ergo sum*. Selfhood is not just a product of inner processes but it expresses the outcome of real or imagined exchanges with Others.

This is a book of astonishing breadth, for Philippe Rochat explores not only different forms of self-awareness, but also the varied settings in which such self-awareness may be evoked. And in the process he leans upon evidence from his own well-known experimental studies of young children, evidence from linguistic theory itself, and evidence from comparative cultural studies of peoples around the world. For him, the evidence is overwhelmingly, "Without others, there is no self-consciousness."

Indeed, it is this other-related nature of self-awareness, with its accompanying fear of rejection, that creates the compelling dynamic of shame that is so much a feature of human awareness. It seems an odd way of putting it, but for Rochat selfhood is as much if not more a human distress maker as a distress dispeller (as it is in Freudian thinking). For him, shame and personal distress are, as it were, inherent in the way we perceive and evaluate our lives. Yet, while this may seem a dark view of the human condition, it is one that leads us to see the human effort to avoid shame and humiliation in a broader, less self-condemnatory way.

Indeed, though this book is strikingly modern, even postmodern, it reflects some ancient philosophical themes, two in particular. The first of these (in the author's words) is that "without others we are nothing."

vii

And the second is that what we think and feel is driven by a fear of being rejected by others. Ancient indeed, for both figure in Greek drama, as in Aeschylus's *Oresteia* trilogy. Yet persistently modern as well, as in post-Vichy France, with Sartre's classic "Hell is the Others." It is admirable how Philippe Rochat revisits these ancient concepts in their modern setting(s) and makes us aware again of their inevitability.

Rochat is most involved with the subjective consequences of our forever "figuring out" what the other fellow has concluded about us. And our conception of ourselves, our selfhood, derives from this figuring out. We do not want to be found too wanting, and if we feel that others find us so, we suffer by a self-imposed reduction in self-pride or self-assurance. In fact, we deal with the balancing act imposed by making up tales to reveal how we "truly" are, and why we need not feel so ashamed. Selfhood, indeed, is a compromise between self-blame and self-praise – the two usually balanced by a narrative that includes them both.

We are all enormously in Philippe Rochat's debt for his having reopened many of these issues – and I choose my words with care, for it is a reopening that we are witnessing. What is interesting to contemplate is where we go from here. Is it a sign of our time that we choose, in these times of trouble, to create Selfhood out of our modern sense of failure to live up to expectations? Where next?

PREFACE

In writing this book, I had in mind anybody interested and sensitive to the question of self-consciousness, how it originates and how it shapes our lives, arguably the most important and revealing of all psychological problems. Why are we so prone to guilt and embarrassment? Why do we care so much about how others see us, about our reputation? What are the origins of such afflictions?

My answer to these questions is that it is because we are members of a species that evolved the unique propensity to reflect upon themselves as object of thoughts, an object of thoughts that is potentially evaluated by others. I argue that this propensity comes from a basic fear: the fear of rejection, of being socially "banned" and ostracized.

From this simple premise, I propose to look at young children and their development, but also at many other intriguing human propensities, to see what they have to tell us about the social origins and nature of human self-consciousness.

I invite the reader to this exploration, an exploration that I value more than just another academic foray. It is an invitation for the exploration of what it means to be human, alive in this world, and how we construe our being in relation to others.

This book is meant to be more than an academic concoction for the few initiated specialists. Based on empirical observations, primarily developmental observations of children, it is a book of ideas guided by strong existential intuitions regarding the human condition. At the core of these intuitions, there is the idea that human psychic life is predominantly determined by what we imagine others perceive of us.

In Sartre's grim terms: "Hell is the Others." But paradoxically, without others we would simply not be, and there would not be any possible paradise. The "good life" is not a solitary, solipsistic existence. We exist and gauge the worth of our existence primarily through the eyes of others. More importantly, others also determine whether *I* am right to feel safe, in particular, safe from being rejected by them.

Feeling safe is part of the "good life," and it is inseparable from the feeling of being affiliated. My argument is that it all depends on the recognition and acknowledgment of self by others.

There are many people who have been instrumental to this project: Britt Berg for her diligent editing of a first rough draft of the manuscript; all my students for stimulating discussions before and during this long project, particularly Meghan Meyer and all my student collaborators at the Emory Infant Laboratory; not to forget my old friend Michel Heller for his constant intellectual jolts and inspiring discussions, and Dan Zahavi for his generous last minute philosophical scrutiny. I express my gratitude to Jerome Bruner, one of my heroes, for the privilege of his friendship, his support over the years, and his legendary enthusiasm and to George Downing for his careful reading and generous comments on a first version of the manuscript. But I am particularly indebted to my Carioca friends Claudia Passos-Ferreira and Pedro Salem of the free spirited, trustful, wild, and warm weekly "séminaire sauvage" in Paris, café de l'Ecole Militaire, during the sweet 2004–5 year. This is especially for you, "Princesse" Claudia and my friend Pedro, for your intelligence, but more importantly, for your warmth, encouragement, and enthusiasm. I learned a lot from you; thank you.

Finally, I express my gratitude to the John Simon Guggenheim Foundation for their 2006–7 fellowship that gave me the freedom to finish this book and start yet another one on the origins of the sense of ownership and entitlement. Thank you for the great privilege and opportunity.

Atlanta, March 2008

Introduction: Main Ideas

Because his own *nature* escapes him, he tries to capture it in the eyes of others.

Jean-Paul Sartre on Baudelaire[1]

Preoccupation with the self is a human propensity, becoming particularly exaggerated in recent human history. For many philosophers and historians, self-preoccupation is the sign of "modernity."[2] It is a syndrome associated with profound political transformations, the ratcheting effects of technological advances that transform the way we live and the way we relate to each other. This book is about this modern syndrome and how it manifests itself in human ontogeny.

As modern individuals, we promote and negotiate our own image via complex acts of self-presentation. We boast of and adorn ourselves. We excel in the promotion of desire, social envy, and seduction. We strive ultimately for our own social ascendance and inclusion by endless attempts at influencing what other people see of us, think of us, represent of us. It is an all-too-human propensity that cuts across people and cultures, hardly the special feature of shy, narcissistic, sociopathic, sexually deviant, or "needy" individuals.

As a species, we evolved a unique sophistication at self-promoting, self-deprecating, and self-spinning games. To be human, particularly in the

---

[1] Sartre, J. P. (1947). *Baudelaire*. Paris: Gallimard.

[2] See Taylor, C. (1989b). *Sources of the Self*. Cambridge, MA: Harvard University Press, and Taylor, C. (1989a). *The Malaise of Modernity*. Canadian Broadcasting Corporation. (1991); and in French, Paris: Les Editions du Cerf, 2005. Preoccupation with the self existed in antique and medieval tales that were produced under ancient aristocratic regimes dominated by loyalty and honor principles. But self-preoccupation appears to have blossomed, at least in Western history of ideas, from the seventeenth century on, from the Enlightenment and all the social and economic revolutions that followed.

modern era, is indeed to care about reputation. We are obsessed with the idea of what is public about us, obsessed with the representation other people might have of us, as persons, but also in relation to the group we identify with, whether family, gang, nation, or culture.

If to be human is to care about reputation, it is to have "others in mind," and the goal here is to explore the origins of this very human propensity. I view this propensity as a cardinal trait and a major determinant of the human psyche.

For some, the property of Man is its ability to laugh. Maybe. But at the origins, what causes laughter and humans' sense of humor are the *ridicule* and the *grotesque* that derive from Man's desperate, often clumsy attempts at asserting and promoting its own person. We do laugh with Molière or the Marx brothers at the pompous, the snob, the inflated, and even the overly deflated, unassuming individual. Humor derives primarily from a preoccupation with the self in relation to others. It derives from what we are as members of a uniquely self-conscious species.

Here, as a developmental psychologist, I ask, "Where does it all come from?" In particular, what are the origins of self-consciousness? What determines our propensity to do, feel, achieve, or think with *others in mind*? What makes us so inescapably inclined to take the perspective of others onto our own person? Why do we care so much about how and what people think of us? To address these questions, I generate ideas from a simple theoretical premise. It is simple, yet constitutive of human self-consciousness.

BASIC PREMISE

Self-consciousness is inseparable from the basic drive to affiliate and maintain proximity with others. From the outset, to be alive implies being with others. I start from the simple fact that without others, *we would not be*. As infants we would not have survived. As adults, we would not have any explicit sense of who we are; we would have no ability, nor any inclination to be self-conscious.

Linked to this simple premise is the irresistible drive to *be with others, to maintain social closeness, and to control social intimacy*. The necessary counterpart of this drive is the basic fear of social alienation, the rejection from others, and the avoidance of such rejection at all costs.

I view the experience of being ostracized, pushed away, bullied, looked down on, isolated, or separated from others as the worst of all possible psychological sufferings. The avoidance of social separation and rejection[3] determines most of what we are and what we do, from infancy on and across the great variety of individual circumstances. From the outset, the drive to affiliate and the avoidance of separation are constitutive invariants that cut across individuals and cultures.

The fear of social rejection is the mother of all fears, the driving force behind most higher-order human psychology, particularly the exacerbated human care about reputation and the control of public presentation of the self. I propose that the need to affiliate and its counterpart, the fear of social rejection, together form the bottom line of what underlies the experience of shame, embarrassment, contempt, empathy, hubris, or guilt. This underlies all the powerful and often devastating self-conscious emotions that are presumably unique to our species. By extension, it is also what underlies the explicit moral sense that can be expressed in benevolence, prosocial behaviors, as well as in revenge and systematic "costly" punishment, all viewed as hallmarks of human self-consciousness.

The definition of self-consciousness is relative to the theory, as for any complex concepts. Here, in its most generic sense, self-consciousness stands for *the representation we hold of ourselves through the eyes of others.* In what follows, I propose that this representation is in essence a social construction, as opposed to an individual elaboration. I try to show that it does not originate from within the individual in the absence of any encounters with others, but on the contrary originates in relation to others.

The main idea is that the origins of self-consciousness are inherently social, that there is no such thing as a "core" or an "individual self." My hope is to debunk the concept of the individual self that would presumably exist and emerge in itself as a conscious object or entity. I propose instead that what develops and is unique to human ontogeny is a sense of self that is *co-constructed in relation to others.*

In short, the premise of the book can be stated in two sentences: We fear the judgment of others, and whatever this judgment might be, good or bad, it determines the representation of who we are in our mind (i.e., our self-consciousness). Once again, the view proposed here is that self-consciousness is in essence a social rather than an individual phenomenon. It depends on

---

[3] Social rejection is viewed here as an active separation caused by others as in bullying or punishing. Social separation is more generic and captures both active but also passive alienation from others, as, for example, in the case of an infant missing her momentarily absent mother who is fetching something in the kitchen or the widower missing his dead wife.

others and does not exist in itself as an individual phenomenon. But how does it all come into place and what kind of psychology arises from such premise?

HISTORICAL QUESTIONS

The issue is not new. Self-consciousness is a classic philosophical conundrum in the Western tradition since the Greeks. Plato and the ancient Greeks began questioning systematically the relation of the mind to the body, extended by a long dualist tradition that culminated with Descartes's famous *Cogito*,[4] which continues to be debated in current philosophy of mind.

Ideas and debates around mind and body as separate entities have dominated Western philosophy. In recent years, however, the mind-body issue has been greatly tempered, even dismissed, by the recent advances in neurosciences that provide abundant evidence of an "embodied mind." The neurosciences provide literal images of a mind incarnated in the neural flesh of the brain. In a way, neuroimages give the hope of grounding and finally naturalizing the phenomenon of consciousness. Presumably, they provide the final blow to the persistent metaphysical idea of the mind as soul hosted in a physical body, an idea that implicitly or explicitly dominated the philosophy of mind since the Greeks.

However, these attempts at reducing the mind to biology do not elude criticisms. They are still considered by many as wishful thinking, a long way from giving the final blow to the dualist ideology of Descartes. These attempts are the expression of a persisting, relentless effort by neuroscientists to reduce higher-order processes and representations to simpler, more parsimonious, and ultimately more predictable causal accounts.

Inseparable to the mind-body problem is the perennial problematic of the self. This problematic rests on the following basic questions: What is *it* that we construe as the self and where might *it* be located? Furthermore, if it exists, where might *it* come from? There are obviously many other ways of stating the problematic of the self, asking, for example: What do we mean when we say "in my mind," "I think," or "I feel"? Who is the subject in such predicaments or ideas? Who is the agent? These questions are far from being resolved and probably will never be. They form an eternal conundrum, a very human conundrum.

---

[4] *Cogito, ergo sum,* "I think; therefore I am," an inference that is often identified as the beginning of modern philosophy of mind, so-called egology, or metaphysical theories about the individuated self.

The ontology and origins of the self form the most difficult of all philosophical conundrums. The reason rests primarily on the fact that "we," who think, feel, perceive, and raise the issue, form the issue itself. In other words, the problem we raise already entails its resolution!

When, for example, I ask, "Who am I?" or "Do I exist and if so, what exists?" I question the existence of something that in my mind already exists and that I refer to with the personal pronoun *I*. It is somehow difficult, if not impossible, to escape circularity. Even when asking "Who is I?" the question presupposes that there is a priori something like an "I." Why ask the question otherwise?

If we assume as Descartes did over three hundred years ago that thinking, by necessity and no matter what, presupposes the existence of a self, hence proves it (I think; therefore I am), then we are left with at least three basic questions regarding the issue of the self that are unanswered: *What is it? Where is it? Where does it come from?* Phrased differently these questions are What is a self? Where is it located? What determines it?

If we accept the existence of a self, the threefold question of its nature, locus, and origins is far from being resolved. It continues to animate fierce debates in the philosophy of mind. It is also a very engaging question for current cognitive and developmental scientists, as well as researchers in the booming field of cognitive neurosciences. But what are the continuing theoretical controversies around this threefold question? Let me try to stake the debate and situate my own ideas in relation to each of the three aspects of the question (nature, locus, and origins).

BASIC PHILOSOPHICAL CONTROVERSIES

The Scottish philosopher David Hume (1711–76), one of the fathers of the empiricist tradition in the philosophy of mind, proposes that if such a thing as a "self" exists, it exists as an illusion, not as a real entity. When introspecting in search of the self, Hume[5] claims that he finds nothing but fleeting feelings and perceptions, no object per se. He concludes that what we tend to consider as self are in fact just sensory and perceptual impressions, not a real or core thing. It might exist, but if it exists, it is not as real as a rock or a chair that can be thrown or sat upon; it is fleeting and impressionistic, a representational construction of the mind.

Varieties of Hume's basic idea are still very much alive today in the philosophical theorizing of the mind, especially by researchers who, well

---

[5] Hume, D. (1928). *A Treatise of Human Nature.* Oxford: Clarendon Press.

informed of the current progress in brain and cognitive neurosciences, deny any ground for the assertion that there is in reality such a thing as a self (see Metzinger, 2003, p. 1, who concludes that "no such things as selves exist in the world: Nobody ever *was* or *had* a self").[6]

To the Humean's skepticism, if not denial of the self, a radically opposite view is espoused by phenomenologists in the tradition of Husserl, Heidegger, Merleau-Ponty, or Sartre, to name a few.[7] Stated in a nutshell, phenomenologists anchor their investigation of the mind in the systematic description of a first-person perspective, the experience of the world through one's own body, which is the primary locus of this experience as it unfolds in real time. The self exists primarily as a preconceptual, implicit entity that arises from the embodied experience of being in the world.

Historically, the phenomenological approach is a deliberate departure that shies away from intellectualism or any kind of purely formal, "disembodied" conceptualization of the mind. In basing their investigation of the mind, in particular the mind-body problem, on a first-person perspective, hence on "subjectivity," the phenomenologists embrace a philosophy that gives a real status of the self, a status contested by Hume and his followers (see the recent book by the phenomenologist Dan Zahavi, 2006).[8]

What I will propose is that, contrary to the strict empiricist argument, the self is real and exists as an object, developing from being implicit and preconceptual to become a representation that is a *social sedimentation*. If there is "pure" subjectivity of first-person perspective, as proposed by phenomenologists, selfhood does eventually develop to become objectified and conceptualized from social interactions. It does not only exist in itself. In development, it is also socially *co-constructed* in interaction with others.

Explicit selfhood emerges as the product of social exchanges and reverberates back onto our primeval awareness of the body, the proto-awareness phenomenologists like Merleau-Ponty insist upon in the realm of perception.[9]

From being first an implicit sense of the body in the world, selfhood eventually becomes objectified, experienced as an invariant entity, something one can label with a personal identity. But this identity does not exist a priori.

[6] Metzinger, T. (2003). *Being No One*. Cambridge, MA: MIT Press

[7] See, for example, Sokolowski, R. (2000). *Introduction to Phenomenology*. Cambridge: Cambridge University Press.

[8] Zahavi, D. (2006). *Subjectivity and Selfhood – Investigating the First-Person Perspective*. Cambridge, MA: MIT Press.

[9] Merleau-Ponty, M. (1945). *Phénoménologie de la perception*. Paris: Editions Gallimard.

It is a by-product (i.e., sedimentation) of social interactions. Hence, in my view, selfhood is neither an illusion as proposed by Hume nor a core subjective reality that phenomenologists insist upon in reaction to and as an alternative to Cartesian rationalism. Selfhood is also socially co-constructed when looking both at child development and at the way we behave as adults across the great variety of human cultures.

INTERNAL VERSUS EXTERNAL LOCUS OF THE SELF

If there is such a thing as a self, where is it? Is it in my body? Can it be superimposed on the physical entity each of us forms, and can it include the material things we own beyond our physical envelope? Once it is acknowledged and ascribed to the individual, delimiting selfhood is another classic puzzler in the philosophy of mind, a continuing debate in today's cognitive sciences and cognitive neurosciences.

In philosophy as in the cognitive sciences, there is an ongoing tension between theories that put more or less weight on the individual and the "internal" origin of consciousness, whether conceptual (explicit) or nonconceptual (implicit). For example, the armchair meditations of Descartes introspecting on his relation to the world and deciphering the proof of his own existence is prototypical of what could be called an *internalist* perspective on consciousness in general, and the experience of selfhood in particular.

Descartes's metaphysical meditations unfold as an introspective process that takes place "within" his person. It presupposes an "interiority" defining the self. The proof of the existence of the self can take place independently of any physical transactions with the "outside" environment, in pure logical thoughts: "I think therefore I am."

Although philosophers in the more recent phenomenological tradition shy away from Cartesian intellectualism, they too put much weight on the private, internal experience of the individual encountering the world.

As already mentioned, contrary to the Cartesian focus on logical thinking and the analysis deriving from a self-reflecting mind, philosophers in the more recent phenomenological tradition describe subjective experience as a preintellectualized "direct" or unmediated encounter of the body with the world. Phenomenologists insist that from this encounter arises a preconceptualized awareness of qualities, that are foundational to mental experience, hence of any subsequent explicit awareness of the self.

In the phenomenological tradition fathered by Husserl and Heidegger, the awareness of what we might be is grounded primarily in a preconceptual, hence implicit private embodied experience that is in essence unalienable. Self-experience happens, in this tradition, from an inside-out vantage point rather than the reverse. The weight is clearly put on the direct experience of what "I" feel encountering the world out there, be it physical or social.

The basic assumption of phenomenology as a philosophical system is that the issue of mind and its relation to the body as well as the issue of selfhood and self-knowledge rests primarily on this preconceptual subjective and first-person experience of the world. The emphasis is on what happens *inside* the individual, not outside. Once again, the phenomenological account rests on the fine description of what is experienced by the individual from "within." It assumes as a given the interiority of experience (i.e., first-person perspective or subjective experience).

As a matter of fact, one could argue that emphasizing the subjective experience as phenomenologists do is an invitation to reinstate some dualism in different, maybe more subtle disguise. It can be seen as an invitation to separate subject and object, to separate the body as locus of experience and the world as encountered by the body that would exist in some kind of independence. Some, including me, are weary of such dualism in disguise and the strong assumption of a subjective experience located inside the individual rather than outside. As an alternative, it is possible to adopt a more "externalist" view of the locus of selfhood and consciousness, a view that I am more inclined to adopt in this book.

From the title, you can see already that my treatment of selfhood is *not* as something just located inside the individual. Rather, I defend the view that within months after birth, *in development*, it has also become increasingly located in the relation of the individual to others, in particular in their mutual evaluation and representation of each other. In general, the idea I will defend is that if there is such a thing as a self, it is not just interior to the individual but rather also at the intersection of the individual as he or she transacts with others. This idea about the nature of the conceptual self is externalist rather than internalist. In development, the weight is quickly shifted away from the individual to the relation of the individual to others.

In short, I will take the stance that within months of birth, the self is increasingly defined in relation to others, not on the basis of an interior subjective experience.

It is common for many contemporary theories in cognitive sciences and neurosciences to circumscribe the study of the mind to the individual and tend to reduce it to "internal" brain features. Language, for example, as well as many other features of conscious life are often seen, or at least alluded to, as "instincts" or "core abilities" that reside from birth within the individual (i.e., its brain) as an evolutionary endowment of the species (see, for example, Pinker, 1994, but see also Thompson, 2007, for a radically different view).[10,11] Such conscious features are tentatively described as innate or prescribed "modules" residing in the brain of the individual.

On the basis of striking accidental brain pathologies and with the advance of brain imaging techniques, neuroscientists are increasingly tempted to capture the nature of selfhood or what constitutes a person in the way the brain of the individual works and the particular ways it is arranged, for example, on the basis of instances of accidental brain damage and correlative personality changes.[12] The interpretative temptation is naturally to construe the locus of self-experience inside (i.e., in the individual brain), rather than emerging from encounters with others interacting from the outside.

The internalist versus externalist controversy is generalized in all cognitive sciences, and now it permeates emerging neurosciences. Some neuroscientists realize that there is something profoundly invalid in studying the brain of the individual to capture the biological underpinnings of consciousness. For example, there is now evidence of a renewed effort to develop techniques to image multiple individual brains simultaneously as they work and communicate with one another.[13]

---

[10] Pinker, S. (1994). *The Language Instinct.* New York: HarperCollins.

[11] Thompson, E. (2007). *Mind in Life: Biology, Phenomenology and the Sciences of Mind.* Cambridge, MA: Harvard University Press.

[12] The most notorious case is the marked change of character and temperament of Phineas Gage, who, in 1848, working on a railroad track, had a one-and-a-quater-inch-thick tamping iron pierce his head. This accident left him with most of the front left side of his brain destroyed. Despite the horrendous accident, the foreman survived and even went back to work a few months after the accident. The originally well-balanced and efficient Mr. Gage became after his accident irreverent, profane, and short-fused with his fellow workers. His employers eventually fired him, his friends lamenting that he was "no longer Gage." This tragic case is typically interpreted as evidence of the equation personality = individual brain configuration and functioning. To my knowledge, such a case is never interpreted as evidence that the brain of the individual participates in ways of relating to others, that the consequences of the brain damage in the case of Phineas Gage are relational rather than internal to the individual. There is little consideration of the idea that personality is social and relational, not a stable intrapsychological entity.

[13] A new, promising technology is being developed and now used to scan multiple brains as they interact. This will certainly change dramatically the field of cognitive, social, and affective neuroscience. It will force neuroscientists to reconsider how the mind works, which is not in isolation, always in concert with other minds. See Frith, C. D., & Frith, U. (1999). Interacting minds – a biological basis. *Science* 286: 1692–1695; also Montagu, P. R., et al. (2002). Hyperscanning: Simultaneous fMRI during linked social interactions. *Neuroimage* 16: 1159–1164, for information of the developing technology.

The brain is indeed adapted and shaped to live in a society of minds. If the brain of the individual can be anatomically described as a distinct entity, it can hardly be described as such at most levels of higher functioning, including self-reflection or self-conceptualization. Most of what the brain allows an individual to perform is done in conjunction with other brains, particularly performances such as thinking and talking, even thinking and talking about the self. This basic fact questions the validity of construing the locus of conscious phenomena in the brain of the individual since most of these phenomena depend on conjugate functioning with other brains.

In the realm of perception, the internalist versus externalist controversy is most evident in the contrast between what can be categorized as reconstructionist (atomistic) and ecological (holistic) theories. For some classic theorists of perception, what we perceive is essentially based on a mental reconstruction of bits and pieces of discrete sensations that are constantly processed by the brain via the various sensory systems. This perspective is eminently internalist as perceptual phenomena happen inside the head of the individual who infers and reconstructs what is out there in the world on the basis of discrete sensations that need articulation to acquire meaning.

In sharp contrast to this view, the externalist approach to perception claims that information or the basic ingredients of perceptual phenomena are contained in the environment, not in the head of the individual.

In his ecological approach to perception, in a radical departure from other existing theories on perception at the time, James J. Gibson[14] proposes that the environment is structured and that the perceptual systems, each the product of a long evolution, are preadapted to harvest directly information that specifies this external structure. Gibson claims the rather odd idea that visual *information is in the light* as it bounces on the objects and hits the eyes of the perceiver. Accordingly, this information is not in the head or the mental product of the individual perceiver but rather exists in the world *outside* the individual. In short, perceptual phenomena are not located within the individual but rather at the meeting of the individual, prepared by evolution, with the organized features of the environment, its resources.

Here, I will propose a view on selfhood that is in resonance with the contrainternalist view of Gibson in the realm of perception. In my view,

---

[14] Gibson, J. J. (1979). *The Ecological Approach to Visual Perception*. Boston: Houghton Mifflin.

the concept of self, qua self, as object of thought and representation emerges from the integration of first- and third-person perspectives. *It becomes objectified in social transactions.*

In the context of the internalist versus externalist debate on the locus of selfhood, I will try to show that in development it becomes increasingly external as it refers more and more to the evaluative eyes of others.

INDIVIDUAL VERSUS SOCIAL ORIGINS OF SELFHOOD

The question of the origins of selfhood and what might determine its development is another classic controversy. The question is: Does selfhood grow from within the individual, or, on the contrary, does it grow from without? Translated differently, does selfhood emerge from an experience that is primarily private, or, on the contrary, from an experience that is primarily public? Does it grow out of an inward process of self-reflection by the individual "à la Descartes," or from the relation of the individual to others in a process that is in essence social rather than individual?

The tendency to construe selfhood as situated within as opposed to without the individual appears to be relatively recent in Western history as Charles Taylor[15] demonstrates in his masterful work *Sources of the Self.* He writes: "Our modern notion of the self is related to, one might say constituted by, a certain sense (or family of senses) of inwardness. . . . We think of our thoughts, ideas, or feelings as being 'within' us . . . we think of our capacities or potentialities as 'inner,' awaiting the development which will manifest them or realize them in the public world." But, Taylor continues, "strong as this partitioning of the world appears to us, as solid as this localization may seem, and anchored in the very nature of the human agent, it is in large part a feature of our world, the world of modern, Western people" (p. 111). Taylor makes the point that inwardness is the privileged metaphor of the Western modern individual who finds his own existential bearing *within* rather than without himself. Taylor's point is echoed by the work of anthropologists and cultural psychologists who demonstrate reliable differences in self-conception across collectivist and more traditional Eastern societies, compared to individualist and more modern Western societies.[16]

---

[15] Taylor, C. (1989b), p. 16.
[16] Triandis, H. C. (1989). The self and social behavior in differing cultural contexts. *Psychological Review* 96(3): 506–520.

This modern Western tendency to anchor selfhood within the individual rather than without is also reflected in theories that have dominated the field of developmental psychology, in particular theories on the ontogenetic origins of the self. How do children develop a sense of themselves, an entity they embody, but also that they eventually objectify and refer to and ultimately are able to conceptualize in a narrative form, capable of statements such as "It is me in the mirror," and "When I grow up I want to become a doctor and heal poor children."

Developmental theories on the origins of the self can be grossly divided along the internalist/externalist dimension. Cognitive theories of child development in the tradition of Piaget reduce self-development essentially to the growth of internal cognitive structures or logical tools that are progressively constructed by the child in interaction with objects and people in the environment. Children construct these internal cognitive tools to create meanings, base their decisions on, and resolve problems encountered in the world. The self of the developing child is equated to these internal cognitive tools. Within this approach, internal logical tools define various levels of cognitive competencies in the child and become a primary object of study. The "internalist" flavor found in such theories is still very much alive and tends to dominate the field of infant and child development.[17]

In addition to focusing primarily on what is growing inside the child, internalist theories tend to attribute mechanisms of this growth to processes that originate within the child rather than without. Such processes include actions that originate in the child and that have the power of structuring and making sense of the environment, as, for example, in Piaget's approach. For other, more current neurobiology-based theories, development is identified in terms of cortical growth in the child, with a particular emphasis on the incremental involvement of orbitofrontal regions of the child's brain,[18] or even the maturation of core representational structures as "modules" coming online at certain moments in development.[19]

---

[17] For a review of these theories, see Rochat, P. (2001). *The Infant's World*. Cambridge, MA: Harvard University Press.

[18] See, for example, Diamond, A. (2002). On normal development of prefrontal cortex from birth to young adulthood: Cognitive functions, anatomy, and biochemistry, in Stuss, Donald T., & Knight, Robert T., eds., *Principles of Frontal Lobe Function*, 466–503. New York: Oxford University Press.

[19] See the presentation and discussion of such accounts, as well as the exposition of an alternative approach in Karmiloff-Smith, A. (1992). *Beyond Modularity: A Developmental Perspective on Cognitive Science*. Cambridge, MA: MIT Press.

In these internalist theories, the environment plays a nonspecific role. In Piaget's theory, for example, the environment plays more of a role of resistance to the structuring actions of the child. These actions are generated within the child and are considered by Piaget as the driving force of development.[20]

In contrast to these internalist views on self-development, other views emphasize a more externalist standpoint, not focusing simply on what changes *inside* the child but what changes in the *relationship* between the child and the environment, the social environment in particular. The origins of the self are brought outside the individual as he or she meets the world with other individuals, rather than alone.[21]

The social environment gains more weight in accounting for the origins of selfhood. The self is externalized in the relation to others. Note that the externalist views I am referring to should not be confounded with the behaviorism focusing strictly on describing the environment while refusing to consider the existence of anything representational or private such as a self. Here, the self as a representation (i.e., the concept of selfhood) is acknowledged as a real phenomenon that needs to be accounted for by putting more weight on the environment, by "externalizing" the problem rather than internalizing it as most developmental theories tend to do.

From an externalist perspective, the origins of selfhood are situated in the transaction of the individual with others. Following the ideas articulated by George Herbert Mead,[22] selfhood is at the intersection of the individual in relation to others. If there is a self, it is *social* in nature. It is at the intersection of multiple perspectives: the first-person perspective (the individual) and the third-person perspective (others). The concept of self originates in the meeting of these perspectives, not primarily in one or

---

[20] Piaget, J. (1936/1952). *The Origins of Intelligence in Children.* New York: International Universities Press. In this seminal book, Piaget has a section entitled "Assimilation, Primary Fact of Psychic Life" (in French, "assimilation, fait premier de la vie psychique"). Piaget states explicitly that cognitive structures are constructed primarily via the propensity to act and assimilate objects to existing action schemas, eventually modifying these schemas to accommodate resistance from the environment to this assimilation. In this view, the environment is nonspecific. Greater weight is put on what originates within the subject rather than without (i.e., the environment), despite Piaget's interactionist claim formalized in his model of equilibration to account for developmental changes.

[21] This point is central to Lev Vygotsky's revolutionary (at the time) Marxist account of child development that emphasizes the dialogical and cultural origins of human cognition; see Vygostky, L. (1978). *Mind in Society: The Development of Higher Psychological Processes.* Cambridge, MA: Harvard University Press.

[22] Mead, G. H. (1934). *Mind, Self, and Society.* Chicago: University of Chicago Press.

in the other. The social theory states that these views are inseparable in relation to self-concept. Without the individual there would be no self to be conceptualized. However, without *others* that surround and are external to the individual, there would be no reasons to conceptualize the self. Both are mutually defining of selfhood.

Following Mead, the developing concept of self originates in the integration of first- and third-person perspectives. He writes, for example: "The 'I' is the response of the organism to the attitudes of the others which one himself assumes. The attitudes of the others constitute the organized 'me,' and then one reacts toward that as an 'I' " (p. 175). This is a view that is close to the social construction theory of self-knowledge proposed in this book.

The general intuition is that the origins of selfhood are to be unveiled neither in the first- or nor in the third-person perspective but rather at their intersection. The rationale for such intuition is that internalist views do not account enough for the rich structure of the social environment that contributes to the specification of the self. It is necessary to conceive the self as neither inside the individual nor simply shaped by outside pressure as behaviorists would claim. Rather, we need to conceive the self – if we accept that there is such thing – as existing in-between, at their intersection.

The general idea guiding this book is that the sense and concept of self cannot be conceived independently of the sense and concept of others. They are both mutually defining as the two sides of a coin. The basic intuition is that when we think of ourselves, we always and inescapably have *others in mind*.

BASIC PREDICAMENT OF THE BOOK

Any intellectual enterprise entails some risks, particularly the risk of being ridiculed, accused of too simplistic conceptual reductions. These are mortal risks in certain intellectual circles, particularly in the world of academia that is mine. The fear of peer rejection is a curse to creativity and intellectual progress. As with any enemy, the best way to tame it is to understand and acknowledge it. Here, I try to consider how the fear of rejection plays in our lives from the outset and shapes what we know about ourselves.

The aim is to explore the unique and convoluted ways humans evolved as a species basically to avoid and control social rejection, a rejection that jeopardizes not only their basic physical survival, but also their psychological well-being. Human well-being is indeed inseparable from the sense of who we are in relation to others, the sense of our relative social affiliation. That is the very basic claim.

The book's predicament is that to be human is primarily to have the propensity to perceive and represent oneself through the eyes of others. If this propensity might exist in other closely related species, the claim that such propensity is *uniquely exacerbated* in humans is central. The goal is to explore the extent of our species-specific exacerbation in the propensity to experience ourselves as evaluated by others, what is commonly thought of as being *self-conscious*.

But why take as a starting point the generalized fear of peer rejection or rejection by evaluative others? Why not take instead the generalized drive to affiliate with others, trademark of any social animal that has to share resources to assure its survival?

The rationale is simple. Social affiliation and basic affiliation needs are what define by necessity any animals whose survival depends on group living and the sharing of resources. Togetherness or the drive to affiliate is a necessary propensity, the constitutive aspect of any social animals and the primal requisite of group living. I start with the premise that the tendency to *approach* others is what drives social animals at the core. It forms a primal attractor and from this core derives the basic fear of losing social proximity, a deep universal anxiety about getting separated from others. This fear is captured by the generalized anxiety attached to separation and even worse, at least in humans, the anxiety about being *actively* rejected by others.

If we share a basic affiliation or approach tendency with all social animals, the point is to investigate and eventually shed a new light on humans' unique expression of such a tendency and its counterpart, the anxiety about being separated from the group. In particular, the goal here is to shed a new light on humans' particular fear of separation and social rejection, both giving rise to exacerbated self-consciousness.

As a premise, the fear of rejection is considered as a derivative of a primal need to affiliate with others, a need that is built in the biology of any social creatures. The focus is on the origins and nature of the human expression of what *derives* from this built-in biological attractor (i.e., drive for togetherness or necessary need to affiliate). My emphasis here is on the generalized fear of social alienation and rejection, not the drive to affiliate that we can posit as a necessary and predetermined need shared by all social animals. Compared to its derivatives, the built-in need to affiliate is arguably less sensitive to species-specific and cross-cultural variations, hence less interesting from the developmental, psychological, and meta-psychological perspective adopted here.

Separation anxiety and the fear of active social rejection are by-products of the basic need to affiliate, a need that is constitutive of all social animals. However, in humans, these by-products have a different meaning. They are processed differently and translate into a radically different kind of psychology.

By nature, humans develop to become evaluative in relation to others, living essentially through the elusive eyes of others. Shame, guilt, and embarrassment are presumably unique human emotions, the experience of others as evaluative entities of the self.

If they are not unique to our species, I would argue, such emotions are at least exacerbated and raised to incomparable levels of representation and symbolism. Such a claim is hard to dismiss. It would be akin to dismissing the fact that humans have evolved language as a special ability to communicate using conventional and creative symbolic systems. Obviously, this is undeniable and the question is how such ability differs from any other ways social animals across species do communicate.

By analogy, this book is about the particular ways humans experience themselves through the eyes of others, and how this experience shapes their psychology in the most fundamental way.

1

Self-Conscious Species

There is only *one man* in a cell in the hole for it to really be "the hole."
Jack Henry Abbott about solitary confinement[1]

What makes us different from any other living things is primarily the self-reflective ability we evolved as a species to unmatched levels of complexity. Unlike all other animals, we grow to deal with, anticipate, and control others' view on the self. To be human is indeed to care about reputation.

It is constitutive of the human psyche to have *others in mind*. It is at the core of human mental struggles, struggles with the representational ghosts of evaluating others. Such ghosts are by definition products or "figments" of the imagination rather than tangible enemies that one can confront and grapple with easily. They are mental creations and more often than not obligatory obsessions. But let us be clear: this kind of ghost does exist! What is ghostly about our representation in evaluating others is only that they have an elusive nature, not that they are products of our very human imagination. Guilt, shame, pride, contempt, or hubris, all are tangible traces of these ghosts that exist universally across human cultures. They are the trademarks of what it means to be human, shadows of something that inhabits our minds, for better or for worse.

But where does the overwhelming concern about how we look and what impact we have on others come from? How do we become such self-absorbed creatures, overly concerned with what we project to the outside world and the impact we have on others?

---

[1] Abbott, J. H. (1981). *In the Belly of the Beast: Letters from Prison*. New York: Random House.

17

FATEFUL LOOP

As a species, we are caught in a unique and fateful reflective loop. We have the privilege as well as the curse of being able to reflect upon ourselves, as an object unto itself, but also through the eyes of others. We can monitor and control our own appearance, thoughts, emotions, using all kinds of means, from the application of cosmetics on our skin, to choosing clothes to wear, words to speak, ways of eating or ways of laying down words on paper. We spend a large amount of our time imagining past and future encounters with others, musing about our own public impact, arranging and rearranging our appearance in the confines of bathrooms in anticipation of future public appearances.

As no other species have, humans have evolved an ability for recursive thinking and self-contemplation, what cognitive scientists call in their jargon "metacognition" and the ability to generate "metarepresentations": the ability to think about thinking, feel about feeling, simulate, monitor, and ultimately control actions by playing them out mentally.[2] In comparison to other animal species, even close great ape relatives with whom we share most of our genetic makeup (close to 97 percent of our genes), humans evolved the cognitive ability to distance themselves mentally from the here and now of perceptual experience and to adopt different perspectives of the self *onto itself,* the self as an object of projection and of evaluation. That does not mean that other animals are not capable of approximating such mental feat.

Animal psychologists, pet owners, and professional animal trainers claim at least some approximation of such ability in nonhuman creatures of the mammalian and even the avian order. It is reasonable to claim some kind of metacognitive control of action in New Caledonian crows when, for example, they use and create tools with an obvious goal of solving a problem in mind, bending soft wires with exquisite precision and dexterity to hook food out of a narrow jar.[3] Closer to us, chimpanzees in their social expertise show signs of complex metacognitive "Machiavellian" intelligence, tricking dominant conspecifics to obtain food, alliance, or

---

[2] For further discussion from a comparative perspective regarding the notions of metacognition and metarepresentations, see Proust, J. (2006). Rationality and metacognition in non-human animals. In S. Hurley & M. Nudds, eds., *Rational Animals?* 247–274. New York: Oxford University Press.

[3] Weir, A. A. S., Chappell, J., & Kacelnik, A. (2002). Shaping of hooks in New Caledonian crow. *Science* 297: 981.

sexual favors.[4] It is not specifically human to display complex adaptation and functioning at levels that transcend the *here and now* of experience.

Most animals can act and strategize according to long-term goals, plans that are projected into the future, arguably requiring some recursive mental process. This said, it is safe to assert that humans have taken mental transcendence of the here and now of experience to levels that are unmatched in animal evolution.

Unmatched is human symbolic ability to produce signs or systems of signs that stand for things in the world. It is hard to argue against the general view that as a species, humans have evolved the unique ability to re-present (present again) things not only for themselves, but also for others: the ability to *produce* systems of signs standing for something else with the *intention* to communicate with others *about* things, be they objects, emotions, states of mind, desires, beliefs, or ideas.

What distinguishes human representational ability from the representational ability manifested in other animals, as sophisticated as it can be, most undeniably is the *intention* to communicate with others about anything, from the mundane to the most abstract and intangible – things as abstract and conceptual as the existence of black holes in faraway, never to be seen galaxies that are just mathematically inferred.

Human symbolic systems are uniquely creative and deliberate in fostering shared meanings about things, especially about the self. No other animals dwell on and cultivate pretense, deception, or simulation for the main purpose of moving, controlling, and eventually seducing the mind of others.

But the human gift for recursive thoughts and intentional, creative symbolic communicative systems comes at a cost. It is associated with a whole range of meta- and existential problems that no other species have to experience. It comes at an existential cost that profoundly shapes human behavior.

POISONED GIFT

"There is only one truly serious philosophical problem: it is suicide." This is how Albert Camus opens "Sisyphus' Myth,"[5] his philosophical essay on

---

[4] For extensive discussions on the topic, see Byrne, R. W., & Whiten, A., eds. (1988). *Machiavellian Intelligence: Social Expertise and the Evolution of Intellect in Monkeys, Apes, and Humans.* New York: Clarendon Press/Oxford University Press. See also the sequel on the same topic by the same editors (1977): *Machiavellian Intelligence. II: Extensions and Evaluations.* New York: Cambridge University Press.

[5] Camus, A. (1955). *The Myth of Sisyphus, and Other Essays.* New York: Vintage Books.

life and absurdity. To be or not to be? That is the human existential question, the expression of a unique capacity to contemplate and choose our own fate, the choice of whether to keep on living or abridge what is left of our life as we project it into the future, sometimes in despair but also sometimes as a last vengeful gesture to get attention from others via hurting and guilt, in order to have a last and long-lasting impact on others. In suicide, ironically, death seems often to be used as a desperate last call for *existence* in the mind of others.

Human ability to act and reflect upon one's own fate is a poisoned gift. It is poisoned because it is associated with profound existential angst. It condemns us to be a uniquely anguished species suffering a panoply of particular mental ills. The worse of all imaginable ills is the disintegration of a sense of self (e.g., hearing voices, losing sense of volition) experienced in psychotic disorders like schizophrenia, which affects on average 1 percent of the human population and is the major cause of internment in mental institutions.

With the aptitude to contemplate oneself as an object unto itself comes also the unavoidable conscious realization of impending death, the absolute certitude that sooner or later there will be definitive severance from others. How could one imagine oneself with no self? It is an impossible proposition that is the main source of human existential turmoil.

Why did humans evolve self-objectification and, by way of consequence, their potential for deep mental turmoil? It is the collateral cost of the ability for self-objectification, ability without which there would be no exploding technologies, arts, and religions; no production of objects for the sake of how they look (paintings), how they sound (music), how they taste (cooking); the fight for ideas (politics), the cultivation of play (sports), or the dwelling in the fancy of simulation and pretense as in novels. Self-objectification is associated with deep turmoil around not only the decision to live and not to live, but also *how* to live life. It is associated with the maintenance of a reputation, the negotiation of values with others, acts of sacrifice, seduction, and shrewd revenge.

Human cultures, as far back as they have been recorded or left traces, frame the turmoil and passion of the self-conscious individual into collective institutions, rites of passage, and rituals. Love and the attachment to others are sealed by marriages and birth celebrations. The tragedy of absolute separation is accompanied by funeral rituals that already existed in the culture of ancestral, now extinct human species other than *Homo sapiens sapiens*. Culture as a symbolic frame that provides shared meanings and values to individuals living together is deeply rooted in human evolution.

Archaeologists find artifacts that are more than forty thousand years old manufactured by *Homo neanderthalis*, including body adornments and systematic ways of burying their dead.[6] Such findings suggest that this extinct human species also followed prescribed collective rituals, relying on symbolic functioning to survive and coexist.

In all probability, like us, *Homo neanderthalis* was already endowed with the poisoned gift of self-consciousness, the ability to contemplate the self as object to itself, ultimately as object of public evaluation through the eyes of others. This gift exacerbates the basic fear of separation and is linked to a unique psychology.

MOTHER OF ALL FEARS

The fear of rejection determines how humans relate to each other. Some simple, universal observations of how we live together and sanction each other support the assertion that the fear of social rejection is the mother of all fears. Nothing is worse than the active rejection by peers, of being deliberately and systematically *ostracized* from the group. Universally, active rejection from the group appears to represent the deepest of human fears.

A case in point is capital punishment, which consists in the absolute severance from the group. Individuals who are threats to the group or have been causing irreversible damage are sanctioned with absolute rejection. In China today, thousands of criminals are executed each year and in the United States hundreds are living on death rows, their lethal punishment pending. The fear of active rejection as central power is no lightweight speculation. The power of deterrence of capital punishment is the argument of those who keep supporting it. We know that this argument is quite debatable on the basis of comparative statistics across cultures. However, even if the threat of death is not the panacea to deter odious crimes, if it is morally questionable, it remains universally the ultimate threat of social rejection for individuals, their absolute dismissal from the group.

Executions can still be a major public event; citizens in some countries are still crowding squares to see beheadings, hangings, and other gruesome public executions of capital punishment. In the United States, major TV networks and newspapers keep running stories on last meal menu details and the last gasps of the executed. The media understand the public fascination.

---

[6] Picq, P. (2003). *Au commencement était l'homme: De Toumaï à Cro-Magnon.* Paris: Odile Jacob.

When crimes are committed within an already punitive environment such as high-security prisons, the scale of punishment is also revealing. First, visitation by friends and relatives is typically withheld. But the worse threat to any infractions by a prisoner is solitary confinement, the isolation from the rest of the prison community. Within the punitive culture, solitary confinement is the toughest punishment prior to death. It is the simulation of death, a temporary death penalty, as delinquents are typically confined to a cell with the dimensions and sensory deprivation of a coffin. All written memoirs of prisoners subjected to such treatment recount the excruciating pain of solitary confinement. The lack of physical and mental contact with others pushes one to madness.

Jack Henry Abbott provides a vivid literary account of his long bouts with isolation within the prison system, where he eventually died. He writes:

> There is only *one man* in a cell in the hole for it to really be 'the hole.'. . .
> you sit in solitary confinement stewing in nothingness, not merely your
> own nothingness but the nothingness of society, others, the world. . .
> Time descends in your cell like the lid of a coffin in which you lie and
> watch it as it slowly closes over you. When you neither move nor think in
> your cell, you are awash in pure nothingness. . . . Solitary confinement in
> prison can alter the ontological makeup of a stone. . . . After a while the
> painful elements begin to throw out shoots and sprout like brittle weeds
> in the garden of memory – until finally, after so long, they choke to death
> everything else in the garden. You are left with wild wasteland of scrubby
> weeds and flinty stone and dusty soil. They call it *psyche-pain*.[7]

Religious people and mystics cultivate social isolation for spiritual elevation. But such isolation is deliberate, not imposed. It is not separation by active rejection from others. It is typically part of a deliberate quest for truth and closeness to supernatural forces. They leave others to meet God, not to be alone.

Teenagers are exaggerations of what we are deep down: anxious to be recognized, accepted, and distinguished by others. The fear of social

---

[7] Abbott, J. H. (1981), p. 43. These letters include the most vivid account of the devastating effects of solitary confinement as extreme punishment within the prison system. Abbott was once Norman Mailer's pen "protégé" and tragic political cause. Mailer sponsored his release from prison and Abbott became a literary success with his support and that of other respectable literary critics. Tragically, only six weeks after he was paroled and the very week his book was favorably reviewed by the prestigious literary section of the *New York Times*, Abbott fell back into crime, killing a young aspiring actor in a brawl over access to a public bathroom. He became the sad embarrassment of those who backed him by putting their liberal credo and political wisdom on the line. Unquestionably gifted but deeply troubled, Abbott hanged himself in his cell in 2002.

rejection finds its root in the basic instinct of attachment, in the basic need to affiliate. We share this need with all other social animals, only to a different extent.

BASIC NEED TO AFFILIATE

Attachment is an instinct or basic functional propensity that allows young-lings to survive by the care of others. But it is of marked importance in human infants, considering their prolonged immaturity and longer reli-ance on others to survive outside the maternal womb. Compared to any other animals, including close primate relatives, humans are born much too soon for self-reliance.

John Bowlby was the first child psychologist to emphasize such instinct, building a theory of personality development that is based on the drive to bond with others, a basic affiliation need or BAN, an acronym I use to remind us that this need is inseparable from a corollary fear of rejection.

Bowlby considered the attachment of infants to their mother as a spe-cial kind of biological need, a need expressed early in life, a need among other basic needs, particularly feeding. His theory was influenced by etho-logical research (the study of animals' behavior in their natural habitat) that blossomed in the 1950s and 1960s with the works of Tinbergen and Lorenz, but also the work of Harlow, who studied young rhesus monkeys in captivity.

Bowlby proposed that the strong bonding between infant and mother rested on a basic need, the need for attachment to one primary caring individual. Such a strong bond does not derive merely from positive reinforcements like food that alleviate physiological needs, as suggested by Freud. The need for attachment is more than a physiological need. It is affective and psychological.

Bowlby's view on attachment as instinct found support from a com-parative and evolutionary perspective in the work of Harlow. Harlow raised infant rhesus monkeys in isolation with various dummy mothers providing either food or tactile comfort to the infant monkey. Harlow showed that the infant preferred to spend more time clinging to the soft cloth dummy mother than to the dummy food provider. In the face of threat or danger, the monkeys clung to the soft mother, searching for protection and comfort. In the long run, they formed attachment and strong bonding with the dummy mother, not with the feeding doll.

René Spitz in the late 1950s provided further support to Bowlby's views in documenting with dramatic footage the psychological deterioration of young children living in a crowded orphanage who were fed but did not receive attention and care from the same individuals. Spitz shows that infants not able to bind with a primary caretaker shut down emotionally. They weaken physically, losing weight while engaging in stereotypic behaviors such as endless rocking in their cribs. These symptoms, which Spitz labeled as *hospitalism*, support Bowlby's general contention that infants need an early affective bond for healthy physical and psychological development. In the context of Harlow's studies, Figure 1 illustrates the chronic fear of a rhesus infant raised in isolation from its mother.

The abundant attachment literature posits the need to bind with others, but the corollary of attachment is the fear of separation, what Bowlby terms *separation anxiety*. The fear of social rejection runs deep into our

FIGURE 1. Devastation of social isolation. Separated from its mother at birth and raised in social isolation in one of the infamous "pit of despair" chambers used by Harry Harlow in the 1970s to establish an animal model of clinical depression, this rhesus monkey ends up spending his days sitting prostrated in a corner of the cage, displaying unmistakable panic fear. This behavior is predictable within days of isolation.

origins. It is the counterpart of attachment as a biological, instinctual, and innate montage. All human self-conscious behaviors are part of this montage and its counterpart: the fear of being socially deaffiliated.

Looking at the development of neonates, it appears that the fear of separation and rejection is a *consequence* of attachment rather than a cause. There is no evidence that babies are born inhabited with the fear of being separated, rejected, or abandoned by others. What is apparent is that they are born with highly organized action systems that allow them to maintain close physical contact with caretakers they depend upon for their survival. These highly organized systems include feeding via sucking and orienting toward sources associated with food and warmth. It all starts with an innate endowment of prefunctional action systems to which caretakers are in turn instinctively attuned in order to dispense the intensive care neonates need for their survival.

A dramatic developmental shift occurs at around six weeks of age with the emergence of socially elicited smiling, arguably the index of the psychological birth of the infant (Rochat, 2001). By then, what infants express is not the automatic or reflex smile triggered even in newborns in the satiation bliss that follows feeding. It is the smiling in face-to-face social exchanges, a smile that is part of a conversation with a social partner that becomes differentiated. Socially elicited smiling is a landmark behavior because it announces the beginning of social sharing and the co-construction of subjective experience with others (so-called primary intersubjectivity).

Prior to this developmental transition, infants are just applying what they are endowed with to interact adaptively toward apt adults who provide food and warmth. As research shows, that is not to say that perceptual learning and discrimination do not exist at birth and even prior, during the fetal period. But this learning has nothing to do with the sharing that starts to emerge by the second month. What is happening psychologically by two months, namely, the unmistakable emergence of shared experience or primary intersubjectivity via smiling and active social coregulation, forms the actual roots of self-objectification and the fear of active rejection by others.

The exacerbated need of humans to affiliate and bind to others probably evolved as an adaptation to their extraordinary prolonged immaturity and helplessness outside the womb. This adaptation is also associated with an exacerbated fear of separation, a fear eventually evolving to become the human fear of rejection, matrix of all human fears. Compared to that in other social species, this fear is exacerbated and taken to new levels by our ways of construing the self as object to itself, what I have presented as the poisoned gift we evolved as a species.

THE IRRECONCILABLE GAP

The very human experience of the self as object of contemplation and evaluation is a complex psychological matter. It is complex mainly because it entails dilemmas and conflicts between first- and third-person perspectives on the self. Such dilemmas and conflicts are at the core of self-consciousness as expressed in embarrassment, shame, guilt, masking, or acting out. It also correspond to the universal experience of an irreconcilable gap between the experience of the embodied self (first-person perspective) and what is actually publicly shared of the self (third-person perspective).

In our contemporary postindustrial cultures that express denial and avoidance of aging as a normal process to come to terms with, it is common to have older people displaying great insecurity, if not depression, in what they realize they project to the public eye. As you get old, there is typically less and less enjoyment in the contemplation of the self in mirrors, an experience that is increasingly depressing in the context of societies that pay little respect and admiration to aging, a process considered more like entropy and self-deterioration than accumulated experience and wisdom. In this context, seeing oneself in mirrors or photographs displaying worn-out and rust-spotted bodies becomes the source of great existential torment.[8]

Older people, do not enjoy the sight of how they actually appear physically to others. For many, mirrors are to be avoided at all costs. But this kind of aversion and torment is not the exclusive psychological mark of old people.

Who is not tempted first to pay attention to the self when looking at group pictures? I remember vividly while riding a subway watching a group of young women very excited and playful while sharing a package of fresh pictures taken at a recent party. They created mayhem on the train, chasing each other to grab what some were editing from the pile: unflattering pictures of themselves, ashamed of how they looked. The behavior of these women was playful, for sure, but the force and tension behind it were remarkably powerful. This force and tension are expressions of the triadic and evaluative nature of selfhood.

---

[8] It is interesting to note that active correction of physical appearance using plastic surgery, even minor surgery like removing aging spots and molds on the face, does not seem to be prevalent in Eastern cultures, even in very advanced industrial, albeit collectivist cultures like Japan. My personal observations in Japan indicate that such physical marks of aging seem to be worn as trophies rather than afflictions, viewed as marks of respect and deference rather than shame and existential torment that can be easily removed by means of a simple surgical procedure. Aging in the East tends to be a source of social promotion and pride; the reverse tends to be true in the West.

There seems to be a universal dichotomy and permanent, ongoing attempts at reconciling two perspectives on the self: a private, embodied first-person perspective and a public, third-person (or second-person in the case of intimate others) perspective. They express a conflict that gives particular dynamic and shapes to outward behavior, be it mirror avoidance or proactive and playful self-editing in the case of the women on the train. It is a conflict in the sense that it reads as a discrepancy or gap between two views on the self. There is a basic *dissonance* between the private (embodied) and the public (social) view on the self, between first- and third-person perspectives.

This dissonance is universal and pervasive. It forms an *irreconcilable gap* that we try endlessly to fill and work out across the lifespan. With old age, in particular deteriorating physical and mental abilities, the gap between the two perspectives on the self becomes increasingly difficult to reconcile.

What I hold in my mind as "me" is always a combination of both perspectives, never the sole representational product of one or the other. In a sense, what we end up representing about ourselves is the result of an elusive and always changing convergence between these two views, the view from within – the embodied, private view on the self – and the view from without – the allocentric view on the self through the evaluative eyes of others. The way we represent what we are is not to be found in one or the other perspective, but at their junction, like the latitude and longitude lines crossing on a navigational map that tells sailors the objective position of their vessel on the ocean.

Likewise, self-knowledge or the representational system that constitutes the person is the product of a crossover between private and public viewpoints. The major problem attached to self-knowledge, however, is that these viewpoints never really overlap. The values each of these perspectives projects onto the self are always dissonant and in need of negotiation as we try desperately to reconcile them. The objectified sense of who we are tends to be always in a zone of uncertainty, in constant need of confirmation and approval.

I argue next that in such a context of uncertainty and disequilibrium, the values carried by the first-person, private or embodied perspective on the self are typically *inflated*. On the contrary, those of the third-person or public perspective on the self are typically *deflated*. In general, more often than not, we tend to overvalue the representations of ourselves compared to the representations we think others hold of us. Obviously, individual exceptions exist, as, for example, in cases of depression where the main symptom is a chronic deflation of self-worth. In general, however, I submit that we tend to be overinfatuated with ourselves, a tendency that is particularly reinforced in contemporary postindustrial cultures.

PERVASIVE NARCISSISM

The irreconcilable gap and the dissonance between first- and third-person perspectives on the self are unsettling and promote actions for their reduction. Attempts at reducing such dissonance correlate with the pervasiveness of self-preoccupation and self-contemplation, particularly prevalent in postindustrial cultures.

Marketing in Eastern and Western industrial cultures, whether rooted in collectivist or individualistic traditions, taps with remarkable success into the pervasive narcissism of potential consumers, serving what amounts to an insatiable appetite to promote their own public image. The list of gadgets is long and always expanding, from cell phones turning into cameras that allow audio as well as visual expression of the self, to an armada of gadgets affording easy to edit images of the self, cameras with pivoting viewfinders providing direct feedback while filming oneself, as well as the raging success of personal Web pages revolving primarily around the management of self-promotion and self-recognition by others in terms of "hit" statistics.[9]

In the United States, it is mesmerizing to see baseball fans spending much of their spectator time, aside from looking at the game, checking the giant screen to see whether they recognize themselves as multiple cameras pan the crowd and zoom more or less randomly at individuals during games. The public display of the self on the large screen seems for many as important and exciting as the game itself. Increasingly, following Andy Warhol's famous predicament, life seems fulfilled in an instant of fame. There is great joy in self-objectification and public recognition of the self, rooted in our basic need to affiliate with others and control our social affiliation by branding ourselves and cultivating our public image. This is particularly obvious in industrialized cultures through just looking at the

---

[9] More than ever, individuals growing up in rich, high-tech societies dream of stardom and limelight, wealth and glamour, that would propel them out of anonymity, making them visible to the largest number. Self-promotion and publicity continue to be today's motto, more than thirty years after Andy Warhol's famous claim that people would just do anything for fifteen minutes of fame. Only a few decades ago, it was the luxury of rich aristocrats to enjoy having their own portraits painted or busts sculpted. It is now available to us, at least in rich countries, via the recent exploding abundance of new media gadgets. The joy and appeal of being seen, and of sharing the public appearance of oneself with others, are part of today's global joy in life. The industry taps into the propensity across cultures to *control what others perceive of the self*. From cosmetics, body alteration, fitness, fashion, to graphic software for personal Web pages, it is a market that proves to have no limits.

evolution of technologies and gadgets available on the market.[10] But this trait echoes deeper in the human mind. It appears to be universal.

FASCINATION AND TERROR OF SELF-RECOGNITION

The image in Figure 2 shows Melanesian children of the island Tanna in Vanuatu (in the South Pacific) contemplating and being very much enticed by their appearance on the pivoted viewer of the video camera filming them live.

I took this picture of my traveling companion while visiting a remote "Kustom" village, a very traditional village with no electricity, nor modern amenities and with a life that has basically not changed since the first settlers arrived more than a thousand years ago in this small, isolated South Pacific island. Aside from the infrequent visits of tourists like us, the life of these children is still very much regulated by stable collective activities and rituals that all seem to promote social fusion of the individual in the group rather than self-promotion. In such small traditional societies, sticking out as an individual from the group is not valued. Yet, the fascination and inclination to contemplate the self seem universal, as demonstrated in this picture. Note that these children never actually asked me to use the camera to film objects or life in their village. There is a universal fascination with the self as an object of contemplation. The nature of this fascination, however, is not only a source of joy as seemingly expressed by the baseball fans in the stadium or the Melanesian children of the picture. It is also a source of great tension, a tension associated with the dissonance between first- and third-person perspectives on the self.

[10] Rich contemporary cultures promote individual development, the individual expression and management of self-presentation. They foster self-idealization. It has been noted for some time that individuals of rich countries seem less and less driven by political group ideals that would promote the collective good. The drive to adhere to collective movements, hence to transcend one's own individual existence via group ideals, is significantly depleted compared to that in recent modern eras. As aptly stated by Lipovestky and other essayists more than twenty years ago, contemporary postindustrial societies are enlarging the trend toward individualism, fostering narcissism in their members. The preoccupation with the self is turning into hypercultivation of the body and its presentation as seen in the exponential craving for tattooing, piercing, or bodybuilding. Tattooing in contemporary modern societies is, among many other meanings, a radical self-branding activity that is among one of the fastest growing small industries in the United States. Contemporary postmodern societies are deeply rooted in individualistic ideologies: "Trust and faith in the future are dissolving, nobody believes anymore in the hopes and radiant days-after of revolution and progress. From now on we want to live immediately, here and now, stay young and not laboring at building a novel Man." Lipovetsky, G. (1983). *The Era of Emptiness.* Paris: Gallimard.

FIGURE 2. Universal fascination with the self. A group of boisterous children from a radically non-Western "Kustom" village on the island of Tanna in Vanuatu (Melanesia) show great delight and act out while contemplating themselves "live" on the pivoted viewer of a video camera.

Over thirty years ago, the visual anthropologist Edmund Carpenter[11] and colleagues visited native Biami tribes living in dense, remote forests of the highland region of Papua New Guinea. At the time, Biamis had no access to mirrors. In addition, because of the murky water of their environment, they could not have experienced any clear reflection of how they looked, aside from directly perceiving visible parts of their own body. The only possible sense of their own physical facial appearance was presumably through the testimony of others, or maybe via the silhouette of their own projected shadow. For them, there were no direct, clear views of their own body as a whole as seen in mirrors, photographs, or any kind of large or small screens.

Introducing video cameras, mirrors, and Polaroid photographs, Carpenter recorded systematically the reactions of adult Biamis when confronted for the first time with a clear view of themselves, in other words when confronted for the first time with the public display of their own physical appearance, what is seen from a third-person perspective.

[11] Carpenter, E. (1975). The tribal terror of self-awareness. In P. Hikins, ed., *Principles of Visual Anthropology*, pp. 56–78. The Hague: Mouton.

Carpenter reports that the Biami adults confronted for the first time with their specular image were terrorized, manifesting a reaction of *great fear*. While transfixed for long bouts of contemplation staring at themselves in the mirror, pictures, or video recordings, they expressed deep anguish and showed all the bodily signs associated with stress and terror. Here is the phenomenon in Carpenter's own words, what he aptly labels *the tribal terror of self-recognition*:

> After a first frightening reaction, they became paralyzed, covering their mouths and hiding their heads – they stood transfixed looking at their own images, only their stomach muscles betraying great tension. Carpenter, 1975, pp. 452–453

The Biamis' expression of terror seeing themselves for the first time in a mirror is much more than anecdotal. It is the ultimate manifestation of their humanity. Carpenter's observations raise a fundamental question from which we can infer an important phenomenon attached to human self-consciousness. Why do the Biamis tend to express terror rather than delight at the clear view of themselves? Why such negative affects?

This response indicates, in the context of the irreconcilable gap between first- and third-person perspectives, a fundamental of human experience in the tendency for *self-idealization* from the first-person perspective. The Biamis would express disappointment and dissonance in the realization of what they actually display to the public eye. But why is it the case? How could such a tendency help us to survive socially? Self-inflation from a first-person perspective is probably the source of important psychological motivation, at the root of social boldness, initiatives, and the inherent self-esteem that help individuals to survive among others. But, paradoxically we have seen that it is also a major source of conflicts and dissonance. This dissonance shapes human behaviors across cultures and is the trademark of a psychology that revolves around reputation. The negotiation of self-image with others is indeed what drives most of our psychology and shapes its dynamic.

THE HUMANITY QUESTION

For centuries philosophers pondered the question of human nature. What does it mean to be human? What makes humans human, and what sets them apart in the animal world? Since the Darwinian revolution and all the evolutionary theories that flourished from the beginning of the nineteenth century, the "humanity" question is irremediably grounded in the continuity of natural history.

From a synchronic perspective, the humanity question began to be considered from a *diachronic* perspective that called for continuity and change. Yet, the question remained a question of contrast (what sets humans apart), a search for some discontinuity, whether quantitative or qualitative. This is a paradox that is still at the core of current theoretical debates in the realm of evolutionary anthropology and allied sciences, including more naturalistic approaches to the philosophy of mind.

There are two broad theoretical camps in today's debate around the humanity question. On one hand, there are theories biased toward an emphasis on continuity. In this perspective, human versus nonhuman differences tend to be minimized. Alternatively, there are theories that tend to emphasize differences and discontinuities between modern humans and their ancestors. The latter theories tend to search more for contrasts and to account for both qualitative and quantitative differences in evolution.

Theories that emphasize continuity ideas (we are very much like our ancestors) resent any attempt at setting humans apart, in particular above any other animal species in evolution. They show, for good reason, contempt for the devaluation of other animals, with humans presented as the apex of evolution, sitting atop the evolutionary "ladder." They fight this *Homo sapiens*–centered view as being both theoretically and politically incorrect, proposing instead that all animal species need to be considered and evaluated in reference to their own particular ecological niche.

Yet, in many respects, it is difficult to resist being politically incorrect. Humans are different from any other species in ways that are striking. Signs of their domination over the planet are conspicuous, for better but mostly for worse. They take over the environment by both controlling and destroying it. The view from a flying plane is good testimony of human invasiveness, if not domination: sea of lights, roads, buildings, bridges, rows of houses, irrigation channels, vast agricultural and fenced animal breeding grounds, ships on every ocean, satellites in the cosmos. All of these are traces of unmatched human psychology and culture.

Traces of humans are indeed conspicuous, particularly since the industrial revolution only a mere 150 years ago, which represents a minuscule blink of time in the scale of biological evolution. It is a minuscule blink in evolutionary time with consequences of gigantic proportion. No other species has had such broad, mostly negative impact on the environment.

Just looking at recent human impact on the environment, it is reasonable to ask what kind of psychology underlies it, in particular what mechanisms might have driven the emergence of such peculiar psychology? Many competing theories exist in fields as diverse as molecular genetics, psycholinguistics, comparative anatomy, psychology, and cognitive neuroscience.

All theories provide hypothetical factors that might have triggered the evolution of modern humans (*Homo sapiens sapiens*) leading to their psychology and unique cultural characteristics. These hypothetical factors range from significant brain growth to the redistribution of brain functions, new ways of physically moving about the environment, the emergence of a particular adaptation for imitation and cultural learning, or the linguistic ability to communicate via complex systems of arbitrary signs.

Closer to the theme of this book, some theories even propose that the ability to recognize oneself in a mirror might be the "acid test" of the particular psychology setting humans and a few of their close relatives apart from all other living species (e.g., chimpanzees and orangutans,[12] and now also dolphins[13] and elephants[14]).

Evidently, it is vain to look for one definite "causal" evolutionary account of the humanity question. Evolutionary accounts are by definition a posteriori speculations. To endorse one or the other theory remains an act of faith. None can elude the necessary precedence of any cause in relation to its effect to be called a causal theory. Was modern humans' brain growth or presumably unique interhemispheric brain specialization *triggered* by new communicative abilities (i.e., language)? Was the evolution of modern humans' ways of communicating and relating to each other *triggered* by new ways of moving upright or in bipedal posture? Or is it the reverse? No one will ever know for sure.

Evolutionary accounts of the humanity question rarely escape circularity. They typically get stuck in what is the cause of what, the chicken and egg question. Such accounts, however, are revealing. They remind us of some important dimensions that constitute humanity, whether it is brain structure, brain functioning, social-cognitive abilities, language, or new

---

[12] Gallup, G. G. (1982). Self-awareness and the emergence of mind in primates. *American Journal of Primatology* 2: 237–248.

[13] Reiss, D., & Marino, L. (1998). Mirror self-recognition in the bottlenose dolphin: A case of cognitive convergence. *Proceedings of the National Academy of Sciences of the United States of America* 98(10): 5937–5942.

[14]).Plotnik, J., & de Waal, F. B. M. (2006). Self-recognition in an Asian elephant. *Proceedings of the National Academy of Sciences of the United States of America* 103(45): 17053–17057.

symbolic ways of understanding each other as well as construing and controlling physical aspects of the world around us. Such theories try to capture the origins of what it means to be human, of the unique human niche that is filled with symbols, rituals, collective representations, traditions, and artifacts: a niche that is associated with unique experiences and unique ways of being and acting in relation to others.

If the evolutionary origins of unique human ways can be traced down to our ancestors, whether monkeys or great apes, that does not elude the question of what constitute human ways of experiencing the world. Continuity in the evolution of species does not indeed elude possibilities of great discontinuity in ways of experiencing the world. Accounting for species-specific propensities to act and experience remains an important task for researchers interested in the humanity question, particularly for anthropologists, but also for developmental psychologists like me.

In this book, I propose a theory that considers humans' unique ways as the particular compulsion of having *others in mind*, the desperate and convoluted human attempt at reconciling first- and third-person perspectives on the self. With broad strokes, my goal so far has been to set the stage for such a theory. In the next chapter, I outline with more precision the basic elements of such a theory, which can be labeled as a social construction theory of self-knowledge.

2

Six Propositions

So far, I have posited basic human traits as behavioral propensities that are constitutive of self-consciousness. These propensities include self-idealization, a basic affiliation need, the fear of rejection, compulsive self-reflectivity, and the universal struggle to reconcile first- and third-person perspectives on the self. All of these human propensities point to the socially "co-constructed" nature of self-knowledge.

I try now to articulate further these propensities in terms of six propositions. These propositions form the theoretical framework that will guide the rest of the book. Together, they account for the co-constructed nature of self-knowledge and ultimately for the social origins of human self-consciousness.

I return first to the general intuition that drives this theoretical framework. I then present and comment on each of the six propositions in turn. I finish the chapter with a succinct narrative summarizing this articulation of ideas from a developmental point of view.

"COGITAMUS, ERGO SUM" – WE THINK, THEREFORE I AM

The origins of self-knowledge are social because without others there would be no such things as a "self," hence no object for self-reflection. This is the basic, commonsense intuition driving my ideas. Self-knowledge has a social background. A self exists in relation to no-self entities, namely, people who coexist in a shared world. Like any forms in the realm of perception, it can only exist in relation to a ground. For self-knowledge, this ground is made of people. We depend on people to come to life and to survive. Other people are the foundation of self-knowledge and of self-consciousness. This statement is basic and essential, too often taken for granted, overlooked by those trying to understand human self-conscious experience.

Without others, we would be nothing, or at least not self-conscious, as we tend to be. It is hard to imagine what kind of sense of self one would have by living alone and interacting only with physical, nonsocial objects from birth on.

As a thought experiment, we can imagine using a device that would automatically feed and dispense basic care to babies who could grow strong and physically healthy without any social contacts. What would be the fate of such infants? They might grow to become active, adapted, and possibly autonomous entities in a world of objects. They would discover that objects afford particular things, that they are source of pleasures such as food, and sometime of displeasures such as a sharp, prickly, or poisonous things. But what else would develop in these laboratory children aside from an implicit, nonreflective sense of self allowing them to survive as active entities in a physical world? What about their emotional and symbolic development? What about self-consciousness?

There are unfortunate approximations of such absurd developmental circumstances in real life. I mentioned already the devastating effects and behavioral disorganization observed in infants growing up in crowded orphanages where they typically lacked even minimal interpersonal care (what René Spitz labeled the *hospitalism* syndrome). Many cases are reported of locked up and isolated children who never totally recover from the psychological ills of the social deprivation they endured sometimes for years. Plainly, these sad case stories demonstrate how devastating social deprivation can be. They show that children are in need of social exchanges, not only to survive physically, but also to develop their intellectual and affective potentials, to develop the intersubjective sense of who they are as persons. Once again, this point is almost embarrassingly trivial, yet it does not seem to have sunk very deep into the minds of many theorists of the self.

In the Cartesian tradition that has dominated Western philosophy, including the more recent history of cognitive sciences, there is the general assumption that we, as individuals, have a privileged access to what we are from "within." In other words, there is a particular emphasis on what philosophers call the authority of first-person perspective.

The idea inherited from Descartes is that although others have access and can construe something about us from "outside," from their own allocentric perspective, it does not equate with what one perceives from within via the direct experience of the own body or via the indirect process of introspection. Descartes's famous conclusion "I think, therefore I am" is existential and constitutive of the self. It is the internal cogitation of individuals that gives them access to the sense of their own objective existence, in other words, an access to an objectified self. But what if a more accurate claim would be instead, or at least in addition, "*We* think, therefore I am"?

SOCIAL CONSTRUCTIONIST APPROACH

In the history of mind study, the views of George Herbert Mead,[1] but also of Lev Vygotsky[2] and Erwin Goffman,[3] are radical sidesteps, marching away from the dominant Cartesian tradition. They offer views that are radically externalist as opposed to internalist in relation to self-knowledge. They define what can be described as a social-constructionist approach to self-knowledge, ultimately self-consciousness.

As the major proponent of such an approach Mead (1934) writes:

> The self, as that which can be an object to itself, is essentially a social structure, and it arises in social experience. After a self has arisen, it in a certain sense provides for itself its social experiences, and so we can conceive of an absolutely solitary self. But it is impossible to conceive of a self arising outside of social experience.

Accordingly, the self as an object to itself is *co-constructed* in interaction with others (hence the suggested *We* think, therefore I am). For Mead, there are a social precedence and a social "communicative" format to self-knowledge.

Once the self is constituted or co-constructed via social exchanges, it can eventually feed into itself as an object of introspection and as part of internal dialogs that are modeled on a social communicative format.[4] This internal dialog (the "I think" of Descartes) is modeled after an original communicative experience with others, an experience that is eventually internalized over developmental time.

---

[1] Mead, G. H. (1934). *Mind, Self, and Society.* Chicago: University of Chicago Press.
[2] Vygotsky, L. (1978). *Mind in Society: The Development of Higher Psychological Processes.* Cambridge: Harvard University Press.
[3] Goffman, E. (1959). *The Presentation of Self in Everyday Life.* New York: Doubleday
[4] See the views of Wertsh, J. (1991). *Voices of the Mind: A Sociocultural Approach to Mediated Action.* Cambridge, MA: Harvard University Press. Wertsh's views are inspired by the theories of the linguist and literary critic Bakhtin on the "dialogical" nature of the self. See also Rochat, P. (2001b). The dialogical nature of cognition. *Monograph of the Society for Research in Child Development*, Vol. 66, 2(265): 133–144.

This interpretation is closely related to the views of Vygotsky and his followers, who proposed that private thinking is the product of an internalizing process of culturally available artifacts that exist first on the outside (i.e., language considered as a cultural tool that exists externally to the developing individual who is acquiring it). Thus Descartes's dialog with himself (his meditations) and from which he infers his own existence would be in Mead's view modeled after the social dialog format attached to the basic and primary act of communicating with others.

Thinking, according to Mead, in particular thinking about the self as one can do in solitary confinement, does not emerge in a social vacuum. Internal thought processes find their roots in social experiences and are shaped by social exchanges.

Yet, in his statement, Mead does not deny the possibility of experiencing a private self, what he calls "an absolutely solitary self," that presumably could have privileged access to an objectified self. Thus, the authority of the first person is not incompatible with Mead's social view on self-knowledge. However, the claim is that such authority is socially constructed. It is formatted by the primacy of communicative exchanges with others. Therefore, for Mead, self-knowledge, including the authority of first-person perspective, does not arise from within. It is external at the origin.

The combination of Mead's idea on the social origins of self-knowledge *and* the authority of first-person perspective is at the core of the social construction theory of self-knowledge I propose here. What this theory adds to former views is the idea of *ongoing representational negotiation* between first- and third-person perspectives on the self. This view rests on a few axioms or six basic theoretical propositions I present next.

THE PROPOSITIONS

The following are simple and basic theoretical axioms arising from the general intuition and rationale I have outlined so far. These propositions posit processes and tendencies that would account for the origins and nature of self-knowledge. Taken together (not in isolation), they specify in psychological terms what – I propose – are the social origins of human self-knowledge, ultimately the origins of human self-consciousness.

Aside from trying to capture the psychological dynamic underlying self-consciousness, these propositions are also intended to clarify concepts such as "self-knowledge" or "self-objectification." This semantic effort will continue in the next chapter, which reviews self-reflective mind states as levels of self-consciousness.

Proposition 1. *Self-knowledge is a system of representations arising when oneself becomes object to itself via the process of self-objectification.*

Self-knowledge is inseparable from self-objectification. It is more than an implicit sense of being alive in a body immersed and interacting in a physical and social environment. Self-knowledge is a complex system of re-presentations that entails evaluation and comparison.

Self-knowledge is, by definition, conceptual and evaluative. It entails much more than the information given by the perception and action of the body acting in the environment. In other words, it entails more than the feeling of being in the world, the implicit sense of being situated, differentiated, and agent. It is more than the implicit sense of aliveness in a body among other bodies.

Self-knowledge is thus the explicit sense of being an object of reflection for oneself, as well as for others. It arises from the decoupling (symbolic) process of self-objectification by which one *stands* for something (see the following discussion).

Proposition 2. *Self-objectification and resulting self-knowledge are a social process.*

In development, self-objectification and deriving self-knowledge arise from social constraints, not from *within* the individual in a social vacuum. They are thus external in their origins. The objectification of the self is an emergent property, the by-product of the way we communicate with each other. Reciprocal social exchanges determine self-objectification. Without reciprocal transactions with others, there would be no self-objectification, hence no self-knowledge as defined earlier. Self-objectification is rooted and formatted in reciprocal exchanges with others. One becomes object to him- or herself by engaging in reciprocal exchanges with others. In short, others form a social mirror that is the necessary condition for self-objectification to emerge and to develop.

Proposition 3. *The origins of self-knowledge are triadic and intersubjective, not private.*

As proposed by Mead (1934; see earlier quote), meanings in general (including objectified meanings of the self) are in essence *triadic*: they arise from the confluence of viewpoints in communication about things, including the self. Thus the nature of conceptual, explicit knowledge that includes knowledge about the self is dialogical. It is always the result of some sort of triangulation. Even when such knowledge develops internally, internal cogitation is rooted in the social format of triadic communication with others; it is external and dialogical in nature, not internal per se. Thus, because of the dialogical origins of self-objectification, the conceptual knowledge arising from such a process is to be located neither within the individual nor in the mind of others. Rather, it is to be located *in-between*, in other words, at their *junction*. Self-knowledge is at the *interface* of the individual and communicating others. By analogy, the meaning of a pointing gesture is at the interface of one individual's attention to a particular object in the environment and other individuals' attention to the same object. It is within neither one nor the other individual's private mind. The meaning of the pointing is shared, not privately owned. The same applies to self-knowledge.

> Proposition 4. *The authority of first- over third-person perspective on the self exists but is short lived in development.*

From birth on, children experience unique sensations that no one else but they can experience. These experiences include listening to their own voice, touching parts of their own body (double touch experience), or feeling their own body move in space (proprioceptive experience). These experiences are privileged and exclusive. They form a unique source of perceptual information from which children can eventually specify themselves as differentiated, situated, and agent entities in the world.

It is primarily because of this privileged experiential source that the authority of the first-person perspective over third-person perspective on the self is real and primary. From birth, the first-person perspective is indeed richer at specifying what we are, at least at an implicit perceptual level. Babies learn more about themselves by focusing on the experience of their own body than by focusing on how people respond to them. However, this authority is short lived as children begin to objectify themselves in the triangulation of reciprocal social exchanges.

With the internalization of thought processes and the emergence of symbolic functioning (i.e., language), third-person perspective on the self differentiates from first-person perspective. From then on, the authority of first- over third-person perspective, although real at the implicit level of self-experience, becomes blurred at the explicit level of self-objectification and self-evaluation.

From the time children begin to objectify their own feelings, their own flaws, their own appearances, their own beliefs, and their own mind states, first-person experience becomes inseparable from what others see of them (third-person, *evaluative* perspective on the self). With the development of self-objectification, the subjective experience of the self begins to lose its intrinsic authority. It begins to depend increasingly on the perspective of others as third-person perspective.

From then on, what develops is an explicit *intersubjective sense of self*, the product of a constant negotiation; first- and third-person perspectives on the self are always fundamentally dissonant, always at odds, forming an irreconcilable gap, as proposed later.

Proposition 5. *There is a dissonance between explicit self-knowledge from the first- and third-person perspectives.*

There is a profound irreconcilability or dissonance between first- and third-person perspectives on the self once objectified and valued. This dissonance shapes behaviors in crucial ways, as individuals try to reconcile their own and others' putative representations about them. These two representational systems are always at some odds or in conflict, always in need of readjustment. It is so because these systems are open, and they do not share the same informational resources: direct, permanent, and embodied for the first-person perspective on the self; indirect, more fleeting, and disembodied for the third-person perspective on the self.

A main property of this dissonance is that it tends to feed into itself and can reach overwhelming proportions in the life of individuals. More often than not, this dissonance is a major struggle, expressed in the nuisance of self-conscious behaviors that hinder creativity and the smooth "flow" of interpersonal exchanges.

To sum up, self-knowledge arising from first- and third-person perspectives forms basic representational systems that are *in conflict* because they do not share the same information. This conflict results in a dynamic that determines most of what we do as members of a self-conscious species.

Proposition 6. *First-person perspective primes inflated values on the self as third-person perspective primes deflated values on the self out of a fear of rejection.*

The privileged source of information and permanence of first-person perspective tends to *prime* an inflated, more positive, and idealized view on the self. In contrast, the third-person perspective (the representation of what others perceive and value of us) tends to prime deflated, more negative values with a general overtone of anxiety from fear of rejection. Attempts at resolving this conflict entail constant negotiation with others and desperate attempts at controlling what we project publicly to the outside world, what Goffman coins the "staging of the self." What underlies such staging is an open-ended, never ending process of negotiation and readjustment between first- and third-person perspective on the self.

The staging of the self results from the constant struggle between what we feel, think, or wish to project to the outside and what we think others actually evaluate feel and think, of us.

RECAP OF THE PROPOSED THEORY

In the perspective of development, the main points of the theory can be summarized as follows:

- Infants are born with an implicit, embodied sense of self that is based on privileged perceptual information. This information is intermodal (visual, auditory, tactile, gustatory, etc.). It includes proprioception, which is the modality of the self "par excellence" (e.g., no one but the self can feel their own body movements).
- This implicit, perceptual sense of self is primary and defines the primacy of an authority of first-person perspective at an implicit perception and action level. However, this primacy is short lived from the time the child becomes explicit about him- or herself in interaction with others.
- As children begin to engage in reciprocal exchanges with others, they objectify themselves as objects of shared attention. They develop an intersubjective sense of themselves, a sense of self that is shared with others. In addition to an implicit sense of self, the self becomes explicit and conceptualized. It is socially "triangulated" or triadic to follow George Herbert Mead.
- From this point on, the authority of the first-person perspective is replaced by a socially negotiated sense of self that is open to evaluation, conflicts, and constant negotiation with others.
- Once explicit, I propose, the sense of self (i.e., self-knowledge) from the first-person perspective is always at odds with the sense of self from the third-person perspective (what we imagine others see of us).
- In general, we tend to idealize ourselves (self-inflation) from the first- and depreciate ourselves (self-deflation) from the third-person perspective.
- Resolving this irreconcilable dissonance is a major factor in how we relate to each other as well as to ourselves. It determines much of what we do and what we are as humans.

3

Varieties of Self-Reflective Mind State

For many scientists, *consciousness* is the "C" word. They avoid it like the plague because it is semantically loose, a concept that covers too much. *Consciousness* is indeed a general term with as many meanings attached to it as there are theories about it. It has been debated for centuries in the tradition of Western philosophy, and the debate continues in the recent wave of cognitive and neuroscience research.

This chapter is an attempt at some clarification regarding the "C" word. I propose a distinction among various states of our self-reflecting mind. These states are construed as forming the variety of mental contexts of our experience of the world in general, and in particular of our experience of the self in relation to others.

The proposed distinction starts with the dichotomy between conscious and non-conscious states. It continues with distinctions among awareness, co-awareness, consciousness, and finally co-consciousness that define the social aspect of knowledge and self-knowledge in particular.

Beyond term clarification, what is proposed here is useful when considering the developmental origins of self-consciousness (see the following chapter). It provides a conceptual tool in the articulation of changes and qualitative shifts that mark the emergence of self-knowledge in human ontogeny.

As a cautionary note, this presentation does not pretend to be a lesson in philosophy of mind. It is the product of a reflection in the context of experimental research that tries to elucidate fundamental "C" questions in the perspective of early development such as, Are infants born conscious? What characterizes newborns' states of awareness? Are infants self-aware? When and how do infants re-cognize themselves? Are they capable of conceptual thoughts? Can they re-present to themselves objects and events that are temporarily out of sight? All these questions have been at the core of my own research for over twenty years, as they have driven a large amount of research on infant behavior and development in the past thirty years.[1]

So here are the conceptual bases for a vocabulary to be used in later discussions. This vocabulary delimits the rules of our investigative game. I will proceed by proposing and defining basic conceptual levels of "consciousness" ranging from its absence, namely, non-consciousness, to what I will propose is its most complex and developed level, termed here *co-consciousness*, what I view as the trademark of our species and our humanity. I will start by discussing (1) *non-conscious* states of the mind, to states of the mind that are (2) *unconscious*, (3) *aware*, (4) *co-aware*, (5) *conscious*, and finally (6) *co-conscious*.

The order of presentation is not random. It corresponds to the proposed chronology of mind states in early ontogeny discussed in the following chapter. I review these six *basic mind states* in turn, closing with a succinct summary.

1. Non-Consciousness

There are many things that we do not know directly, things we know via the testimony of others or indirectly by being taught about them. We know these things exist although we never experience them directly. For example, I know that I have a brain. I know also that as I am typing this text, millions of neurons are firing inside my skull that I do not feel, not even as passing tickles or itches. My liver, bones, or stomach might hurt occasionally, but most of the time they do what they do with me totally oblivious of their vital job. Most of what happens are transparent, invisible phenomena to our minds. We are like most drivers, oblivious of what exactly is happening under the hood of our vehicle.

The actual mechanics of my experience, the neural networks involved, and the complex patterns of firing underlying what I feel and think, all exist and happen unbeknownst to me. I am like the passengers of a cruise ship who are having cocktails while totally oblivious of the huge pistons and greasy transmissions propelling their vessel over the ocean. Of course, they might decide to go visit the engine room below and could have access to the mechanics of the ship. But it would be like my getting a brain scan to witness what is happening in my head as I think and type these lines. Such witnessing is feasible but unlikely. It would be a rather unusual experience.

---

[1] Rochat, P. (2001). *The Infant's World*. Cambridge, MA: Harvard University Press.

Most of the time, we are *non-conscious* of the biological and computational phenomena that underlie our experience of being alive and sentient individuals. We become aware of it typically when something goes wrong, typically through pain as in headaches or indigestion. We are also *non-conscious* when we are in deep sleep. This is not insignificant considering that we typically spend more than one-third of our life in this state, with no direct access to dreams or memory traces of the time spent sleeping. If something happened during deep sleep, it is all transparent, hence invisible to our mind or a conscious void. Yet, paradoxically, when we sleep we are still alive. Thus to be alive does not entail necessarily to have access mentally to what is happening. Someone plunged in a coma is *non-conscious*, yet still alive. It is still possible, however, that the comatose individual is registering something. This is the hope of visitors who still talk to their loved one in a totally nonresponsive comatose state. If such registering does occur, then the person would not be non-conscious as defined previously, but possibly unconscious, aware, conscious, or even co-conscious, in a variety of other mind states.

To summarize, in talking to a totally nonresponsive comatose yet still alive person (with basic vital signs), the talker is assuming that the person in question is not *non-conscious*. To be non-conscious is to be alive, yet not responsive and totally oblivious of what is happening around or within our own body. We might add that what characterizes non-consciousness as opposed to any other states of the mind is that when eventually coming out of such state, one has absolutely no memory of what it was like to be in it. To be non-conscious is to be alive, yet absolutely oblivious of being. It is a state of the mind by negation, like a cosmic black hole of antimatter, a thing of nothingness. It is as difficult for us to construe non-consciousness while conscious as it is to construe death while alive, nothingness while being in the world. However, non-consciousness does exist as a reality that is necessary, if not by direct inference from experience, at least by logical deduction.

2. Unconsciousness

There is another state of the mind with no traces of explicit awareness as in the state of non-consciousness presented earlier, yet clearly distinct from it. Contrary to being in a non-conscious state, in being unconscious one can eventually become aware and conscious of it.

Unconsciousness characterizes the state of the mind that was taken into full consideration for the first time by Freud in his psychodynamic theory

of personality and mental life in general. It is a state that can only be
understood in the way it manifests itself, after the fact, and often in non-
obvious, disguised ways. In the clinical world, it is the main object of the
psychoanalytical method invented by Freud. According to this method,
one has access to unconscious meanings via theories and interpretation,
typically retrospectively and through reconstruction by way of techniques
such as temporary induced hypnotic trance or free association in the
context of affective transference with the analyst. Psychoanalytic techniques allow for the reenactment of painful experiences that were at one
point repressed or dissociated from conscious content of the individual in
self-defense.

Outside the psychoanalytical cure, unconscious phenomena are ram-
pant in our lives, manifesting themselves in the strange things we recall
spontaneously from long lost memories, to the sudden pulls and pushes
we experience toward things and people for unknown reasons. These
reasons are unknown to us, yet they are real. Why does this particular
person trigger such a strong affective pull in me? Why does this specific
smell put me in some erotic spin and this other irritate me to the bones,
rubbing me the wrong way and turning me into a time bomb? Unknown
to us, from the earliest time of our lives, we bury experiences and memories of the kind that are seemingly lost but still exist as they reemerge to
influence what we are and how we behave in the here and now. It also
influences our choices and decisions as advertisers know well. It is a
reliable and widely applied fact that brand names influence future
choices and purchases. Exposure to things, even as an unattended background, makes them more palatable. This is an expression of our unconscious state of mind whereby we store and compute facts without being
aware that we do and are influenced by them in what we experience
wrongly as willful decisions.

3. Awareness

The English language is advantageous in the context of this discussion. In
English, as well as in its sister language German, which is also traditionally
the language of modern philosophy, words such as *awareness* or *to be
aware* exist, allowing for a contrast with the word *consciousness* or the state
of being *conscious*. French, for example, does not provide such a distinction. Curiously, in the same way, no word exists in French that stands for
the English word *self-consciousness* (*Selbsterlebnis* in German), a word that
captures the sense of being looked upon or the experience of being on

public display. More than once, the absence of such a word in French made me think that this book was not meant to be written in my mother tongue. In French, we are conscious, or we are not ("on est conscient ou on ne l'est pas"). English as well as German offer terms qualifying an additional kind of state of the mind, the state by which one is not conscious in the sense of having the knowledge of knowing (see later discussion), but yet is in a state of *awareness.*

Awareness is a state in which one is neither conscious, non-conscious, nor unconscious. It is a state in which one is, for example, aware of being alive in a sentient body in the world. It corresponds to what phenomenologists like Husserl and Merleau-Ponty capture as the sense of being present in the world: "le sentiment de sa présence au monde" (the feeling of one's own presence in the world).

To be aware is distinct from being conscious. It is different because awareness does not have to be conceptual. It is preconceptual or implicit. To be aware of something is different from conceiving, thinking, objectifying, or being explicit about this thing. One is aware of something typically prior to being able to communicate about it to others via language or any kind of intentional gestures. Any explicit account of the awareness of being alive, for example, is very difficult since it is an experience that, in essence, is implicit and preconceptual. As adepts of phenomenology insist, it precedes and is the foundation as well as the necessary condition of any explicit experience of the self in the world.

One way to justify as well as to clarify awareness as a particular state of the mind distinct from any "C" states is to refer to the situation we typically face every morning as we wake up.

As we emerge from deep sleep, there is a moment when we are aware of being alive and present in the world, yet not sure where we are and what we are looking at. We are not yet grasping our situation in a world that is objectified. We are awake yet in the state preceding the explicit contemplation that it is nine o'clock, the alarm did not go off, I will be late to my appointment, better rush to the bathroom before the kids, where are my slippers, and so forth. The state of awareness is a state that is not made of intentions, with no target objects to be reflected upon. Once again, awareness is a nonobjectified state. It is different and needs to be distinguished from non-conscious or unconscious states because it provides a clear sense of being alive, an experience that is "opaque" (i.e., not transparent) to the subject in the sense of a mentally accessible experience that can eventually become explicit via further elaboration. It corresponds to a subjective or *first-person perspective* on the experience of being alive in the world. This distinct state of awareness is important, particularly when trying to qualify what is happening in the mind of the very young infant during the first six weeks of life (see next chapter). Newborns, for example, appear to be aware in the sense described, as do most animals and any perceiving (not merely sensing) complex systems. Yet, they are not conscious in the sense of knowing that they know (see later discussion).

To drive the nail further and consolidate the distinction of awareness as a specific state of the mind, it is helpful to refer to a distinction made sometimes in the realm of perception between *seeing* and *looking*. This distinction captures two fundamentally different ways of perceiving, one that is peripheral, the other that is focused or oriented toward particular features of the environment.

Seeing has no other object than to perceive, whatever it is. In contrast, looking is oriented toward a target in space. In essence, it is intentional following Brentano's idea that all mental, hence conscious phenomena have a target, an object to which they tend: "We can define mental phenomena by stating that they are phenomena containing an intentional object inside themselves."[2,3]

So we might *look* at a face, trying to identify or recognize it. In this case we are engaged in a conscious act (intentional or representational in Brentano's terms), a profoundly different state of affairs compared to being aware of the face via seeing.

In a state of awareness, we *see* the face but without any intentions of gathering certain kinds of information to fulfill a particular task. We see it because it is in front of us, we are awake, and our eyes are open. We are just aware of a face. We can clearly discriminate it from other nonface entities, yet we are not conscious of it. This state of the mind is, I will suggest, what characterizes the earliest stage of mental life, when infants are awake and perceiving, when they are just aware as opposed to conscious in the sense that will be described further. But, before getting into the consciousness levels, it is important to consider another kind of awareness that is distinct from the awareness state considered so far: it is the awareness of being with others, a state that is not easy to describe. Yet, it is a mind state that is crucially important to distinguish from any other.

[2] Brentano, F. C. (1874). *Psychologie vom empirischen Standpunkt* (Psychology from an empirical standpoint). Leipzig: Duncker & Humbolt; book acute 2, chapter 1, p. 102 of French translation cited by Jacob, P. (2004).

[3] Jacob, P. (2004). *L'intentionalité, problèmes de philosophie de l'esprit.* Paris: Odile Jacob.

4. Co-Awareness

When I am eating at a restaurant on my own, reading my paper while digging seemingly absentmindedly into my plate, could I say that I only enjoy my own company? I do not think so. Although I do not pay particular attention to the people around me, I am not particularly interested, and ultimately will not know what they eat or talk about, I am still very much aware of their presence. After my meals, I would not recognize any of these people in a police lineup, nor could I reconstruct any of their conversation or meals. I certainly have some fleeting moments of attention, but this is not my main focus, and any knowledge I might accumulate about people and things around me is unstable and quickly gone out of my mind.

If I look up from my plate and paper, I see people more than I am actually looking at them. I am basically on my own, reading my paper at a public place, not in the seclusion of my kitchen. But there is something fundamentally different between the public and the private situations in which I might choose to eat and read, aside from obvious sound and other movement stimulation levels.

At the restaurant, I might not look at or pay any particular attention to the people surrounding me, but I am certainly not oblivious of their presence: I am aware of it and in particular of my presence in the world *with them* ("mitsein," in Heidegger's vocabulary). Inversely, I can assume that as much as I am aware of their presence, they are also aware of mine, though they probably do not pay particular attention to me. They probably see me fleetingly, without particularly looking at me.

Anonymous people like me eating at a restaurant cannot escape being *co-aware* of each other's presence. It is inescapable regardless of our immersing activities, whether reading, eating, chatting with a friend, or listening to stories.

Co-awareness is an extension of the awareness state presented earlier. As for awareness, it is not an objectifying, intentional state of mind; nor is it non-conscious or unconscious. It is experientially accessible to us, not just transparent. Yet, it is different and needs to be distinguished from the state of awareness discussed in the preceding section because it is more than an involuted (self-oriented) process. In essence, it is a mind state that is social, an awareness projected outward toward the presence of other individuals. It pertains to the sense of being aware of one's presence in the world with others, not alone in a solipsist way. Co-awareness is the awareness that our presence in the world is communal rather than individual, a presence that is simultaneously shared with the presence of others: that one's presence in the world is not alone but rather together with the presence of others. As elusive as it might sound, it is crucial to emphasize *co-awareness* as a specific state of mind, distinct from either awareness per se or any other conscious states.

In general, we tend to behave and experience the world differently when we feel or do not feel part of a community, when we feel or do not feel the presence of other individuals. Co-awareness is, more often than not, a source of comfort and reassurance. Comfort accompanies the awareness of being copresent in the world and there is indeed something reassuring in being *co-aware*. Co-awareness contributes to our well-being as we all tend to express some need to be with others without having to know or interact directly with them.

Co-awareness transcends the state of individual awareness discussed previously. It enlarges it by including the awareness of others who are simultaneously aware and present in the world. It is reassuring and can be a source of comfort to the extent that others are in an analogous state of mind. My state of co-awareness at the restaurant eating alone would not be a source of comfort and reassurance if all other people, rather than chatting and eating, would be, for example, dead drunk and snoring around me, hence would not show any signs of co-awareness. Nor would it be reassuring if people were staring at me while I was reading my paper and eating, not simply existing for themselves around me, showing instead objectified "consciousness" of me, a state of the mind that carries with it the potential for reasoning and identification, ultimately judgment and evaluation.

5. Consciousness

In common language, the word *consciousness* connotes multiple things, from a particular alert or awake state of the mind ("he is conscious") to the representation of good or bad deeds ("he has bad consciousness"). Sometimes it has a moral meaning or connotation; sometimes the word is used to capture one's state of explicit (objectified and communicable) knowledge about things in the world, including the self. Here, and for now, I will focus primarily on the latter, which is actually closer to the etymological sense of the word.

The word *consciousness* derives from the Greek *suneidesis* meaning "communal knowledge" or knowledge that can be shared with others. *Suneidesis* was eventually translated in the Latin word *conscientia*, which articulates the preposition *con* (with) and the substantive *scientia* (knowledge). Thus literally, and if we stick to its etymological meaning, the word *consciousness* can mean either one of two things, and eventually, both. In reference to its Greek roots, *consciousness* could mean literally that to be conscious is to have knowledge *with others, knowledge in common,* or *shared knowledge.* In this sense, *consciousness* refers to the social nature of all we know of knowing. This meaning dominated up to the seventeenth century and as long as consciousness continued to be considered primarily in the realm of ethics and in relation to shared morality.[4] This meaning changed with René Descartes's new epistemological stance toward this state of the mind. From Descartes on, the word *consciousness* started to mean primarily "with such knowledge" rather than "such knowledge with." The inversion is quite consequential as it marks a change from an ethical and *social* focus to a more epistemological and "egological" or individual focus. It marks the beginning of an individualistic rather than collective approach to consciousness. In the Cartesian tradition, cognitive psychologists and researchers in artificial intelligence continue to construe consciousness as the knowledge of what one (whether an individual, a machine, a robot, a program) knows, does, has done, and will do. It is removed from the ethical, cultural, and collective domain.

Historically, prior to the seventeenth century, one could say that consciousness was primarily understood as a phenomenon that could not be conceived independently of the collective, not independently of others or some social rules or goals. For example, all heroes in Homeric tales consult their *thumos* or heart (not their brain) before they act at major junctures of their lives. With Descartes, this consultation becomes a mental meditation that is self-serving, proving one's own existence and the limits of one's own knowledge about things independent of the collective. With Descartes, consciousness becomes an individualistic, more private and solipsistic state of the mind that is opaque, not transparent, accessible to itself through self-reflection. The rationalist tradition launched by Descartes introduces a transition from *cogitamus, ergo sum* (we think, therefore I am) to Descartes's famous *cogito, ergo sum* (I think, therefore I am). This tradition was followed and enriched by many other philosophers in the following centuries, including influential thinkers such as Malebranche, Spinoza, Leibniz, and Kant.[5] Descartes's solipsistic, self-reflective view of consciousness has had an enormous impact and continues to prevail in current cognitive and neuroscience research.

---

[4] Simha, A. (2004). *La Conscience – du corps au sujet* (Consciousness – from the body to the subject). Paris: Armand Colin.

[5] Jacob, P. (2004), pp. 25–42.

It is now difficult to dissociate the solipsistic, self-reflective aspect of consciousness from its meaning, yet it should not occlude the collective aspect of knowing with others, the shared knowledge that is also entailed by this state of the mind.

However, the Cartesian, rationalist, and individualistic outlook on consciousness captures a distinct state of mind, real enough to be distinguished from the collective aspect of consciousness, namely, all matters that I know you know and that we share, a state of mind I will call *co-consciousness* (see later discussion).

Consciousness is the state of mind where one knows that he knows, and that what he knows knowing is not just transparent, but rather opaque and objectifiable. It can become explicit in terms of propositions, predicates, or any other kinds of mental representation, be it simulation, pretense, or memories. These representations are for oneself but also eventually for others, when formatted in words, in texts, or in any other public formats. The crucial point and what gives the specificity of consciousness is that it is the result of a process that depends primarily on the individual's self-reflection and thinking. It acknowledges the fact that there is a state of mind where we can think primarily for ourselves, making discoveries on our own and seemingly for ourselves, not primarily for others. At least it acknowledges the possibility of such a state of mind. For example, when I wake up and I emerge from the mere awareness of being alive in my body and the awareness of my presence in the world, when I look at my alarm clock to realize that it did not go off and that I will be late for my appointment; when I begin to wonder where I left my slippers, I am becoming conscious for myself (although I contemplate being late to my appointment therefore factor others in my thoughts). However, I grasp my situation on my own and under the spell of my own reflection. I become conscious in the Cartesian sense of "with knowledge."

As I am typing these words, in the seclusion of my room, I might have the audience of some elusive readers in mind but, unquestionably, I am primarily struggling with my own thoughts, trying to make sense first for myself, then rereading to see whether it is intelligible for others. There is something intrinsically solipsistic in my state of mind, which is primarily a conscious state in the Cartesian sense.

Another, more existential reason to consider consciousness as distinct from the more collective co-consciousness I will introduce next is the fact that it is *embodied*. It exists and vanishes with the body. In this sense, consciousness depends on our very own individual existence, not the existence of others. This delimits consciousness as primarily an individual phenomenon, assuming, of course, that once dead, the body goes as well as the knowledge of knowing. If this is true, then consciousness depends on and is delimited by the temporary existence of the individual itself.

In summary, in the Cartesian, solipsistic tradition, consciousness stands for the state of mind by which one knows of knowing on his or her own. It is different from being aware. In Brentano's sense of intentionality and representation, in consciousness one's mental activities tend to mental objects or re-presentations of things that are *objectified*. They can be mentally manipulated, becoming eventually the source of communicable, hence explicit discoveries or realizations, albeit new thoughts, decisions, proofs, sudden understandings (insights), or novel predictions. In this sense, consciousness corresponds to what cognitive psychologists have labeled as *metacognition*: the knowledge of knowledge and the knowledge of knowing, or not knowing (i.e., of being ignorant).

Consciousness entails a self-reflective loop and an introspective process dealing with mental objects or objects that are re-presented. The nature and format of these mental objects are the main topic of today's abundant cognitive science research. Some claim that these mental objects are mainly symbolic and propositional in nature. A growing number of other researchers claim that they are mainly embodied simulations.[6] Whatever these mental objects might be, they are considered mainly as mental objects generated by the solitary conscious individual, not enough, in my opinion, as mental objects co-constructed and elaborated in interaction with other individuals.

There is indeed something profound missing from the mainstream conceptualization of our capacity to be conscious, and it is necessary to acknowledge what I see as an even more evolved state of mind, a state of mind that is not taken enough into consideration by current cognitive and cognitive neuroscientists. This state of mind is what I call *co-consciousness*.

6. Co-Consciousness

Since it is necessary to qualify the solipsistic state of mind put forth by Descartes and that is generally acknowledged as consciousness, it is also necessary to qualify another state of mind that eludes the Cartesian conception. It is the state in which we not only know of knowing, but, more

---

[6] See, for example, the simulation- and perception-based views on cognition proposed by Barsalou, L. in his 1999 article Perceptual symbol systems. *Behavioral and Brain Sciences* 22: 257–660, in sharp opposition to the artificial intelligence and amodal views of Pylyshyn, Z. W. (1984). *Computation and Cognition*. Cambridge, MA: MIT Press.

importantly, *know of sharing knowledge with others.* Here the knowledge of knowing is not just individual but collective.

In contradistinction to the Cartesian, solipsistic conception of consciousness, the knowledge of knowing coexists in multiple minds and in a way transcends the individual who becomes only one part of a whole. The knowledge that the individual knows is not of the conscious kind described prior. Why? Simply because it will survive individuals.

This knowledge will eventually be retained in the mind of other surviving persons as well as in institutions (marriage, justice, schools) that the passing individuals helped shaping during their lifetime whether by abiding by it, transgressing it, or rebelling against it. Rather than embodied in the individual, this metaknowledge is embodied in the group, including the family, the society, and the culture where the individual evolves.

Furthermore, the mental objects or re-presentations of co-consciousness are not within the individual, but rather *outside.* In particular, they are between the individual and others, not in one of them taken separately. They exist in the social transaction. The mental objects of co-consciousness are at the interface between an individual and other individuals with whom he or she is sharing the experience of being in the world.

This distinction, quite abstract as it stands, is crucial, especially in the context of this book. It might help to return to my late waking up example. I left myself realizing that the alarm did not go off, that I would be late for my appointment, and could not figure where I left my slippers, maybe also that the bathroom I needed to use in a hurry was currently occupied. All this corresponds to self-realization, a step beyond the mere awareness of being alive. But it is still very much determined by my own action and situation. It is real, in essence solipsistic, but does not capture what should naturally happen next.

In taking my shower, I may decide to call the person I am supposed to meet. In calling this person, let us say my boss, who tends to terrorize me, I will adopt an apologetic, polite, and submissive voice that is a clear masking of the irritation and frustration I might be actually experiencing deep down in my stress. Such masking marks an important transition in mind state, the transition from consciousness to co-consciousness proper. It is in contrast to the conscious experience of situating myself in my bedroom, looking at my alarm clock, searching for my slippers, and heading to the shower. At this point I do not think about what I know through my own devices, but what I know with *others in mind*: I become *co-conscious.*

In this new state, the content of the knowledge that I know, in other words, the mental objects I represent (e.g., beliefs, doubts, certitudes), emerges from the particular relationship and rapport I have with my boss. This rapport is mutually monitored, constantly revised and renegotiated as a function of our ongoing relationship.

My mental representations and the knowledge that I know of knowing do not depend anymore on my solipsist cogitation. They become fundamentally codependent on others' mental representations that I share or at least try to figure. So, if my boss is in a good mood, showing lenience and understanding, my conscious experience of the situation will change accordingly. This dynamic is far removed from Descartes's metaphysical meditations.

Metacognition is not only the solipsistic, self-reflective process that takes place in the individual, in some kind of social vacuum. For the most part, it takes place in the context of social exchanges and shared representations. These shared representations are always changing, the product of a constant negotiation among individuals, what can be labeled as *intersubjective negotiation* or the negotiation of shared experience. Ultimately, it is this negotiation that shapes what we know of knowing (our metacognition), what should be called our *co-conscious* experience.

Co-conscious experience is the source of the universe of knowledge that guides our behaviors. It is what constitutes our ideas and conceptions of the world and particularly the representations we hold about ourselves in relation to others. The content of this experience is inseparable from the necessities of relating to and coexisting with others.

As a case in point, most of what we hold as true we receive from the testimony of others whom we trust to tell the truth or at least convince us that they do. Knowledge and representations are mainly learned in negotiation or from the testimony of others. What do I know that I can honestly claim I learned and discovered on my very own? The answer is, very little. From the earliest age we rely on what others tell us about things, explain to us what to think and what to believe. We discover relatively little on our own, in spite of the young scientist and active discoverer metaphor that has dominated and continues to dominate theories in child development since Piaget.

We know that the Earth is round not because we have discovered on our own that boats vanish behind the horizon while building sand castles on an early childhood beach. As we did for most of our knowledge, we acquired it through the testimony of others, from the observation of others, and in negotiation with others. Rare is the knowledge one can claim having discovered in the solipsistic and solitary vacuum of his mind, like Descartes's proving his own existence by thinking. Even in this case, thinking is typically formatted in a social dialog between imaginary voices that play the game of contradicting each other until a solution or agreement is found. We emulate this game of imaginary voices in an effort to recreate the emulation and the benefit of teamwork in the quest for a solution.

This shows how much, deep down, we know that without others we do not amount to much. Co-consciousness does play a major role in what we know, but also in what we feel, the way we think, and what we do as individuals whose autonomy is for the most part illusory. All this applies to the self as self-consciousness stands for *co-consciousness about the self*, a mind state that is of particular interest to us in this book.

DYNAMIC OF MIND STATES

Considering the various kinds of mind state as separate, fixed, and well delimited entities is very much incomplete. It does not capture how these mind states relate to each other and how, in the reality of our mental life, we are constantly transiting through them. Rather than static, the repertoire of our wakeful mind states is indeed dynamic. It forms a varied landscape in which we navigate.

We sleep, we dream, we are wakened by nightmares or delicious fantasies, we think, we talk, and we manage our person for public display. All these activities and other happenings that make up our lives correspond to and are accompanied by at least one of the five particular mind states I have described. In fact, aside maybe from when we are plunged in deep sleep, most of the time these states interact and switch as we are engaged in one kind of activity or immersed in one particular situation. There is a complex dynamic among mind states that cannot be overlooked. As an illustration of this complex dynamic, I will use a concrete, albeit mundane and totally made-up example just for demonstration's sake.

It is Sunday and some friends come to my place for brunch. We sit around the table and enjoy each other's company while eating, telling stories, and chitchatting. It was my initiative to set up this invitation, yet I could not tell what drove me to do so because in all honesty, I cherish my Sundays on my own, unshaved and unwashed, reading the paper and blasting the music that most people hate. Yet I chose to socialize for reasons that were unclear at the time. In fact, I realized afterward that somehow it might have been related to a phone conversation I had weeks ago with my mother, who worried about my living a life with no wife and kids in sight, dominated by the shameless pleasures of extended bachelorhood. I never thought about my life in these terms and Mom shed a new light on it. Lo and behold, at the time, I did not think much about it. Yet, as I was cleaning up the dishes and the guests were gone, ready for resuming the old habit of Sunday nap and music, I recalled my mother's phone conversation and realized, deep down, that it played a role in my setting up this brunch.

In this simple anecdote, we see all the complex interplay of the various kinds of mind states I as the protagonist go through. In particular:

All through the event, processes unknown to me are taking place within me, in my brain and in my mouth and stomach as when, for example, I chase the eggs Benedict with a Bloody Mary. My non-consciousness was at work.

In the meantime, what originated this invitation was buried in the lost phone conversation with my mother that managed to return alive, unknown to me, to trigger a habit change. My unconsciousness was at work.

Preparing the invitation, choosing the guests, cooking, shopping, and cleaning up my bachelor den entailed some planning and reflection: the evaluation of what was reasonable, appropriate, and what was not; how much food and how many could be fed. My consciousness was at work.

Finally, but not least importantly, in the actual happening of the invitation, the stories told, the gifts received, the promise of more to come, the birth of new affinities, and maybe even some phone numbers exchanged, all that form the shared social space and new social knowledge that emerge from the encounter of individuals negotiating a good time and trying to align experience with each other, the ultimate function of such social gathering: my co-consciousness was at work.

What we see is that all these mind states are interacting with each other at all times. They form a complex dynamic and our navigation through them is not a linear or clean transition path as they coexist and are mutually defining of each other. Yet, they correspond to different levels of wakeful mental processing and can be distinguished as such.

Each mental state can be considered as representing a finite number of layers piling on top of each other, like geological layers. Here I would like to draw an analogy with the way we tend to process images and extract meanings from artifacts such as a photograph or a painting. In this process, a viewer can take different stances that are, to some extent, analogous to the different states of mind.[7]

[7] Rochat, P., & Callaghan, T. (2005). What drives symbolic development? The case of pictorial comprehension and production. In L. Namy (ed)., *Symbol Use and Symbolic Representation: Developmental and Comparative Perspectives*, 25–46. Mahwah, NJ: Lawrence Erlbaum Associates.

In recent research, my colleagues and I tried to seize the developmental emergence of pictorial stances adopted by young children between birth and four or five years. These stances resemble to some extent the states of mind I discussed earlier, except that they have a specific content, namely, responding to and making sense of a picture.

First, we can be oblivious of a picture presented to us, as when we drive in a busy city, concentrating on the road in the midst of the typical jungle of flickering billboards that are trying to distract us with new products and urging smiles. We might not see these pictures or might see them, but at a subconscious level as probably intended by the advertisers.

We can also look at a picture as a physical object, overlooking the image it supports, perceiving, for example, a photograph as a three-dimensional physical piece of paper, oblivious of the image it supports. Another way to contemplate a picture is possibly to take the image represented on the picture as a real, not a represented thing. So if the image portrays a cup, I might confound this cup for a real, substantial three-dimensional object that it is not. We can take the picture for what it is, a representation of something that might or might not exist.

Finally, and in our account that would be the final, "higher" level of picture contemplation,[8] we might see in the picture not only the two-dimensional representation of something that might exist, but also and more importantly, the way the picture has been produced or taken. In this *intentional stance* toward the picture, the viewer of the picture is using it to figure out the person behind the picture, namely, its producer. By adopting an intentional stance, the viewer tries to figure out who took or made the picture and why. What was her intention? What did she try to convey by representing the way she did the thing she chose to depict?

In our work, we used these levels to capture the development of picture understanding in the young child, our research suggesting that there is a developmental order leading the child toward an intentional stance and theories of mind in picture understanding. More to the point of this discussion, we proposed that as adults, we tend to *oscillate* between these pictorial stances that unfold in an orderly fashion in the course of the first five years. We adopt alternatively one of these stances as a function of the particular circumstances of our encounters with pictures: while driving, when skimming through magazines, or during the guided tour of a

---

[8] Callaghan, T., & Rochat, P. (2008). Children's theories of the relation between artist and picture. In C. Milbrath & H. M. Trautner, eds., *Children's Understanding and Production of Pictures, Drawing, and Art: Theoretical and Empirical Approaches*, 187–207. Cambridge, MA: Hogrefe & Huber.

museum. The general theoretical intuition is that we are constantly oscillating or switching among these distinct levels of pictorial awareness and
meaning making, all developing in the first five years of life. The question
as to what triggers such oscillation and switching remains, however, wide
open, notwithstanding the fact that a clean transition from one level to
another is probably not typical.

The direct use of this intuition to account for the dynamic of mind
states is too simple and would fall into the caricature depiction provided
by psychology textbooks discussing states of the mind in a hierarchic,
orderly fashion following the successive sleep states we go through during
the night, oscillating from deep to active (rapid eye movement) sleep. Such
an analogy implies too much order and hierarchy. It does not capture the
actual mess and interference of wakeful states, not giving enough room for
the chaotic and random aspect of what William James called *stream of
consciousness*.

In reality, states of mind as well as the variety of our contemplative
stances toward pictures do not wax and wane in a regular, predictable
fashion as in sleep. We might be wide awake and alert, in a state of hyper-
consciousness and co-consciousness, or in a state of great reconstruction
in relation to a picture, then suddenly blank or even pass out. We can jump
from one state to any of the others, without having to pass through a
predictable order. The dynamics of mind states as well as of pictorial
stances are essentially stochastic, with no absolute determinism. Indeed,
it is hard to predict what state of mind will follow the current one and
whether the preceding one continues to interfere and influence the one we
are currently in.

Interference is typically the rule, not the exception. The unconscious state
I was in just before the alarm went off influences my sudden awareness of
being alive, and eventually my state of consciousness or co-consciousness
with others. Whether I was, in my dreams and as the alarm went off,
immersed in a musing landscape made of pleasure and plenty, or on the
contrary in a landscape of dire and dread, affects my emerging awareness of
being alive, eventually waking up on either the right or wrong side of the
bed. By analogy, the guided tour of the museum changes the way we
respond to paintings.

So, once again, it is important to emphasize that the dynamic of successive mental states is bushy rather than orderly, linear, and predictable. It
is made of interferences and for the most part, unpredictable qualitative
jumps. Yet we navigate through these states that are phenomenally distin-
guishable and that correspond to highly contrasted ways of being mentally

engaged and alive in the world. In the dynamic system jargon, in the midst of chaos and unpredictability, these ways correspond to specific momentary stable or attractor states.

These ways of being range from obliviousness, to being aware and co-aware of our presence in the world, to being intentional and dealing with an objectified, embodied world and body. Ultimately, these ways also include the state of *co-consciousness* in which one is dealing with a shared knowing that transcends individual consciousness. At the level of co-consciousness, the knowledge of knowing is defined in relation to others. This is the constitutive level of self-consciousness.

Assuming that the various mind states are not just a given, in the next chapter we consider how co-consciousness and other mind states do unfold in early development.

4

Mind States in Development

In the preceding chapter, I distinguished a variety of six general mind states that capture, at minimum, what is happening in the adult mind when awake. This distinction is not purely abstract and theoretical, not the result of mere introspection and armchair speculation. It is empirically based, informed by developmental observations and a natural history of mind states as they appear to emerge in the first months of life. Here I review these observations in support of the proposed mind state distinction.

The question of interest here is what constitutes the states of the mind at the beginning of life and how do these states unfold eventually to reach the state of *co-consciousness* (i.e., *self-co-consciousness*).

You can see already that co-consciousness is not construed here as any kind of acquired mind state but rather the culmination of a development, possibly unique to our species. Be reminded that the main argument of this book is that co-consciousness is at the root of what makes us human, and in particular the self-conscious species we are, a species that is unique for its obsession with others as *evaluators* of the self.

On the basis of selected developmental research, I will discuss the emerging signs of co-consciousness in the developing child. The goal is to understand what co-consciousness is made of by looking at how it develops as children engage in increasingly complex transactions with people and things in the world. Looking at this development will help in specifying further the various mind states presented in the preceding chapter. It will also aid in "naturalizing" these mind states by looking at how they unfold in ontogeny, providing a natural history of co-consciousness in the perspective of development.

I consider the earliest evidence of the states of awareness, co-awareness, consciousness, and eventually the developmental signs of co-consciousness as flourishing by the middle of the second year with language and other uniquely human symbolic developments. But, first, I consider the origins of this natural history, where it all begins, discussing the wakeful mind states of newborns. The question is, What are the range and nature of newborns' mind states when not asleep?

BORN TOO SOON

As adults, we typically spend close to 30 percent of our life sleeping. Newborns, in contrast, spend close to 90 percent of theirs. If not fast asleep, newborns spend their time fussing, crying, sometimes in moments of calm wakeful state. But these moments are rare and fleeting. With eyes open, the infant stares around with sometimes gentle writhing and orienting movements engaging the whole body.

Newborns' rare calm and wakeful moments form a narrow window of time in their life. This window is precious because it can inform us on the starting state of the mind. For example, is this starting state a *blank slate*, as radical empiricists would claim, or is the mind of the newborn already full of a priori concepts and representations as proposed by nativists?[1]

Over forty years ago, Montagu[2] aptly termed the first weeks that follow the nine months of human in utero gestation as exterogestation. It is an apt description in terms of recent progress in infancy research, and in particular fetal research showing a remarkable behavioral continuity between prenatal and postnatal life.

New ultrasonic technology allowed for the unambiguous demonstration that at least during the last three months of gestation, fetuses display the same behavioral and state repertoire as the one displayed by newborns immediately after birth and during the first six weeks of postnatal life. In other words, from a behavioral standpoint, we now know that there is a remarkable continuity between pre- and postnatal life.

In comparison to other primates, human infants appear to be born too soon. As a case in point, to reach the growth level of other great ape species at birth, in particular our closest relatives the gorillas or the chimpanzees, human newborns would have more than to *double* their gestation time!

Various theories are proposed as to why humans are born too soon in comparison to other closely related species. One speculation is that the growth of the human brain demands the rich sensory stimulations

---

[1] Pinker, S. (2002). *The Blank Slate: The Modern Denial of Human Nature*. London: Allen Lane.

[2] Montagu, A. (1961). Neonatal and infant immaturity in man. *Journal of the American Medical Association* 178(23): 56–57.

provided by the environment outside the uterus. Another tentative explanation is that human brain growth requires more nutrient and energy resources than can be supplied through the placenta. Another interesting evolutionary account is linked to the evolutionary emergence of the unique human vertical posture and bipedal locomotion. Accordingly, the emergence of bipedal locomotion in human evolution changed the configuration of the pelvis bone and as a consequence narrowed considerably the birth canal. This, in turn, limited the maximal cranial growth of the fetus in order to pass through the canal safely. All this might have channeled a precipitated human birth and an adaptation toward a continuing gestation outside the womb.

As discussed at length in a former book[3] and following the ideas put forth by Bruner[4] in a seminal article on the nature and uses of immaturity, the fact that humans are born too soon has had cascading effects. It contributed to the uniqueness of the human mind and what humans tend to achieve in their mental development. These cascading effects are evident, whatever remote causes contributed to their emergence in evolution. Co-consciousness and self-consciousness are among these effects. However, they are not yet present at birth, relying on extensive learning outside the womb, in interaction with objects, but also with people, in the context of rich reciprocal exchanges.

ARE NEWBORNS AWARE?

So what is on the mind of human newborns in their rare moments of wakefulness, when not crying or fussing? What do they see, hear, and feel? In relation to these questions, the past forty years of abundant research on infant behavior and development has seriously shaken major myths and assumptions put forth by philosophers and early childhood psychologists. To make a long story short, babies were thought to be born cognitively *incompetent* and behaviorally *disorganized*. But this assumption does not meet new research scrutiny.

Pioneer psychologists such as William James or Wilhelm Wundt regarded infants as born in a blooming, buzzing confusion or as highly unpredictable; thus, they were not suitable as objects of reliable scientific investigation. In fact, a lot of research provides evidence that infants are born *aware* and behave in ways that are organized and predictable, not random.

---

[3] Rochat, P. (2001a). *The Infant's World*. Cambridge, MA: Harvard University Press.
[4] Bruner, J. (1972). Nature and uses of immaturity. *American Psychologist* 27(8): 687–708.

It is safe to say today that newborns are aware of the body and of the objects they sense via the multiple sensory channels. They do not seem to be merely "passive sensory recipients" à la William James, bombarded by nondescript, meaningless, and on the whole *confusing* stimulations. It is now clear that from birth on, infants are perceivers and actors in a meaningful environment. For example, when in an alert and quiet behavioral state, infants who are less than twenty-four hours old will orient to sounds they hear and even show first signs of manual reaching behavior toward objects they see passing by close to them. They systematically move one of their hands to the mouth following intraoral sucrose stimulation and some researchers found that despite the fact that newborns are still greatly impaired visually, they do perceive objects as being substantial and belonging to a continuous spatial layout. All these findings show that newborn infants are perceptually aware of segregated, distal objects. They do not simply feel: they also perceive; they do not simply see: they also look; they do not simply hear: they also listen.

Following the mind states' vocabulary proposed in the preceding chapter, empirical evidence shows that hours after birth, newborns are aware, perceiving objects, hence *having a sense of their presence in a world furnished by distinct entities or things.*[5] But are they nothing but aware of their presence in the world?

CAN NEWBORNS BE UNCONSCIOUS?

Aside from showing fleeting, reliable awareness, newborns are for the most part in a state of non-consciousness, typically sleeping. Remember that I referred to the state of non-consciousness as the state in which one is oblivious (i.e., unaware) of what is happening around or within the own body. But can newborns be unconscious when not either aware or non-conscious? This is a difficult question that would deserve research scrutiny that I am not aware exists yet. Is there a mere exposure effect (the unconscious effect of being exposed to something, unbeknownst to us) and implicit long-term memories in newborns? Interesting question but with no clear answer yet. In this respect, future brain imaging research on newborns will be decisive in trying to answer this question.

For now, we can only speculate that if these phenomena exist at birth, even prior to birth, they must be very limited, probably insignificant.

---

[5] See Rochat, P. (2001a), pp. 37–42, for a more detailed discussion of the research supporting these ideas.

However, matters clearly change within a few weeks after birth, as testified by well-established behavioral research on early memory. In general, from at least three months of age, there is convincing evidence of long-term implicit procedural memory, hence evidence of an unconscious mind state if we follow my definition.

Research shows marked development in memory capacity and retrieval ability starting at two or three months, suggesting the existence of an unconscious mind state. There is long-term storage of information that influenced infants' behavior, unbeknownst to them, weeks, and sometimes even months, later.

For example, three-month-old infants learn to kick a mobile suspended above their crib with a ribbon fastened around one of their ankles and demonstrate clear recall in subsequent test sessions occurring sometimes weeks later, presumably without any opportunity for rehearsal. This is evidence of implicit memory and the unconscious processing of information.

At the explicit level, however, we know that our earliest memory rarely goes back further than our third, or maybe second birthday. We all suffer from so-called infantile amnesia. It suggests that if implicit procedural long-term memory is an early fact of life, at least starting two or three months after birth, information is not encoded and retrieved in the same way at two or three years of age. There is a marked developmental shift when children begin by two to three years of age to function at an explicit level, producing images and narratives about their own experiences that can be recalled years later when reaching adulthood. Infantile amnesia suggests that the explicit format of memories changes their nature, making them retrievable years later at an explicit level.

In summary, infants from at least two to three months after birth manifest an unconscious mind state, acquiring for the long term proce-dural actions without any need of particular rehearsal. These procedures (e.g., kicking of a mobile) are implicitly acquired and stored by the infant, readily reactivated in the appropriate context, sometimes months later. Very young infants do show traces of unconscious processing that can be retrieved to become explicit in action, hence showing evidence of an unconscious mind state as discussed in the preceding chapter.

ARE NEWBORNS CO-AWARE?

I have suggested that newborns are for the most part non-conscious with glimpses of awareness and probably little, if any, unconsciousness. We have seen that clear evidence of unconscious processing exists in infants aged two to three months, not prior. If newborns, by glimpses, show awareness of a meaningful environment in which they are perceivers, actors, and learners,[6] do they show evidence of co-awareness with others? The question is, Do newborns show any signs of a distinct awareness of their presence *with others,* namely, another person or other people as opposed to anything else furnishing the environment?

One way to demonstrate co-awareness at birth would be to show that infants are particularly attuned to people, that they respond differentially to people as opposed to any other entities in the environment. However, there is a major hurdle to such demonstration in the fact that people are, for the child and particularly for the highly dependent newborn, the most attentive, caring, nurturing, hence rewarding feature in their environment. So, whether they show co-awareness or no co-awareness, newborns will spend most of their wakeful hours fed and cared for typically by one person who becomes a central focus of attention, but particularly a central focus of learning and adaptation.

From day one, infants learn their mother's smell, the particular shape of her nipples, the particular vitality of her gestures, her voice, vocal expression, and overall moods at playtime and during routine care. The timing of her responses, her overall consistency in more or less ritualized, structured daily routines, notwithstanding her attention to behavioral changes of her infant form invariant perceptual information that is readily picked up by the infant from birth. Clearly, caretakers, and particularly the primary caretaker, are, for the newborn, privileged objects of attention and learning during fleeting times of wakefulness. But does this privileged attention and learning of the mother from birth entail co-awareness?

One is inclined to infer "co-awareness" in moments of calm fusion. For example, newborns latch to the nipple, sucking and feeding their heart out with eyes closed, one of their tiny hands gently fingering and stroking the round surface of the bosom with the mother often looking down and smiling at her progeny. It is also hard not to read mutual comfort in an infant's abandoning herself in sleep over a shoulder or curled into the adult's arms.

But these compelling instances of comfort do not warrant ascribing "co-awareness" to the child. They are by-products of feeding and sleeping within the highly adapted care systems of adults who provide nurturance

---

[6] See Rochat, P. (2001a), pp. 130–141, for further discussion.

and indispensable postural support and scaffolding. These instances do not show that the infant would behave differently if a programmed robot would take care of him or her. I think the child would adapt to the robot as much as he or she adapts to the mother. If the robot is well designed and simulates the complexity of mother's attention and care to the child, I do not see why the child would not develop normally in the first four to five weeks of postnatal life. I understand that this statement might horrify some, but there are no hard facts demonstrating that infants early in life are co-aware, having a particular sense of their presence with others in the world.

Co-awareness, I suggest, starts to be evident only by *six weeks*, when infants show first signs of shared experience in face-to-face interaction via *smiling*, a response that is by this age socially elicited and not simply associated with satiation. There, infants seem to behave and respond in specific, mutual ways to the presence of others. In the reciprocal stance they take toward others, they become in all evidence "co-aware" proper.

Another fact that could be interpreted as evidence of co-awareness in neonates is a phenomenon well known to nurses working in the newborn ward at maternity hospitals. When a newborn begins to cry in his bassinet, typically other infants in other bassinets join the chorus. This contamination phenomenon of crying among newborns is well documented.[7] But does that qualify as "co-awareness" and possibly the basic foundation of "empathy" or the feeling for others?

I do not think so. It probably stands merely for what it is: emotional contagion of the other child inadvertently wakened by the crying room-mate(s). The contagion phenomenon is real and certainly the expression of a basic sensitivity to others that will channel development toward states of co-awareness and even empathy, but at this stage it does not qualify as such. Much development is still needed for co-awareness to emerge. I would assume that at birth the mere recording of other infants' cries or any kind of comparably persistent high-pitch sound would probably trigger the same kind of contamination in the neonate. This assumption, which is still up for experimental grabs and could be easily tested, would disqualify any claim of co-awareness associated with emotional contagion at birth.

---

[7] See the original findings by Simner, M. L. (1971). Newborn's response to the cry of another infant. *Developmental Psychology* 5: 136–150; also the replication of the phenomenon of emotional contagion in newborns by Sagi, A., & Hoffman, M. L. (1976). Empathic distress in the newborn. *Developmental Psychology* 12: 175–176.

TWO-MONTH REVOLUTION

Probably the best way to support my claim of a lack of co-awareness mind state at birth and in the course of the first month following birth is to describe what is happening next, sometimes called the "two-month revolution" (Rochat, 2001). What is happening at approximately six weeks of age is a radical new stance toward the world taken by the infant. At the interpersonal level – and we will have ample opportunity to return to it later in the book – infants begin to manifest socially elicited smiling. This smiling is an unmistakable expression of positive affect in the presence of another individual, either interacting with the child or adopting a calm frontal presentation. It is different from the automatic or so-called reflexive smiles expressed by the neonate during sleep, particularly after feeding.

Newborn smiles are linked to satiety and associated with the engagement of opioid (endorphin) systems for which there are good animal models.[8] Newborn smiling is of a radically different kind compared to the smiling expressed by six weeks in the social context of intimate face-to-face exchanges. By six weeks, evidence of socially elicited smiling indicates for the first time the child is unambiguously *co-aware* of his presence with another. It is the first unambiguous sign of a sense of a socially shared experience, what is labeled in the infancy literature as *primary intersubjectivity*.[9]

Accompanying the emergence of socially elicited smiles and the unambiguous sign of co-awareness (sense of being with others) at around six weeks of age, there is a host of profound changes in the behavioral organization of the infant. Most noticeable is the fact that the child becomes increasingly awake and, when awake, begins to spend significantly more time in an alert and *active* state in comparison to an alert but inactive state.[10]

Immediately after birth and during the four weeks that follow birth, newborns spend the majority of their wakeful time with eyes open. However, they do not seem to pay much attention to what is happening around them. This behavioural state is typically referred to as an alert but *inactive* state of wakefulness. In this state, infants are staring (seeing) but not

---

[8] Barr, G., Paredes, W., Erikson, K. L., & Zukin, S. R. (1986). Opioid receptor–mediated analgesia in the developing rat. *Developmental Brain Research* 29: 145–152.

[9] Trevarthen, C. (1980). The foundations of intersubjectivity: Developments of interpersonal and cooperative understanding in infants. In D. R. Olson, ed., *The Social Foundations of Language and Thought: Essays in Honor of Jerome S. Bruner*, pp. 316–342. New York: W. W. Norton.

[10] Wolff, P. H. (1987). *The Development of Behavioral States and the Expression of Emotions in Early Infancy*. Chicago: University of Chicago Press.

looking, to use a distinction proposed before. For example, although awake and with eyes open, the infant does not show any inclination toward tracking an object slowly moving in front of her eyes. Newborns happen to be often in this inactive wakeful state despite the fact that they are known to be highly sensitive to the movements of objects they see, despite their low visual acuity and rather "fuzzy" vision at birth and in the first weeks of postnatal life. Although research shows that when awake, newborns can discriminate objects as discrete three-dimensional entities, they do not do so systematically. Most of the time they do not pay much attention to objects and do not seem to engage in much learning about them. If their eyes are open they seem to see something rather than look at objects. If they do look at objects – and we know they do – it is rather fleeting as opposed to frequent and systematic.

By six weeks, however, active exploration becomes markedly more common. When in an alert, wakeful state, infants now spend the majority of their time actively tracking and exploring objects. As they stare at the world, they look "at" significantly more than they just see "through." In the social realm, they pay new attention to people in the context of recip-rocal exchanges. From this point on, they also become newly capable of co-awareness.

CONTEMPLATIVE STANCE BY TWO MONTHS

This change in wakeful state marks the emergence of a new mental stance toward the world, the *contemplative stance,* which is the mark of the two-month revolution. I consider this developmental transition as the psychological birth of the child, to contrast it to the biological birth, when the child transits from intra- to extrauterine life (Rochat, 2001). Before six weeks, infants can be described as essentially "stimulus bound," highly dependent and opportunistic in their transactions with the surrounding world. There are no clear signs that they are deliberate in their exploration and orientation toward the resources of their environment. There are no clear signs that newborns are intentionally oriented in Brentano's sense of having a representation of the target of their actions. There are no signs of intentionality in the very young infant. However, conditions change six weeks post partum.

Infants begin to show unambiguous signs that they are actively explor-ing and seeing the consequences of their own action. This is what I call the contemplative stance. It is different from mere operant or instrumental conditioning that is evident in newborns, even in fetuses. For example, in validated and often replicated studies, a few hours after birth infants turn their head in anticipation of an interesting spectacle: a voice from a loudspeaker placed to the side or a rewarding outcome such as the delivery of sweet food. However, this kind of learning does not entail the contemplative or protointentional stance observed by two-month-olds. But how can we show that? Here is an example.

Some time ago, we systematically recorded the oral pressure that infants applied on a "musical" pacifier introduced in their mouth for a few minutes. Each time the infant pressed the rubber nipple above a certain (low) threshold, she heard a perfectly contingent succession of discrete sounds generated by a computer.[11] These sounds, from speakers close to the infant, varied in pitch (more or less high tone). In one condition, each time the infant sucked above threshold, the pitch variation of the sound was commensurate to the pressure variation the infant applied on the pacifier with her mouth. In other words, the infant experienced an auditory *analog* of the oral pressure applied on the pacifier. In a different condition, passed in succession and in a counterbalanced order, each time the infant sucked above threshold, she heard a succession of sounds with a pitch that varied randomly. In this condition and as before, the infant experienced a contingent sound, but now what she heard was a *nonanalog* of the oral pressure on the pacifier.

We systematically analyzed the oral response of the infant in each condition to establish whether the infant detected any differences between the two. The rationale was that such discrimination would demonstrate that infants are not simply reinforced in their sucking by a contingent sound as in any straightforward operant conditioning experiments, but that infants systematically attend and explore the perceptual consequences of their own action. Stated differently, instead of responding directly by being reinforced by contingent sounds, such discrimination would show that the infant adopted a contemplative stance toward the quality of the contingent sounds. The infant would not merely demonstrate sensitivity to the temporal co-occurrence of the sound (any kind of sound) with sucking. Such discrimination would indicate that infants are like trumpet players who do not simply learn to play by blowing air into their horn but by modulating the airflow to affect the quality of the sounds they produce. And this is exactly what we found with two-month-old infants. They sucked very differently in the analog compared to the nonanalog

---

[11] Rochat, P., & Striano, T. (1999a). Emerging self-exploration by two-month-old infants. *Developmental Science* 2: 206–218.

conditions, demonstrating clear discrimination between the two. By two months, infants appear to explore in systematic ways and to be sensitive to the overall quality and relative matching of the auditory consequences of their own oral action on the pacifier. They demonstrate the adoption of a contemplative stance.

We tried to replicate this experiment with healthy newborn infants, less than forty-eight-hours old, who, like two-month-olds, are perfectly capable of sucking and hearing the range of sounds presented to them. Interestingly, we did not find any evidence of discrimination between the analog and nonanalog auditory conditions with the group of newborns.

This research provides empirical evidence that between birth and two months, infants develop a new contemplative stance in their wakeful exploration of the world, a radically new level of awareness that entails the beginning of some sort of mental decoupling (i.e., the contemplation of what my actions do, hence the dissociation between my actions and their consequences). This early sign of decoupling is a precursor of the metacognitive dimension that eventually will define and is constitutive of consciousness (i.e., the knowledge of knowing; see preceding chapter).

CONFIDENCE, MASTERY, AND TRUST BEYOND TWO MONTHS

The adoption of a contemplative stance by two months is a major step in early development. It is from then on that infants begin to develop expectations and representations about what should happen next. They become less bound to the immediacy of their perceptual experience, the here and now of their sensations. From this developmental departure, infants develop a perspective on what is happening around them, as well as in them, beginning to enjoy what some philosophers like Dennett call "elbow room." But what is happening in this room at such an early age? I propose that it is first and foremost the building of mastery and trust.

By the second month, when viewing a moving object behind an opaque screen, the way infants track such an object with their eyes shows that they are beginning to expect to see this object either present behind the screen once lifted, or reappearing on the other side after traveling in a certain way while out of sight. The infancy literature offers multiple experiments demonstrating that by two months infants expect objects to move and interact in certain ways. For example, there is much evidence that in the mind of the two-month-old, objects exist as substantial entities occupying continuous space.

Other research points to the fact that from this developmental time on, infants become astutely sensitive to regularities in their environment. They begin to expect certain things to happen and others not to happen. They show surprise and apparent dismay when they are not confirmed in their expectations. In some sense, their experience with objects and people begins to form norms of expectation. One could say that between birth and two months the memory of the child develops from mere traces to become normative. It becomes arranged into explicit (in the sense of behaviorally expressed) representations of what should happen next. Infants become more than spectators of what they see, anticipating outcomes and showing budding signs of intentionality in what they do. Here I use the term *intentionality* with caution, in the minimal sense of a differentiation between means and end (e.g., systematically moving one leg in a particular way to kick a mobile and then contemplate its motion).

In support of this interpretation, experiments suggest that infants by two months are probabilistic in their learning. They begin to form expectations about future events based on the quick processing of the successive occurrence over time in terms of conditional probability (if event A occurs, what is the probability that event B will follow?).

For example, after being exposed to episodes of discrete lights flashing at regular intervals (either to the right or to the left of the child, perhaps three flashes to the right followed by one to the left), infants quickly anticipate when the side switch happens, tracking the light with anticipatory eye movements toward the location where the next flash will happen.[12]

More recently, research shows that by eight months, infants learn to parse continuous strings of speech sounds (i.e., phonemes) into words by picking up the relative proximity or succession of these sounds over time.[13] Infants pick up the relative regularities by which one phoneme precedes or follows another. In this remarkable experiment, infants appear to parse the stream of phonemes in terms of the probability of what is going to happen next on the string. This enables them to form larger chunks, which in turn will allow them one day to become linguistically competent. The comprehension and production of speech do indeed entail such parsing: the parsing of successive speech sounds into words, words into sentences, and eventually sentences into narratives.

[12] Haith, M. M., Wass, T. S., & Adler, S. A. (1997). Infant visual expectations: Advances and issues. *Monograph of the Society for Research in Child Development* 62(2): 150–160. Oxford: Blackwell.
[13] Aslin, R. N., Saffran, J. R., & Newport, E. L. (1998). Computation of conditional probability statistics by human infants. *Psychological Science* 9: 321–324.

Infants from two months begin to engage in probabilistic learning of what will happen next by experiencing recurrent events in the environment. From two to three months they begin to expect and anticipate certain visual events to occur depending on certain signaling conditions. In relation to language, by at least eight months infants manage to detect the high probability of one particular phoneme that immediately follows another, detecting a meaningful link between the two. With probabilistic learning (also called statistical learning), infants do transcend the here and now of perception to form what will become concepts or explicit representations.

In short, starting by the second month, infants begin to have perspective and a budding mental distancing in their experience of the world, projecting and connecting forward and backward in time, transcending the here and now of perception and action. By adopting a contemplative stance they become more exploratory in their transactions with the environment, more proactive and less stimulus bound.

The progress represented by the adoption of a contemplative stance entails prediction and anticipation, but also room for major affective development: the development of confidence, trust, and a sense of mastery. All of these psychological pieces emerge from an ability and inclination to predict. By definition, predicting is like betting. One takes relative risks depending on degrees of confidence. Confidence, on the other hand, is directly connected to how one masters a particular situation and how one trusts his or her judgment in making the prediction.

As infants become less stimulus bound and more contemplative by two months, they also become increasingly evaluative in their perception of objects, people, and themselves. They begin to expect some events or things over others; their perceptions become increasingly normative. This development opens new avenues for long-term changes, including the development of self-consciousness, which is by definition a deeply evaluative phenomenon.

In summary, way upstream in development, consciousness finds its source in the early evaluative and comparative abilities infants manifest starting at two months when they begin to adopt a contemplative stance toward the world. To become the self-conscious individuals we are, this stance is eventually turned toward the self in reference to others. But this new orientation requires much further development.

BIRTH OF CONSCIOUSNESS

In the preceding chapter, I discussed consciousness as metacognitive: the knowledge of knowledge and the knowledge of knowing. In the Cartesian tradition, consciousness corresponds to an introspective process, a self-reflective loop that deals with mental objects that are represented. Stated differently and following the vocabulary I have proposed, consciousness entails an objectification or the contemplation of something that becomes the object of thoughts. When I wake up from deep sleep, to take the example I used, I transit from a first state of awareness by which I experience being alive and not sleeping. This happens when I first snap out of sleep and wake up. I become more than aware, namely, conscious, from the moment that, looking at the alarm clock, I realize that I am late for my appointment.

The attention to the time displayed on the clock and the set of representations following this target of attention *objectify* my situation in space and time. My situation becomes an object of contemplation, and, once again, I become conscious as opposed to merely aware.

When infants begin to show signs of taking a contemplative stance (by two months), do they qualify as becoming conscious? This is a thorny question. With adults, such determination is much more simple because of language and all the explicit propositional formulations that are possible regarding the state of knowing to know. But what about the nonverbal infants who cannot talk but who nevertheless show some explicitness in the way they learn, explore, and expect certain things to happen? Does that qualify for consciousness in the sense we understand it here? Do infants at this stage know of knowing things that are *objects* of mental reflection?

My view is that by taking a contemplative stance, infants assemble the necessary ingredients required by consciousness: they become less stimulus bound, manifest elbow room for reflection and exploration, and clearly expect particular outcomes they have somehow stored as representations. All these necessary ingredients come on line by at least two months. Yet they are not sufficient. They are not sufficient to make infants at this early stage *conscious* per se, at least not in the sense of my looking at my alarm clock and objectifying my situation in time and space eventually to recognize that I am late. This takes further development.

So, if they are not conscious per se, what is on the mind of two-month-olds as they explore, learn, and expect things to happen? Do they become "meta" by taking their first contemplative stance toward the world?

When young infants first become contemplative and less stimulus bound, they have little to no control over it. They are still very much opportunistic, and not yet deliberate as to what should be the focus of their contemplation. The "elbow room" of decision is still too narrow to give the infant the distance required for consciousness proper. I am now walking on thin ice, aware of how complex and difficult the question is.

The empirical research I used to illustrate the two-month revolution, in particular the sucking study in which we recorded infants sucking for sounds they produced that were either analog or nonanalog in pitch variation, shows that they are attentive to the auditory consequences of their own oral action. Infants appear, by then and not prior since we could not replicate the findings with newborns, contemplative and discriminating of such self-produced auditory consequences. But the interpretation stops there.

There is no claim that infants, in paying attention to their own sound production and by exploring the oral-auditory loop of what they do with the pacifier are actually objectifying or identifying themselves as the agents of such a loop, that they are *conscious* of causing the various sounds.

Likewise, when infants are building expectations and learning to chunk streams of arbitrary speech sounds on the basis of conditional probability, it is not reasonable to claim that what they do is objectified in their mind, in other words, that they are *conscious* of what they do. Rather, we could say that they have the new propensity to engage in this kind of learning and exploration; that both entail some *decoupling* with the here and now of perceptual experience. It is this new propensity that opens the way toward consciousness proper.

In the sucking for sound experiments or the parsing of speech sound stream, it is thus doubtful that the infants already know they are producing the sounds or that they are learning to parse the sound stream. No "explicit" first-person perspective is necessary to manifest such discrimination and learning. As we will see, one has to wait until the end of the first year to see clear signs of emerging consciousness proper.

So, when and how can we say that consciousness, the knowledge that one knows, emerges beyond the two-month revolution? When can we say that children are more than aware of things around them, that they can objectify these things as representations, that they can manipulate these representations mentally, knowing that they can refer to real things and events in the world? In short, when do children demonstrate that they know of knowing?

These are among the most difficult and perennial questions in developmental psychology. According to the definition, it is when children objectify their experience as re-presentations. As construed here, consciousness entails a self-reflective loop and an introspective process dealing with objects that are literally "re-presented" or "thought of," somehow

reenacted in the theater of the mind beyond the here and now of perception. Only then experience becomes conscious, not just an awareness.

As infants take a contemplative stance toward the world, they are
not at once conscious of knowing that they know, at least not explicitly,
not at a communicable level. If there is budding evidence of a self-reflective
loop, it is only at a very basic *implicit* perceptual level, not at an explicit,
higher-order cognitive level. As a matter of fact, there is evidence in the
literature of very basic metacognitive abilities in implicit decision making
and problem solving even in monkeys.[14] It is thus necessary to distinguish
levels of metacognition (levels of knowledge of knowing) that are more or
less explicit and that involve different levels of cognitive engagement.[15]

At two months, with the adoption of the contemplative stance, infants
clearly begin to show first rudimentary signs of metacognitive abilities.
However, we are months away from when children understand at an
explicit level that they know; that they are conscious of knowing.

Evidence of higher-order explicit consciousness can only be revealed
in the context of intentional communication with others. It is only in
relation to others that young children begin to reveal that they know of
knowing. If not to communicate with others, why should a child become
explicit about his or her conscious mind state? We will see that infants
typically start to communicate with intentions and become explicit about
their conscious mind state by the second half of the first year with the
emergence of secondary intersubjectivity (i.e., social referencing, joint
attention, and intentional communicative gestures).

From a more dynamic or motivational ("intrapsychological") point of
view, I propose that infants are *emotionally pushed* toward the explicit
revelation that they know of knowing. My intuition is that they are pushed
toward metacognition about the self and constrained toward consciousness, primarily because they have to deal with the basic anxiety of being
separated from their mother.

In concrete terms, basic separation anxiety accompanies progress in
autonomous locomotion and young children's autonomous ways of
exploring the world, away from the secure base of the mother. This anxiety
is the trade-off of such motor progress. At this critical juncture of development (eight to nine months), the child has to find balance between the

---

[14] Smith, D., Shields, W. E., & Washburn, D. A. (2003). The comparative psychology
of uncertainty monitoring and metacognition. *Behavioral and Brain Sciences* 26: 317–373.

[15] Proust, J. (2007). Metacognition and metarepresentation: Is a self-directed theory of
mind a precondition for metacognition? *Synthese* 159: 271–295.

comfort of symbiosis and the need for seeking novelty away from the primal comfort zone of the mother. This is an eternal and universal existential dilemma that we carry all through the lifetime, a dilemma that is acutely expressed for the first time at around eight months of age.

Up to about eight months, infants typically do not mind being picked up and interacting with strangers, people they do not know. Starting around eight months, however, infants begin to show marked distress and expressions of shyness and overall behavioral inhibition in contact with strangers. Often they cry and start desperately searching for another, known individual, typically the mother, for comfort and proximity. This is a robust phenomenon that transcends culture and the particular family situation of the infant.

By eight months, stranger and separation anxieties thus appear to be a universal landmark in development, not unlike the emergence of social smiling by the second month after birth. Infants respond and resolve first stranger and separation anxieties in various ways that some view as stable markers of personality traits over the life span. These anxieties are particularly interesting in relation to the question of the origins of consciousness.

Following Bowlby's pioneer theoretical approach,[16] the expression of stranger and separation anxieties indicates that infants have achieved the construction of a working model of their mother or the primary caretaker with whom they have developed comfort, trust, and a complex safety network. This representation is primary and a cornerstone in the mental life of the child. According to Bowlby, the working model of the mother derives from an instinctive drive toward attachment that humans inherited from mammalian evolution. Note that Bowlby's idea is based on ethological and comparative works of the 1950s and 1960s, particularly the seminal work of Harry Harlow demonstrating a basic instinct toward attachment in young animals, particularly infant rhesus monkeys, an instinct that is shown to be independent of basic survival needs such as feeding.[17] At the time, Bowlby's ideas were controversial, flying in the face of basic Freudian assumptions on the primary role of physiological rather than attachment needs early in life.

The distress and uneasiness infants generally manifest in the presence of strangers indicate that they compare these new people to what they represent as familiar. The new people facing the child are not simply

---

[16] Bowlby, J. (1969/1982). *Attachment and Loss*. New York: Basic Books.
[17] Harlow, H. F. (1958). The nature of love. *American Psychologist* 13: 673–685.

triggering automatic fear responses toward the unfamiliar in the same way that the vision of a charging grizzly bear makes us run away. They trigger an anxiety about separation from the mother. They remind them that they are away from their secure base. In expressing anxiety, children demonstrate that they objectify their own situation in the world as being away from their mother. They show signs that they are explicitly conscious of their separation from her. How to justify such rich interpretation? Simply by the fact that prior to eight months, children typically do not show any clear signs of stranger anxiety. Therefore, the developmental transition and the robust emergence of such a phenomenon by eight months call for the involvement of higher mental processes in the child, processes that are conscious.

The fact that stranger anxiety is among the earliest explicit signs of consciousness proper is not surprising. It entails a strong emotional content for young children, therefore a high degree of motivation to develop a new perspective in the contemplation of the situation they are in. Developmental breakthroughs and major ontogenetic progresses have to be connected with high emotional content. This high-strung emotional content would provide the necessary motivational boost for developmental breakthroughs. By analogy to adult life, most people would concur that progress and major breakthroughs in our lives are associated with highly charged emotional dramas and situations, including separation, whether imposed or chosen. The same applies to child development, in particular the origins of self-consciousness. Behind self-consciousness, there is indeed a deep, emotionally loaded fear of separation, the fear of losing proximity with significant and securing others.

BIRTH OF CO-CONSCIOUSNESS

The time infants typically begin to manifest separation and stranger anxieties (eight to nine months) is also the time of marked progress in other developmental domains, particularly the motor domain, which is of special interest. By eight months, as infants show explicit attachment and stranger anxiety, they also gain great postural freedom to roam around the world, typically starting to crawl and to engage in self-propelled locomotion. This coincidence is not fortuitous, and I think it is quite significant.

On one hand, the child is developing attachment and clear discrimination among people, whether they dispense comfort and intimacy or, on the contrary, are a threat. This clear discrimination leads the child to search for and maintain proximity with those who fit their working model of comfort and intimacy. On the other hand, the child is developing new postural means, methods of self-propelled locomotion, to allow him to become increasingly independent to explore the environment alone and away from close physical contacts with the mother or any other secure figures.

There is a fundamental tension between the drive to roam and the drive to maintain closeness and proximity that arises at this juncture of development. This juncture is particularly crucial. It marks the emergence of an existential dilemma that the child will carry all through life, particularly if growing up in the context of a Western lifestyle: the dilemma of achieving individual goals that entail exploration and risk taking while maintaining proximity with those providing comfort and intimacy. Such maintenance is fundamentally antagonistic to the enticement of exploring and taking risks.

Infants are constrained to resolve this dilemma, and they do so mainly by trying to include others in their irresistible foray into the object world.[18] They learn to share, and particularly to share attention with others. They are constrained to do so. If they roam away from the mother, they will turn around to check not only whether she is still there, but also whether she is with them at the level of her attention. Infants begin to manifest so-called joint attention, checking back and forth between the object of exploration and the gaze of the mother or anybody close to them. The emergence of shared attention corresponds to what some describe as the "nine-month revolution,"[19] marking the development of secondary intersubjectivity.[20]

From nine months of age, the child begins to share attention with others *about* objects in the world (secondary intersubjectivity), not only in emotional, face-to-face exchanges (primary intersubjectivity). A new attention triangle is formed among the child, others, and the object of exploration that becomes a topic of communication.[21]

---

[18] Rochat, P. (2001a).

[19] Tomasello, M. (1995). Joint attention as social cognition. In C. J. Moore & P. Dunham, eds., *Joint Attention: Its Origins and Role in Development*, 103–130. Hillsdale, NJ: Lawrence Erlbaum Associates.

[20] Trevarthen, C., & Hubley, P. (1978). Secondary intersubjectivity: Confidence, confiding and acts of meaning in the first year. In A. Lock, ed., *Action, Gesture and Symbol*, 183–239. New York: Academic Press.

[21] See Bruner, J. (1983). *Child's Talk*. New York: W. W. Norton, and *Acts of Meaning*. Cambridge, MA: Harvard University Press, for clear and in-depth discussion of what emerges with the development of joint engagement.

At this juncture, children become, for the first time, *referential* in their interaction with others. This new triangulation, like the navigational triangulation sailors use to objectify their situation on the ocean, is the source of further objectification for the infant, hence further consolidation of consciousness as defined here. It is also the origin of the *co-consciousness* that develops beyond nine months, and particularly starting at the middle of the second year, as we will see.

In trying to incorporate and monitor the attention of others while exploring the world around them, infants get their first active entry into the mind of others. More importantly, they get their first entry into the mind of others *in relation to them*, as much as in relation to the object they are jointly attending to.

When infants begin to check back and forth between the object of interest and another person, they monitor whether the other person is also attending to the object, but they also check whether the person is attending to *them* as they explore the object. In other words, the motive behind infants' budding joint attention is not only communicative, but also *selfreferencing*. The self-referencing aspect of joint attention is probably even primary in the context of the dilemma of proximity maintenance, the need to explore, and the emergence of separation anxiety.

In checking back and forth whether someone else is engaged jointly with them, infants begin also to check for their own existence in the mind of others. This process parallels the referential act of joint attention that is accounted for in the literature. I see here the birth of co-consciousness. It is the first sign that infants begin not only to know that they know, objectifying their own knowledge and representations as we have seen before in relation to consciousness, but also that *they know that they share knowledge with others*.

While engaging in joint attention, (see Fig. 6, p. 161, for an illustration) infants become for the first time not only explicitly conscious of the object they are attending to, but also explicitly co-conscious of this object. In other words, they show explicit understanding that they are not alone in their knowledge of the object, that there is the possibility of shared knowledge and values. Explicit co-consciousness gives infants new means of assessing how people relate to them, whether they are more or less willing to share. This is obviously a crucial social tool for the child, a tool that is related to the emergence of self-consciousness since it is evaluative of the self in relation to others. This is evident when infants begin to be insistent by gesturing and showing initiatives to share and engage others' attention in what they do. The relative response of the others is a good gauging of how they relate to the child. Children appear frequently to provoke such gauging, assessing their social situation, in the same way that we are constantly doing it as adults in our relationships, particularly with intimate others. We find signs of such initiatives from seven months of age.

Here is an example. In one study,[22] we analyzed seven- to nine-month-old infants, as they begin to show joint attention, in a situation where they faced a friendly adult experimenter who surreptitiously interrupted her interaction with the child to adopt a still face. We observed that by seven months of age, rather than looking away and manifesting negative affects, infants try actively to reengage the experimenter. They work at capturing her attention via deliberate gestures such as clapping and poking at her. In comparison to younger infants, they show a new initiative in trying to change actively the social mirror provided by others. At younger ages, infants are mainly avoidant and distressed in such still face circumstances. By seven to nine months, infants work at actively gesturing and presenting themselves in a way that would transform the experience of the other from frozen to becoming friendly again.

The behavioral changes emerging at around nine months (both in terms of stranger and separation anxieties and in terms of the emergence of secondary intersubjectivity via joint attention) mark a new step taken by infants toward their contemplation of the world and in particular the way they construe others.

By nine months, when you hand the infant an attractive toy and as he reaches for it you suddenly retrieve the toy out of his reach, the infant will begin to look up toward your face presumably to check what you are up to and disambiguate the situation. The infant begins to detect in such behavior a violation of what was intended in your original gesture. In gazing toward you, the child is wondering what is going on in your mind that might transpire on your face with a particular expression: smile if it is playful, neutral face if it is more on the vicious side.

We made the same kind of observations with infants who by nine months tend to look up to an experimenter facing them to disambiguate a situation when a mechanical toy suddenly starts to bark and move about close to the child. Interestingly, by this age infants

---

[22] Striano, T., & Rochat, P. (1999). Developmental link between dyadic and triadic social competence in infancy. *British Journal of Developmental Psychology* 17(4): 551–562.

FIGURE 3. True intentional imitation. An 18-month-old child from the island of Upolu in Samoa imitates the exact gestural means by which an adult model (top panel) turns on a battery-operated push-on light by bending forward and pressing on its switch with his forehead. Consequently, the child (bottom panel) shows no hesitation in reproducing the same awkward gesture to produce the desired effect of turning the light on. By this behavior, the child demonstrates an attunement not only to what things are produced by others, but to how they are produced. This is an index of newly emerging identification with others and an ability to project oneself into their shoes.

---

tend to refer significantly less toward the experimenter if she is not attentive, absorbed in reading a book in front of the child, oblivious of the barking toy, as if nothing happened.[23] This observation suggests that the infant chooses to refer socially when the other is attentive and engaged, factoring whether she is sharing engagement in the situation or not.

From such empirical evidence, we conclude that infants already by seven months begin to understand what others' intended looking means, as opposed to distraction or absentmindedness. These kinds of observations suggest first rudiments of mind reading in the young children. They begin to behave as if they know that they share or do not share knowledge with others. It is the first sign of co-consciousness as defined here.

Beyond nine months, and certainly by at least fourteen months, infants show clear signs of construing others as intentional, behaving with plans and representations in mind. By fourteen months, multiple experiments demonstrate that children begin to imitate, not only to emulate the result of an action performed by others, but to reproduce their plans, namely, the way they decided to do an action, whether economical or not. There is clear evidence of children taking the perspective of others, projecting and identifying with others. As shown in Figure 3, if an adult presses a push-on switch to turn on a light by bending forward to hit the switch with his or her forehead, a rather cumbersome way of doing it, the child will do the same.[24]

---

[23] Striano, T., & Rochat, P. (2000). Emergence of selective social referencing. *Infancy* 1(2): 253–264.
[24] See the original experiment by Andrew Meltzoff (1995). Understanding the intentions of others: Re-enactment of intended acts by eighteen-month-old children. *Developmental Psychology* 31(5): 838–850.

By at least fourteen months, children are explicitly attuned to the intentions or rational action[25] plans of an adult, even though it would be much more economical simply to press the push-on light switch by using one hand, an action the child would be perfectly capable of performing.

In social interaction, there comes a point in development when children manage to transcend the surface reading of others' behavior, starting to read the mental design behind gazes or other public expressions and behaviors. They begin to construe the behavior of others as standing for mental states: whether, for example, others' behaviors are intentional or accidental, oriented toward them or not.

More importantly, by their first birthday, children become attuned to others' behaviors in terms of whether or not they reflect knowledge sharing about a particular situation or event in the environment. This is the beginning of a co-construction of knowledge and representations by which the young child enters the world of co-consciousness.

Starting at nine months and increasingly by the middle of the first year, children begin to show active comparison between what they hold as representation of a particular aspect of the world and what others hold as representation of the same aspect of the world. In the context of this book dealing with self-consciousness, we will see in the next chapter how this comparison is turned toward the self.

Most significant is the fact that by their first birthday, children start to utter their first words, words that are quickly followed by a noticeable period of vocabulary explosion at around eighteen to twenty-four months.

Language comprehension and production entail shared knowledge of knowing, in other words, explicit co-consciousness. In learning to talk and to comprehend language, children do not only learn to communicate with signs and gestures as other animals do. More profoundly, they learn to share the concepts that underlie the meaning of each word. For example, when children learn the word *tree*, they quickly understand that it stands for the class of bushy, branchy, leafy, vegetable things with large trunks existing out there in the world, and nothing else (mutual exclusivity principle) – not for color, texture, or the fruits it might bear. The word *tree* only stands for a class of the same thing, despite great variations in the make of its members.

---

[25] Gergely, G., Bekkering, H., & Király, I. (2002). Rational imitation in preverbal infants. *Nature* 415: 755.

In short, learning to talk and to comprehend language rests on the construction of a conceptual knowledge that is shared with others. Developing linguistic competence is a clear indication that the child is born to co-consciousness. In development, co-consciousness finds its roots when infants begin to construe others as intentional, hence as holding representations that guide their behaviors, representations that can be compared and shared. Beyond imitation, joint attention, and social referencing, hence beyond the nine-month social-cognitive revolution, co-consciousness blossoms with language development.

5

Birth of Self-Consciousness

The self has always been an elusive, difficult, and still highly controversial concept in the realm of both philosophy and psychology. It continues to be elusive in the context of the new wave of cognitive neurosciences. In this chapter, I would like to discuss this concept from a developmental perspective, in particular in light of new research on the self in infancy. This research is irreplaceable in discussing the self in relation to the various states of mind I reviewed earlier, in particular in relation to consciousness and co-consciousness.

Developmental facts point to the basic ingredients of self-knowledge as it unfolds in the course of early ontogeny. Developmental research provides empirical ground and is a privileged terrain of reflection on what it takes to be self-conscious, the psychological implications of self-consciousness, which are of interest here.

When do children have a sense of themselves as a differentiated and unique entity in the world? When and how do they become self-conscious and co-conscious of themselves in relation to others? In response to these questions, it is judicious to discern various levels of self-knowledge as they appear to unfold chronologically from the moment of birth to approximately four to five years of age. The focus here is on this emergence as a way of deconstructing the meaning of human self-consciousness.

The developmental approach allows us to observe how basic competencies emerge and come online. By analogy, it is comparable to observing the construction of a skyscraper via daily photographs taken during the process showing what it took to get to the final product. I have in mind an old postcard depicting the Eiffel Tower in the various phases of

Ideas in this chapter were originally outlined in Rochat, P. (2003). Five levels of self-awareness as they unfold early in life. *Consciousness and Cognition* 12(4): 717–731.

its construction and revealing what it is made of in the sequence of its construction.

In developmental psychology, such a construction process can be observed over and over again. Children repeat patterns of growth that prefigure what is intrinsic to the life of grown-ups, such as self-consciousness. What does it mean and what does it take to recognize oneself in a mirror? Children provide crucial elements of response in their development.

We will see that prior to the expression of explicit signs of self-consciousness, such as self-recognition and self-identification in a mirror or in a photograph, infants from birth manifest an implicit sense of themselves. The questions of interest here are, What are the contrasted levels of self-knowledge unfolding in early development? and What does this development tell us about the nature of self-consciousness in general?

SELF-CONSCIOUS EMOTIONS IN DEVELOPMENT

There is a general consensus on a few major landmarks in young children's psychological development such as the manifestation of the first social smile, the first independent steps, or the first words. All parents also notice an important change at around two years of age when children manifest "self-consciousness," the so-called secondary emotions such as embarrassment or pride in very specific situations such as mirror exposure or competitive games.[1]

Prior to the second year, an infant placed in front of a mirror will typically smile, coo, and explore in apparent delight at the perfect contingency between acted and seen movements bouncing back at him or her from the polished surface of the mirror. By two years, the specular image is associated with radically different behaviors. Toddlers become typically frozen and sometimes behave as if they want to hide themselves by tucking their head in their shoulders or hiding their face behind their hands. They show embarrassment.[2] This is a robust phenomenon and one is naturally tempted to ask what it means psychologically for children in their development. The following literary quotation captures this important transition:

> There is a thing that happens with children: If no one is watching them, nothing is really happening to them. It is not some philosophical

---

[1] See Lewis, M. (1992). *Shame: The Exposed Self.* New York: Free Press; also Kagan, J. (1984). *The Nature of the Child.* New York: Basic Books.

[2] See Lewis, M., & Brooks-Gunn, J. (1979). *Social Cognition and the Acquisition of Self.* New York: Plenum Press.

conundrum like the one about the tree falling in the forest and no one
hearing it: that is a puzzler for college freshman. No. If you are very
small, you actually understand that there is no point in jumping into the
swimming pool unless they see you do it. The child crying, "Watch me,
watch me," is not begging for attention; he is pleading for existence
itself. M. R. Montgomery, *Saying Goodbye: A Memoir for Two Fathers*[3]

The poet Arthur Rimbaud claimed that "I is someone Else" (Je est un
autre), suggesting that we experience ourselves as another; oneself through
the eyes of anotherself. It appears indeed that by two to three years young
children do start to have *others in mind* when they behave. The expression
of embarrassment that children often begin to display in front of mirrors
at around this age is the expression of such "self-consciousness." Their
behavior is not unlike that of criminals hiding their face from the cameras.
Their behavior indicates a drive to vanish from the public eye, as they
come to realize via the experience of their own specular image how they
present themselves to the world. Not only do they discover in the mirror
that it is they; they also realize that it is they as *perceived by others*. The
malaise might result from the realization of a fundamental discrepancy
between how the child represents himself or herself from within, and how
he or she is actually perceived by others as reflected in the mirror. Note,
once again, that this interpretation is consistent with what the visual
anthropologist Edmund Carpenter reported in adults of an isolated Papua
New Guinea tribe (the Biamis) confronted for the first time with their
own clear facial reflection (see section entitled "Fascination and Terror of
Self-Recognition" in Chapter 1).

Remember that the Biamis of New Guinea presumably did not have any
mirror experience and the rivers in the Papuan plateau are typically too
murky to provide clear reflections, unlike the rivers of ancient Greece
enjoyed by Narcissus. Carpenter and colleagues recorded their reactions
when they looked at themselves in a mirror for the first time and viewed
themselves in video recordings or in Polaroid photographs. They reported
generalized reactions of terror and anguish.

If children begin to have "others in mind" by the age of two or three
years, how does this self-consciousness come about? I will suggest that
there are at least six steps to this progression, each corresponding to a
different level of self-awareness. I will first describe these six levels of self-
awareness in terms of various reactions to the mirror that I will use as

[3] Montgomery, M. R. (1989). *Saying Goodbye: A Memoir for Two Fathers*. New York:
Random House.

illustrations. In a second part, I provide some empirical evidence of how these levels of self-awareness unfold chronologically between birth and early childhood.

What do children see when they see themselves in a mirror? Do they see that it is they or do they perceive someone else facing them? When do mirrors and their reflection begin to be considered as what they are, namely, a solid polished surface that reflects? We can surreptitiously place a yellow Post-It paper on a child's forehead, as shown in the photograph. We then play with him to confirm that the child is oblivious that his forehead is now holding such a yellow mark. If we now place the child in front of a mirror, what does he see and what is he inclined to do? There are six possibilities, ranging from self-obliviousness to self-consciousness, each corresponding to a particular level of self-awareness. I describe these levels in the order of their relative complexity.

Level 0: Confusion

This is the degree zero of self-knowledge, the level at which the individual is oblivious of any mirror reflection, thus oblivious of the mirror itself. The specular image is confounded with the reality of the environment it reflects. It is perceived as a mere extension of the world, not a reflection of it. Birds flying into mirrors would exemplify this level, as they sometimes accidentally crash into windows. They mistakenly perceive mirrors as an extension of the environment, not as differentiated objects. Pet owners know that placing a mirror in a canary cage is a substitute for companionship and triggers in the bird a melodious courtship song. It is also the level expressed by dogs, cats, or monkeys facing mirrors and posturing endless aggressive displays to their own specular image as if they were confronting a creature other than they.

Level 1: Differentiation

This is the first sign that the individual is not oblivious of mirrors as a tool for reflection. At this level, there is a sense that what is perceived in the mirror is different from what is perceived in the surrounding environment. More specifically, when perceiving their own specular image, individuals pick up the fact that there is something unique about the experience, namely, that there is a perfect contingency between seen and felt movements. Beyond the confusion of the preceding level, this level entails some basic perceptual differentiation, differentiation between the experience of own bodily movements as reflected in the mirror and the direct experience of other moving entities in the world. This is a first level of self-world differentiation: a differentiated self is expressed.

Level 2: Situation

Beyond the differentiation of the uniqueness of self-produced movements seen on the surface of the mirror, the individual now is capable of systematically exploring the intermodal link between seen movements on the mirror surface and what is perceived of the own body proprioceptively. In other words, individuals now go beyond the awareness of matched surface characteristics of seen and felt movements. They also explore how the experience of their own body relates to the specular image, an image that is out there, projecting back at them what they feel from within. As compared to the preceding level, this can be viewed as first signs of a contemplative stance toward the specular image, a sort of *protonarcissistic* stage guided by self-exploration on a projected surface. At this level, there is no confusion. The individual is aware that what is seen on the mirror is unique to the self. In addition, the individual is also aware that what is seen is "out there," on a surface that is spatially situated in relation to the body: a situated self is expressed.

Level 3: Identification

At this level, the individual manifests recognition, the fact that what is in the mirror is "Me," not another individual staring at and shadowing the self. There is more than differentiation and situation of self in relation to the specular image. This level is expressed when children refer explicitly to the self while exploring their own specular image. As illustrated in Figure 4, in the case of the Post-It sticker surreptitiously placed on the

---

FIGURE 4. Mirror self-recognition. A Samoan child discovers in the mirror that a Post-It sticker was surreptitiously put on his forehead (top panel). Looking at himself in the mirror, within seconds, he reaches toward his head to touch and eventually remove the Post-It. This is considered by many as the "acid test" of self-concept, the demonstration that the child knows it is he in the mirror, nobody else.

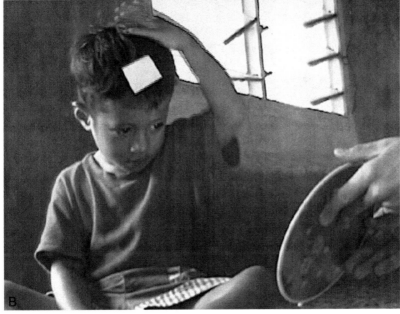

child's forehead prior to mirror exposure, the child discovers it in the mirror and reaches for it for touch or removal. This behavior is considered by developmental psychologists as the index of an emerging conceptual self[4] but also as a major cognitive landmark by evolutionary psychologists.[5,6] At this level, the individual is capable of referring the specular image to the own body, the latter being the referent of what is seen in the mirror. There is an identity relation between the self as experienced from within and what is displayed on the polished surface of the mirror: an identified self is expressed.

Level 4: Permanence

The self is identified beyond the here and now of mirror experience. It can be identified in pictures and movies taken in the past, where the self might be significantly younger, at a different location, and dressed in different clothes. In other words, the identification of the self is not tied to the temporal simultaneity and spatial coincidence of the body and its reflection, whether in live videos or specular images. The individual manifests a sense of self that persists beyond the immediacy of mirror experience. A permanent self is expressed: an entity that is represented as invariant over time and appearance changes.

Level 5: Self-Consciousness or "Meta" Self-Knowledge

The self is now recognized not only from a first-person perspective, but also from a third person's. Individuals are not only aware of what they are but of *how* they are in the mind of others: how they present themselves to the public eye.[7] The public outlook on the self is simulated for further evaluation of how one is perceived and valued by others. The result of this evaluation, more often than not, is either a devaluation or a delusion, linked to so-called self-conscious emotions or attitudes such as pride or shame. A self-conscious self is expressed: an entity that is simulated and projected in the mind of others.

---

[4] See Lewis & Brooks-Gunn. (1979).
[5] See Gallup, G. G., Jr. (1982). Self-awareness and the emergence of mind in primates. *American Journal of Primatology* 2: 237–248.
[6] Parker, S. T., Mitchell R. W., & Boccia, M. L. (1994). *Self-Awareness in Animals and Humans*. Cambridge, MA: Cambridge University Press.
[7] See Goffman, E. (1959).

SELF-WORLD DIFFERENTIATION AT BIRTH

Recent empirical findings suggest that infants do not enter the world with the exclusive expression of self-obliviousness corresponding to *Level 0*, the degree zero of self-awareness as described earlier. It appears that immediately after birth, infants already demonstrate a sense of their own body as a differentiated entity: an entity among other entities in the environment (*Level 1*). This is evident, for example, when observing the rooting response of newborns and what triggers it. When one touches the cheek of newborns, they tend to orient their head toward the touch stimulation. This response is highly predictable and part of the routine neurobehavioral assessment of neonates.

In a study, we compared such a response in twenty-four-hour-old infants following either a tactile stimulation originating from the index finger of the experimenter or from self-stimulation, as infants spontaneously placed one of their hands in contact with a cheek. Systematic comparison shows that neonates do root significantly more to external compared to self-stimulation.[8] From birth, infants differentiate between self- and nonself touch, between stimulation originating from either the own body or an external source. Contrary to the assumption of many classic theories of child development, infants are not born in a state of fusion or confusion with the environment (the "booming, buzzing, confusion" proposed by William James). They do show some rudiments of self-world differentiation. What might be the origins of such innate capacity? The answer is that from birth and possibly even prior, there are distinct perceptual experiences that are *uniquely specifying* the own body as opposed to the experience of other entities in the world.

When infants experience their own crying, their own touch, or the perfect contingency between seen and felt bodily movements (e.g., the arm crossing the field of view), they perceive something that no one but they can perceive. There is an authority of first-person perspective for this unique category of perceptual experiences. The transport of their own hand to their face, very frequent at birth and even during the last trimester of pregnancy, is a unique tactile experience, unlike any other tactile experience as it entails a "double touch": the hand touching the face and simultaneously the face touching the hand. The same is true for the auditory experience of the own crying or the visual-proprioceptive experience accompanying self-produced movements. These basic perceptual (i.e.,

---

[8] Rochat, P. & Hespos, S. J. (1997). Differential rooting response by neonates: Evidence of an early sense of self. *Early Development and Parenting* 6(3–4): 105–112.

multimodal) experiences are indeed self-specifying, unlike any other perception experienced by the infant from birth and even prior to birth in the
confines, of the maternal womb.

Young infants appear to pick up the invariant information that specifies
the own body as a differentiated entity, an entity that is experienced differently from other physical bodies or objects that are *out there* in the environment. Aside from our own research, there is an abundance of
experimental studies with newborns and very young infants that suggest
the existence of early self-world differentiation.[9]

SITUATED SELF FROM TWO MONTHS OF AGE

By the end of the second month, infants show clear signs that in addition
to self-world differentiation, they have a sense of how their own body is
situated in relation to other entities in the environment (*Level 2*).

If infants from birth show a propensity to imitate facial expressions such
as tongue protrusion[10] or basic emotions such as joy or sadness,[11] by the
second month they demonstrate systematic matching that denotes a novel
sense of how they relate to the model they imitate. In a one experiment[12]
researchers showed, for example, that six-week-olds tend to copy systematically the orientation of the tongue protrusion of an adult model pulling
her tongue either to the right or to the left, as opposed to midline. This
imitative response of the infants indicates that not only do they reproduce
the global tongue protrusion act, something they are capable of from birth,
they also approximate the directionality of the modeled tongue movements.
This entails that in addition to differentiating their own actions from those
of the model, they are capable of mapping their own bodily space to the
bodily space of the model. With this sophisticated imitative behavior,
infants appear not only to differentiate themselves but also to situate themselves in relation to the perceived model. What is particularly striking in
the observations reported is the fact that by the second month infants
are actively approximating the tongue orientation of the model, engaged

---

[9] See multiple chapters in the edited volume by Rochat, P. (1995). *The Self in Infancy:
Theory and Research.* Amsterdam: North-Holland/Elsevier.

[10] Meltzoff, A. N., & Moore, M. K. (1977). Imitation of facial and manual gestures. *Science*
198(4312): 75–78.

[11] Field, T. M., et al. (1982). Discrimination and imitation of facial expressions by neonates.
Science 218(4568): 179–181.

[12] Meltzoff, A. N., & Moore, M. K. (1992). Early imitation within a functional framework:
The importance of person identity, movement, and development. *Infant Behavior and
Development* 15: 479–505.

in active exploration until they map the target action. On the basis of microanalyses of the videotapes, infants typically start to pull their tongue at midline, slowly and with apparent effort moving it to the side while staring at the model. This active exploration is an index of both differentiation and situation of the infant in relation to the adult model facing her.

In a related perception-action study that I discussed in the preceding chapter, we find that by the second month, infants become actively involved in exploring and contemplating the auditory consequences of their own sucking actions.[13] As a reminder, we recorded young infants' oral activity while introduced to a pacifier connected to a sound producing device. Each time the infants applied oral pressure on the pacifier above a low threshold, they heard a perfectly contingent succession of discrete sounds with a particular pitch variation. In one condition, the pitch variation was an analog of the oral pressure applied on the pacifier, with an ascending and descending pitch variation mapping the increase and decrease of oral pressure. In another condition, the pitch variation was a nonanalog of the oral pressure, varying randomly. We found that the infants' oral activity on the pacifier was markedly different in the analog and nonanalog conditions. When trying to replicate these findings with a group of newborns we did not find any evidence of such differential activity, as these younger infants demonstrated no sign of discrimination between the two conditions.

By the second month, infants thus appear to be newly exploring the perceptual events they produce in the environment adopting what was described as a contemplative stance.[14] Presumably, this developing stance implies both differentiation (*Level 1*) and situation (*Level 2*) in relation to the object of contemplation.

In the social realm, and corresponding also to the emergent contemplative stance, infants, by the second month, begin to smile when playfully engaging in face-to-face interactions with another person. As discussed before, the infants are expressing a novel sense of shared experience with others. It is also at this time that infants begin to engage in protoconversations with others via turn taking, imitation, affective mirroring, and mutual monitoring, all implying a sense of self that is differentiated and situated in relation to the conversing partner who is sharing experiences.

Finally, probably the least ambiguous demonstration of Level 2 self-awareness occurs when infants start systematically to reach for objects they

[13] Rochat & Striano (1999).
[14] Rochat (2001).

see, deliberately putting their hands in contact with objects. By four months, normally developing infants become "touch all," or "touche à tout," as the French say. They express systematic eye-hand coordination. However, they do so selectively.

We observed that from the time they are capable of reaching, infants are sensitive to the situation of their own body in relation to the object they reach, namely, the distance that separates them from the object.[15] In addition, they calibrate their decision to reach in relation to their postural degrees of freedom, whether they are more or less able to move forward toward the object without losing balance and falling onto the ground. Infants are capable of eye-hand coordination long before they are capable of maintaining postural stability during sitting. Early reaching is therefore challenging to the infant's overall body balance.

For example, in a series of studies, we found that four- to six-month-old infants' decision to reach toward an object placed at various distances and locations in front of them was determined by their own sense of situation and postural ability. For objects presented at the same distance, the propensity of infants to reach for these objects varied according to their sitting ability. We also found in infants of comparable sitting ability, hence with comparable postural degrees of freedom, that their attempts to reach for an object varied with whether we attached weights to their wrists. These weights restored the center of mass of their body, therefore adding to their balance problem as they reached forward toward the object. We found that in the weighted condition, infants are less inclined to reach, despite the fact that they have no problem moving their arm around with the loaded bracelet. In short, these observations clearly indicate that infants have a sense of self not only as differentiated (*Level 1*) but also as situated in relation to what the environment affords for action (*Level 2*).

THE BIRTH OF "ME" BY THE SECOND YEAR

Until the middle of the second year, when linguistic and symbolic competencies start to play a major role in the psychic life of children, self-awareness remains *implicit*. It is expressed in perception and action, not yet expressed via symbolic means such as words. Prior to approximately fourteen to eighteen months there is no clear evidence yet that the children perceive traces of themselves, as *standing for* themselves, only themselves,

---

[15] Rochat, P., Goubet, N., & Senders, S. J. (1999). To reach or not to reach? Perception of body effectivities by young infants. *Infant and Child Development* 8(3): 129–148.

and no one else, such as the footprints they might leave in the mud or the image they see in the mirror.

Infants do, however, months earlier, discriminate between their own image and the image of another infant. Preferential looking studies show that by five or six months infants tend to be significantly more captivated by a video recording of another, same age infant, compared to a video recording of themselves wearing an identical, same color outfit.[16] It appears that by this age, and presumably via previous exposure to mirrors and other self-reflecting devices, infants pick up invariant features of their own face. It does not mean, however, that they construe these features as standing for them. It is the product of perceptual learning of subtle invariant facial features they quickly become familiar with. When placed in a situation where they have the choice to explore either their familiar face or the face of another child, they show a typical preference for novelty. Although certainly a necessary precursor and a sign of remarkable perceptual learning ability, this preference does not mean yet that infants do *recognize* themselves on the TV.

The same kind of interpretation applies to our findings that four- and seven-month-olds show clear discrimination between seeing themselves live on a TV while moving around in their seat versus seeing a live experimenter on a TV engaged in the systematic imitation of what the infant is doing.[17] In our experiment, the experimenter shadowed the infant as mirrors do. We found that infants smiled, vocalized, and looked differentially at the imitating experimenter seen on TV compared to the self. In addition, infants tended to react differentially in either condition when the image was suddenly frozen in "still-face" episodes.

In all, young infants demonstrated once again their perceptual ability to distinguish between the familiar sight of themselves and the novelty of an experimenter shadowing them.

Despite all this remarkable ability to discriminate perceptually between what pertains to the self and what pertains to others, up to the middle of the first year infants are oblivious that some rouge has surreptitiously been smeared on their face or that a yellow Post-It might appear on their forehead when looking at their own specular image. It is only by eighteen months that infants start to reach for the mark on their own body, often in order to remove it (*Level 3*). Most developmental and comparative psychologists

[16] Bahrick, L. E., Moss, L., & Fadil, C. (1996). Development of visual self-recognition in infancy. *Ecological Psychology* 8(3): 189–208.

[17] Rochat, P., & Striano, T. (2002). Who is in the mirror: Self-other discrimination in specular images by 4- and 9-month-old infants. *Child Development* 73: 35–46.

consider this behavior the litmus test of self-awareness. It is often viewed as
the evidence of a conceptual or "represented" sense of self in any organism
behaving like this in front of mirrors, whether human or nonhuman primates, avian, mammals like elephants, or even cetaceans like dolphins.

But why might it be the case? It is mainly because by showing this
behavior, individuals demonstrate the ability to refer to the specular image
as referring to their own body. In other words, they refer the silhouette
they see reflected in the mirror to precise regions of their own body they
cannot see directly (e.g., their forehead). This would be impossible without
some kind of a representation of the own body that is mapped onto what is
seen in the mirror. Therefore, this behavior indicates that the individual
sees the mirror reflection as standing for this representation (*Level 3*). It is
identified as referring to the body experienced and represented from
within, not anybody else's. *Identity* is used here in the literal, dictionary
sense of "recognizing the condition of being oneself, not another" (*Random House Unabridged Dictionary*).

In relation to the preceding formulation, mirror self-recognition
expressed via the "successful" passing of the mark test is predictably linked
to major progress in symbolic (referential) functioning of the child in
other domains, in particular language development.

By eighteen months, infants also start to emphasize differences between
them and other people in their verbal production. They express semantic
roles that can be taken either by them or by others.[18] An explicit, hence
reflective conception of the self is apparent at the early stage of language
acquisition, at around the same age that infants begin to recognize themselves in mirrors. This chronological link in development provides indirect
validation of the mirror test and the interpretation outlined earlier.
Indeed, language acquisition requires a preexisting conceptual or represented sense of self as "Me" as opposed to simply "I": "a theory of the self
as distinct from other people, and a theory of the self from the point of
view of one's conversational partners" (Bates, 1990, p. 165).

THE BIRTH OF ME EXTENDING OVER TIME

If infants identify themselves in mirrors starting at eighteen months, they still
demonstrate that the *Me* they identify in the specular image remains enig-
matic and ambivalent. They still appear to oscillate between an awareness of

[18] Bates, E. (1990). Language about me and you: Pronominal reference and the emerging
concept of self. In D. Cicchetti & M. Beeghly, eds., *The Self in Transition: Infancy to
Childhood*, 165–182. Chicago: University of Chicago Press.

the self and an awareness of seeing someone else facing them. Identifying oneself in the mirror is a major feat, not only for the referential mapping between the mirror reflection and the own body schema, but also because what the child sees in the mirror is the way he or she always sees others: in an "en face" posture often with eye contact. In relation to this basic experience of social encounters, what the child experiences in the mirror might be "Me," but it is also what others typically look like. The child therefore has to suspend and override the overall visual experience of others, the specular image standing for "Me as an other," the Me but not Me dilemma[19] (see also from a psychoanalytical perspective Jacques Lacan's account of "the mirror stage" and his views on ego formation in development).[20]

The mirror experience of the self carries this fundamental ambiguity and children struggle with it, as we will see, until at least their fourth birthday. Note that this ambiguity is pervasive all through the life span. As adults, we look at ourselves in mirrors, working on our presentation by simulating or representing the looking of others on our own body. What we are seeing is de facto our appearance as seen by others, hence the pretense of someone else.

In his seminal observations of his own children, Piaget[21] reports anecdotes that pertain to the mirror dilemma. Jacqueline, aged twenty-three months, announces to her father as they are returning from a walk that she is going to see her father, her aunt, and herself in the mirror. Piaget observes that Jacqueline, who is perfectly capable of identifying herself in the mirror as "Me" when prompted by her father's asking, "Who is there?" also at times provides a *third-person* account of what she sees in the specular image. Likewise, she tends to oscillate between claiming that it is "Me" or that it is "Jacqueline" when viewing photographs with her in them (Piaget, 1962, pp. 224–225).

More recently, as part of a series of ingenious studies on the developmental origins of self-recognition, Povinelli[22] reports the commentary of a three-year-old viewing herself on a TV with a sticker on her forehead. She says, "It's Jennifer . . . it's a sticker" and then adds, "But why is she wearing my shirt?" (Povinelli, 2001, p. 81).

[19] Rochat (2001).
[20] Lacan, J. (1953). Some reflections on the ego. *International Journal of Psychoanalysis* 34: 11–17; Lacan, J. (1966). *Ecrits*. Paris: Seuil.
[21] Piaget, J. (1962). *Play, Dreams and Imitation in Childhood*. New York: Norton.
[22] Povinelli, D. J. (2001). The self: Elevated in consciousness and extended in time. In Moore, C., & Lemmon, K., eds., *The Self in Time: Developmental Perspectives*, 75–95. Mahwah, NJ: Lawrence Erlbaum Associates.

In all, these observations illustrate once again the Me but not Me dilemma, which children struggle with months after they show signs of self-identification in mirrors. The recent research of Povinelli and colleagues demonstrates that children slowly progress past the Me but not Me dilemma when viewing live or prerecorded videos of themselves. For example, three-year-olds and younger children do tend to reach for a large sticker they see on top of their own head while viewing a live video of themselves. In contrast, they do not do this when viewing the replay of the same video taken only three minutes prior. Furthermore, when asked who was on the TV, it is only by four years that the majority of children say, "Me" rather than their proper name, suggesting a first-person rather than a third-person stance.[23]

The careful empirical work of Povinelli and colleagues on delayed self-recognition shows that it is not prior to the age of three years that children begin to grasp the temporal dimension of the self; that the self pertains not only to what is experienced now but also to what was experienced then, what can be seen in a mirror now or in a movie tomorrow: the same enduring self (*Level 4*).

OTHERS IN MIND: EVALUATIVE AND METACOGNITIVE SELF-KNOWLEDGE

By the time young children begin to express and recognize themselves as enduring entities, they also begin to show major advances in their under-standing of others. By four to five years, children begin to be capable of holding multiple representations and perspectives on objects and people. They can, for example, infer the particular age, relative sentience, tempera-ment, and emotionality of a person by merely looking at the quality of a simple drawing. By this age, children infer the mind and affects of the artist behind a graphic symbol.[24] This ability is linked to the developing child's ability to construe false belief in others, as well as to grasp the representa-tional status of graphic and other symbolic artifacts such as maps, photos, or scale models.[25,26]

---

[23] Povinelli (2001).

[24] Callaghan, T., & Rochat, P. (2003). Traces of the artist: Sensitivity to the role of the artist in children's pictorial reasoning. *British Journal of Developmental Psychology* 21: 415–445.

[25] DeLoache, J. S. (1991). Symbolic functioning in very young children: Understanding of pictures and models. *Child Development* 62(4): 736–752.

[26] Olson, D., & Cambell, R. (1993). Constructing representations. In C. Pratt & A. F. Garton, eds., *Systems of Representation in Children: Development and Use*, 11–26. New York: Wiley & Sons; Perner, J. (1991). *Understanding the Representational Mind.* Cambridge, MA: MIT Press.

The development of representational abilities, in general, and theories of mind, in particular, corresponds also to evidence of metaawareness in relation to the self (*Level 5*). For example, when children begin to understand explicitly that another person holds a false belief, they necessarily understand that they themselves hold the right belief. In the same way, when infants demonstrate some construal of object permanence, they also demonstrate their own permanence in relation to objects.[27] These terms are inseparable.

The expression of embarrassment in front of mirrors by the second year can be interpreted as the first signs of young children's awareness of their public appearance and how others perceive them. As proposed earlier, by this age children begin to experience the basic fear-generating realization of a gap between how they perceive themselves from within and what others perceive from the outside.

An alternative interpretation would be that young children shy away from their reflection in the mirror not because they are "self-conscious," but rather because they wrongly construe the presence of another child staring at them with some kind of a persistent still face. But this is doubtful, considering that at an early age, infants discriminate between seeing themselves and seeing someone else in a video.

By showing embarrassment and other so-called secondary emotions, young children demonstrate a propensity toward an evaluation of the self in relation to the social world. They begin to have others in mind, existing "through," in addition to "with" others.

Secondary emotions, such as the embarrassment children begin to express by two to three years of age parallel, and are probably linked to, the emergence of symbolic and pretend play. Such play entails, if not at the beginning, at least by three to four years, some ability to simulate events and roles, and to take and elaborate on the perspective of others.[28,29]

The process of imagining what others might perceive or judge about the self, whether this imagination is implicitly or explicitly expressed, is linked to the cognitive ability to run a simulation of others' minds as they encounter the self. There are fantasies and phantasms involved, the imaginary stuff that tends to feed the self-conscious mind and characterizes the metacognitive level of self-awareness (*Level 5*).

[27] Rochat (2001).
[28] Harris, P. (1991). The work of the imagination. In A. Whiten, ed., *Natural Theories of Mind*, 283–304. Oxford: Blackwell.
[29] Tomasello, M., Striano, T., & Rochat, P. (1999). Do young children use objects as symbols? *British Journal of Developmental Psychology* 17(4): 563–584.

SELF-KNOWLEDGE AS INFORMED BY EARLY DEVELOPMENT

The development of self-knowledge early in life reveals layers of processes that expand from the perception of the body in action to the evaluative sense of self as perceived by others. It reveals also what mature self-awareness is made of. I propose that the self-knowledge experienced by adults is made of the six basic levels discussed here.

Self-awareness is a dynamic process, not a static phenomenon. As already mentioned in a preceding chapter, we are constantly oscillating in our levels of mental awareness and mind states. The same applies to the self: we oscillate from dreaming or losing awareness about ourselves during sleep, to being highly self-conscious in public circumstances, or in a state of confusion and dissociation as we immerse ourselves in movies or novels. In fact, our oscillation among these states of self-awareness can be construed as a constant transition among the six levels unfolding early in life. These levels form the basic degrees of freedom of self-awareness, a phenomenon that is dynamic, revealing itself in the constant fluctuation from one level to another.

Borrowing from dynamic systems jargon, I construe these levels as forming a collection of basic *attractors* in the process of self-awareness. These attractors are universal, shared by all mature individuals (i.e., individuals who have reached Level 5 of metacognitive self-awareness) who are fluctuating among the six levels just described in the perspective of development. What might differ from individual to individual are the rhythm and fluctuating patterns of oscillation among these basic levels of self-awareness. Some people are more prone to dwell in states of confusion while abandoning their embodied self in the saga of a novel or a movie. They are particularly inclined to enjoy the projection of themselves into another (nonself) being, reacting as if they were part of a scene on the screen, on the stage, or in the book. This state corresponds to a mature expression of Level 0 (self-world confusion), albeit expressed in a state of hypervigilance. Likewise, but in a radically different way (a difference that would deserve much more scrutiny), we transit through Level 0 when sinking into a non-REM sleep state of hypovigilance with no consecutive dream recollection.

As adults, we do indeed manifest all of the depicted levels of self-awareness that develop early in life. We lose ourselves in actions that entail a great deal of implicit self-awareness as in sport (Levels 1 and 2). Interestingly, if one rises to the next levels of explicit self-awareness (Level 3 and above) while engaged in skilled actions such as playing tennis or golf, this transition is associated with dramatic changes in performance, typically a deterioration.

Tennis and golf players will tell you that if they step into explicit self-consciousness, erring into explicitly thinking and reflecting on what they are doing, their game tends to collapse. There is nothing worse for tennis players than self-reflecting on the shape of their backhand. Explicit meta cognition about the self, in this instance, is maladaptive. The same applies for people engaging in meditation. People meditating and teachers within the Buddhist tradition will tell you that certain mind states cannot be attained without emptying oneself of explicit self-reflecting mental activities.

Adult meditation techniques revolve around the control of explicit self-conscious awareness, in particular the control of undesirable slippage from one level of self-awareness to another. Movie directors, by attempting to enthrall their captive audience, also try to control such slippages in actually fostering them. In general, and maybe with the exception of avant-garde movies that apply to the letter Berthold Brecht's distancing principles by which spectators should not leave their "intelligence" at the cloakroom of the theater, movie directors' goal is typically to captivate spectators, inviting them to lose grip with themselves. If a movie is successful, spectators will abandon themselves into the screen, becoming the protagonists of the story they follow. The screen becomes not only alive with moving pictures, but a simulation of a reality where spectators become "another" in an imaginary realm that is supported by vivid images, through a sophisticated editing language that provides syntax to these images and reinforces their "hypnotic," absorbing power of dissociation on the spectators.

The heuristic value of the proposed dynamic account of self-awareness is limited when considering that individuals are more often than not self-aware *with others*, not aware of themselves on their own. The social dimension of self-awareness has not been treated here, and we need to acknowledge the fact that we are rarely, if ever, aware alone. As discussed in the preceding chapter, infants and children develop to become "co-aware" and "co-conscious" of the world, including themselves. They develop awareness with others, not on their own. The lonely awareness of the physical or social world is a myth, too often upheld by cognitive theories that tend to isolate conscious experience from the social realm.

In this chapter, I have not referred to the fact that self-knowledge is primarily co-constructed in interaction with others, the central thesis of this book. The rather "nonsocial" account of developing self-awareness just outlined has, however, heuristic merits that deserve to be underlined.

For one, this account is informed by empirical observations as to how the awareness of the own body develops early in life. Second, it shows that what emerges chronologically in development are qualitatively different levels of self-experience. I have proposed that these levels might constitute the basic attractor states of mature self-consciousness. This said, the mechanisms of this development are conceived as social in origin.

The heuristic value of this simple ontogenetic model is that it supports the account of a fundamental, often overlooked aspect of self-awareness: the fact that self-awareness is not singular, but multiple; the fact that it is dynamic, in constant flux among levels of various experiential qualities all through the life span. Infants and young children, in their development, tell us what these levels of self-awareness are.

To end with a garden metaphor, self-awareness develops as onions do, layer after layer, in a cumulative consolidation. The main idea I have tried to convey is that self-awareness is essentially the experience of one's own fluctuation through these layers as we act, perceive, and think in the world.

As we will see in the next chapter, self-awareness refers also and maybe in a more crucial way to the experience of the self in relation to others that are inescapably evaluative, often the source of great anxieties such as those expressed in the emotion of *shame*.

6

Shame and Self-Knowledge

> Through shame, we endow others with indubitable power.
>
> Jean-Paul Sartre, *Being and Nothingness*

The knowledge that derives from the contemplation of the self can be a source of great anxiety, often associated with a "self-conscious" experience of fear and devaluation. But why is that? Why is human self-knowledge so often associated with terror and negative experiences, rather than awe or admiration? What is the big fear?

The negative emotional connotation of self-knowledge is revealing of the constitutive nature of the human psyche, a psyche that is primarily determined by the pervasive propensity to have others in mind, others who are represented as judges and evaluators of the self.

In the context of such propensity, *shame* is a central emotion, the epitome of *self-consciousness*. The aim of this chapter is thus to discuss the foundations of human shame in relation to self-knowledge. What does such a basic evaluative emotion tell us about the way we represent ourselves?

The word *shame* captures a profound, complex, and too often neglected emotion: the experience of self in relation to others. Such an emotion has, by definition, some negative affective tone. *Shame* is "the painful feeling arising from the consciousness of something improper, ridiculous, dishonorable" (*Random House Unabridged Dictionary*).

I have already mentioned the terror of self-recognition observed by Carpenter and collaborators in the adult Biamis of Papua New Guinea. When confronted for the first time with their own specular image, they show many bodily signs associated with the experience of great fear. Such explicit signs of embarrassment are also often associated with early mirror self-recognition, starting in the middle of the second year.

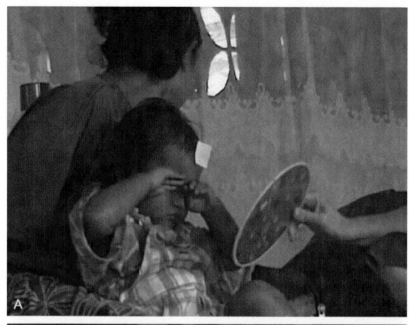

FIGURE 5. Universal ambivalence and embarrassment of self-recognition. A two-year-old girl from Samoa and a four-year-old boy from rural Kenya face themselves in the mirror with marks that were surreptitiously placed on their foreheads. "Self-conscious" in the literal sense, the girl looks down, showing embarrassment and clear discomfort, hiding her face behind the back of her hands, a frequent response observed in children all over the world. The Kenyan boy sits frozen and subdued, side glancing at himself in the mirror.

Children tend to freeze, look away from the mirror, bury their head into their shoulders, looking down sometimes with a coy smile. Or, alternatively, after freezing for a while, they might start to act out and behave boisterously as a proactive expression of self-consciousness. Figure 5 illustrates such behavior found in children across cultures (here a Samoan and a Kenyan two-year-old and four-year-old).

The question is why is there such generalized disturbance, to a large extent negative in tone, associated with the knowledge of the self, in particular one's own physical appearance discovered on the polished surface of the mirror or any other pictorial/media representations? Why such powerful inhibitory effects, which tend to reduce performance and disorganize behavior? From engaged and smooth, behavior becomes suddenly avoidant, or exaggerated, the result of unmistakable anxiety or concern. This is a striking phenomenon. I propose that it raises an existential question with profound ramifications at all levels of human psychological functioning.

GENERALIZED PHOBIA OF PUBLIC EXPOSURE

A recent survey shows that when people are asked to rank their personal fears, from worst to milder, a large majority of them considered the fear of *public speech* the worse.[1] This might be a trait of our rich Western cultures, which promote personal careers by putting much emphasis on individual, rather than group performance. In most valued professions, individuals are primarily judged and sanctioned on the basis of how they package themselves to become public with their ideas.

Public speech is bread and butter not only for teachers, lawyers, writers, or people in academia, but also for the growing number of people working in the corporate world. On the job, people are increasingly put on stage, and, more often than not, they hate it. Only a few "natural" individuals

---

[1] Furmark, T. (2002). Social phobia: Overview of community surveys. *Acta Psychiatrica Scandinavica* 105(2): 84–93.

claim actually to enjoy public speech. Most people are either terrified or plainly paralyzed, incapable of articulating their ideas in front of a captive audience. Typically, it takes a lot of training and practice to overcome and eventually manage the fear of public performance, if it is manageable at all.

One of my university professors who eventually became a colleague of mine confessed to me that in his thirty-plus years of teaching large psychology classes, prior to facing the students, he always visited the bathroom to throw up. This is not an unusual anecdote. Many seasoned actors recount the same kind of stories about untamable stage fright: fear of memory lapses, fear of mental and physical paralysis. In fact, stage fright becomes a companion and a need to actors. They worry when they do not experience it, as it serves as a reality check, boosting alertness and engagement before a performance, providing a sort of necessary sympathetic response and memory warmup. Performers often comment that the fear vanishes almost immediately once they step on stage. In a puff and with hidden resources, off goes the fear of forgetting lines; dissipated is the horrendous fear of losing words and the train of thought. In actuality, it is rare to witness performers suddenly frozen on stage. It happens, but the audience is generally lenient. If such an episode happens and is noticed by spectators, it tends not to be perceived as a major failure. Not so for the performers, who tend to moan, inflate, get obsessed, ruminate, and get depressed over such a mishap. From their own perspective, these lapses are construed as catastrophic, jeopardizing their reputation. They know their gig and see much more failure than novice audiences can see.

There is a profound discrepancy between first-person and third-party perspective, a major gap in expectation between spectators and performers. The audience generally keeps a fish eye on the global plot, more interested in what is going to happen next than on the details of what is happening. The audience tends to be oblivious to the details that upset performers. Performers, more often than not, assume either that everybody notices their flaws or that their performance could have been much improved if such flaws did not occur. This occurs even if there is an overwhelming consensus among critics that the performance was a triumph. Most visual artists tend to feel very uncomfortable at the opening of their own show: everybody congratulates them while they only see shortcomings in their work. They typically have bypassed it, immersed in a continuous creative process of changes and refinements.

Often, there is a profound discrepancy between what one feels from within and what is public to the outside, between what one perceives as self-presenting and what he or she thinks or is actually perceived by others.

It is the irreconcilable gap between the actor and the spectator views, of the painter and the guests at the gallery opening. This gap forms the core issue of self-consciousness.

We are all actors of all trades, always having to perform, most of the time to familiar, trustworthy publics, but also to new publics whose judgments we fear. As do professional artists, we experience stage fright and discrepancies between what we perceive of ourselves performing and what others perceive and how they ultimately evaluate our public appearances. This is a paralyzing, often unforgettable traumatic experience. Rare are those who, prior to a public intervention, never felt that they were going to the guillotine, never experienced the feeling of being mocked and depreciated by others while performing, and depressed for a long time afterward. I can remember reading papers at conferences like a cattle auctioneer, nose down, as if in a tunnel with the echoing of my own voice in my head, totally shut off from the audience. This is not an uncommon recollection in my profession and others.

It is hard work to get comfortable speaking and articulating ideas to others, particularly when others have the power to sanction and to judge. When our elusive reputation is at stake, we experience such situations as life or death. In general, the threat of others is overly inflated to the point of paralysis. We cannot help but smell danger and the question is, What is the nature of this obligatory perception? What might cause such seemingly universal, debilitating human fright about public exposure? What causes such a general trend of social phobia and insecurity?

Obviously, the unrest and potential paralysis caused by public performance come from a conception of the audience as threatening. We surrender to its sanctioning power. The question is, What might be the perceived sanction that plunges us into such a submissive and debilitating condition? What is the ultimate threat that causes us such predictable and endemic anxiety attacks?

I submit that behind all this there is a generalized fear of being ostracized and severed from the group, the fear of social rejection. It all boils down to the expression of the basic affiliation need (BAN) and its corollary, the fear of isolation, the separation from others. The tension between these opposite poles is a source of great anxiety, the generalized threatening experience of pending social disapproval and rejection. The force of such an experience is commensurate with the force of our basic affiliation need, a motivational system that is hard-wired with deep roots in mammalian evolution, as implied by current attachment theories in the footsteps of John Bowlby's seminal work.

THE FEELING OF SOCIAL REJECTION

On the street I am currently living on, there is a beggar. He is sitting on the sidewalk with an empty yogurt box in front of him, his head down, always holding the same torn cardboard sign, on it, a shaky, handwritten message that reads, in fading blue ink, "Jobless and hungry." Every time I pass by him, I vicariously experience social cruelty, probably as most people maneuvering around the collapsed body and paying attention to his sign do. Passing by the beggar, you either feel for him or ignore him. Either way, you respond to the unavoidable fact of social rejection.

Despite the obvious tragedy, and whether this beggar is a fake or not, the man is carefully putting his life in a nutshell in a sidewalk display. He is staging something we can all relate to, something that deep down has a fearful echo we all can empathize with.

The self-display by this man connotes that he is an honest worker who lost his job and has to beg as a last resort to feed himself and maybe his family. Collapsed on the sidewalk, head down as a sign of resignation, avoiding the fast passing gazes that might fall upon him, the man is exquisitely staging his misery and humiliation. His self-presentation forces us to empathize and eventually act upon his experience of social rejection by dropping a coin or two into his cup.

Presumably forced by extenuating life circumstances and not to diminish the tragedy behind it all, the genuine humiliation of begging (who gets a kick out of begging?), one cannot help but noticing how well planned and staged this man's whole self-presentation is. He chose the exact location where he plops down daily with his cardboard sign, near a church visited by large crowds of devout Catholics in a rich Paris neighborhood, where the Virgin Mary is supposed to have appeared. His overall body posture, the avoidant and depressed gaze down, the materiality of the sign he is holding, the writing on it, although certainly constrained by a lack of means, all is to a large extent *staged*. It is intended to have some communicative impact on others, to convince and eventually cause a generous gesture from passersby like me.

In essence, what the beggar on my street is staging, as are most individuals pushed to such a performance of themselves, is the deeply tragic and painful feeling of being *left out*: the feeling of being pushed out from the protective enclosure of others. It is the shared tragedy of all involuntary outcasts, stigmatized because temporarily unemployed, incarcerated, victimized, or persecuted for political and racial reasons. It is the tragedy of all those who are abandoned by their peers, who are mentally ill, born grotesque according to whatever standard, or simply too old. Socially stigmatized, these individuals share the feeling of rejection and lack of recognition by others expressed in the specific emotion of *shame*.

Shame is inseparable from and an integral part of self-consciousness. In many ways, it is the explicit, inescapable emotional expression of self-consciousness. It arises from the comparison and devaluation of the self in relation to others and their judging eyes. Ultimately, it entails a debilitating form of *co-consciousness*.

Shame is considered here as the primary self-conscious emotion from which all others derive, including envy, pride, guilt, and empathy. Shame, in my view, is the direct behavioral expression of social rejection and separation, what I have presented as the matrix of all other fears. But before discussing this idea further, we need to agree on what the concept of emotion means. It is indeed necessary to clarify some terms too often mixed up and confounded with the concept of emotion.

FEELINGS, AFFECTS, AND EMOTIONS DEFINED

What is an emotion? If you look at the psychological literature, you will soon realize that there are probably over a hundred answers to this question, each theory (and they are many) providing its own definition.

The word *emotion* is derived from the Latin *emovere*, which means "to move out." So, literally, *emotion* means the expression of things we feel inside, namely, feelings. In the literature, we find great confusion of terms such as *feelings*, *emotions*, and *affects*. Here I propose a simple vocabulary defining these important psychological constructs. *Feelings* stand for the perception of what is experienced from within, namely, mood and fluctuating affective climates, which oscillate between elation and depression, intense pleasure and pain. *Affects* stand for constantly changing, distinct internal climates or moods that are perceived via feelings. *Emotions* are the behavioral expressions linked to the feelings of affects. Emotions are what other people can read, what is on public display (literally what is *moved out*) on the own body's theater stage. With this definition, emotions are in principle readable by others, having a primary communicative function.

I reproduce in the following the proposed definitions as they were originally published (Rochat & Striano, 1999b). We considered feelings, affects, and emotions as concepts too often confounded in the literature, in need of being distinguished as they form three basic categories of subjective experiences determining social exchanges from birth.[2]

---

[2] Rochat, P., & Striano, T. (1999b). Social cognitive development in the first year. In Rochat, P., ed., *Early Social Cognition*, 3–34. Mahwah, NJ: Lawrence Erlbaum Associates.

- *Feelings* are the perception of specific private experiences such as pain, hunger, or frustration. In comparison to affects, this category of subjective experiences generally lasts for a shorter time in duration and ends following particular problem-solving actions such as feeding for hunger, comfort for pain, or fulfilling a goal for frustration.
- *Affects* qualify the perception of a general mood or perceived private tone that exists as a background to both feelings and emotions (see below). Affects are diffused and protracted in comparison to feelings. They fluctuate along a continuum, from low general tone (depression) to high tone (elation). To use a weather metaphor, affects are the perception of the global pressure system, as it fluctuates from high to low pressure, and vice versa, over time.
- *Emotions* are the observable (public) expressions of feelings and affects through movement, postures, and facial display – as in the behavioral expressions of pain, joy, disgust, sadness, surprise, or anger. As shown over a century ago by Darwin, emotions have specific, identifiable features that communicate the private experience of feelings and affects.[3]

THE EMOTION OF SHAME

Shame, as an emotion, is the public expression of the feelings and affects associated with social rejection. In its prototypical expression, it is avoidant in the sense of a general propensity *to hide* away and *flee* from public scrutiny.

In shame, one looks down, hides the face, turns away, tugs the head into the shoulders, curls in a ball, runs away, and, in short, expresses urges to vanish from the public eye, to withdraw from any social transactions. Criminals tend to hide their faces behind papers and raised collars as they are being arrested, hiding from journalists scavenging for sensational pictures. Recent published photographs from China show a long row of criminals, all equally looking down in shame as they are presented one last time to the public before facing the firing squad.

Less dramatic, but equally expressive, is the young child discovering his own image in the mirror and shying away from it (see Figure 5). All these behavioral expressions are unmistakably avoidant in nature: individuals fleeing an audience, hiding and withdrawing from the pain of public scrutiny. Shame is indeed associated with painful feelings, and it is read

[3] Darwin, C. (1872/1965). *The Expression of the Emotions in Man and Animals*. Chicago: University of Chicago Press.

as such by others when not taken as fake. No one enjoys shame. Sado-masochistic inclinations do exist, as do pleasures associated with pain, but these are special cases and as far as I can tell, do not apply to shame. No one enjoys being socially rejected – no one.

Shame is thus an emotion associated with the avoidance of some deep pain, but what pain? It is the pain of being seen. Shame is *the avoidant behavioral expression of being exposed to public scrutiny.* Evidently, behind such expression lies the fear of being judged, hence disowned and ultimately rejected by others.

In French, the word *honte* stands for *shame* in English. Interestingly, *honte* derives from the same roots as the verb *honnir*, which means literally to denounce or to condemn to public contempt. In other words, in the French sense, it is inseparable from the social banning of the individual. *La honte*, in the literal sense of the word, captures the psychology behind it. It is the feeling of and the avoidant response to social banning. It is an emotion that is the behavioral expression of the feeling of being socially rejected.

This feeling is associated with pain and a depressed affective mood that the beggar on my street puts on display by holding with head down his timid and feeble cardboard sign.

THE DERIVATIVES OF SHAME: CONTEMPT, EMPATHY, AND PRIDE

The emotion of shame, as the behavioral expression of the painful feeling of being socially rejected, is not only expressed in gaze avoidance or the hiding of the face. Opposite forms derive from it, in particular the self-conscious emotions of *contempt, empathy, and pride.* I consider these other self-conscious emotions as derived forms of shame.

Contempt, empathy, and pride correspond also to the painful feeling of being either fearful of rejection or actually rejected by others. They are different, derived expressions of basically the same feeling. Although the primary behavioral propensity associated with the emotion of shame is withdrawal, these more proactive (as opposed to avoidant) emotions share an identical experiential primitive. Pride, hubris, contempt, and empathy represent different forms of the same social fear, the fear of being rejected. In the view proposed here, they all derive from shame.

Pride and hubris as expressions of a sense of superiority put a psychological distance between self and others. By definition, these emotions are expressions of self-attributed empowering in relation to others. They are also expressions of social withdrawal, or at least social distance. They are proactive posturing and behavioral buffers against social rejection. They are shields against social judgments, expressions of self-reassurance as social insurance.

Putting distance between self and others, trying to raise the self above public scrutiny is another, more proactive form of social withdrawal. It is, in fact, analogous to the primary propensity to vanish from the public eye that is explicit in the expression of shame. All put *distance and estrangement* between self and others. In the case of pride and hubris, noncrossable distances are put between them.

The same can be said for contempt, which is an emotion that clearly also puts a distance between self and others, an active dissociation by rejection. Contempt turns social rejection the other way around: now it is the self that rejects others. In psychoanalytical terms, contempt is a *reaction formation* to social rejection, an inversion by which contempt is the tendency to reverse onto others the social rejection we experience for ourselves.

The contemptuous individual is expressing at a deeper level a fear of social rejection, distancing himself via the expression of superiority and dissociation. It is the opposite of withdrawal, yet gets the same regulatory result. Contempt shares deep down the same shameful root, the same social fear of being ostracized, and the same basic expression of a need to affiliate and to fuse with others. From this viewpoint, social insecurity is expressed equally in withdrawal and contempt, except that it is an inverted form.

We do not only experience shame for ourselves. We also experience it vicariously or by contamination. Shame, as the primary emotional expression of the feeling of being socially rejected, pertains also to the *rejection of others*. Teenagers are often ashamed of peers' seeing them in the company of their parents. Likewise, parents can be ashamed of their children. To be shameful does not have to involve us alone. We have the propensity to be ashamed by proxy.

We are ashamed of being associated with others whom we do not endorse, afraid that their reputation might rub off on us. The contamination of a poor reputation is a threat of social rejection by proxy, a fear of being judged and ultimately rejected by people we try to gain respect from and affiliate with.

Empathy, as an emotion, also entails vicarious and projected feelings from third- to first-person perspective. Somehow, we perceive and can relate to what others are perceiving of their own mood and affects from within the privacy of their own bodies.

I do feel and express empathy for the person who is neglected, rejected, or in pain, but particularly, and I would say, in the deepest, most conspicuous way, for the person who is ostracized, rejected, and socially persecuted. We can feel for someone experiencing a mishap, something that happens by surprise, by a loss of control or a bad twist of fate. But we empathize particularly for people who are deliberately ostracized, humiliated by others, innocents who are abandoned and neglected. All enticing traditional tales and stories that have endured the passage of time tend to have as core conflict social separation and the rupture of intimacy. It is the universal fear we try to conjure by reenacting it in fiction and movies. Love stories are the epitome of such conjuring, always finding their force against the backdrop of treacherous separation and difficult destiny. A love story without the drama of separation is not a story; it is just a boring anecdote. A story does not exist without a conflict, and usually a conflict revolves around social separation, be it war, death, withdrawal, or divorce. We are enticed by stories that conjure our deep fears, particularly the fear of social separation, the loss or absence of intimacy.

Empathy is also an emotional derivative of shame, as for pride and contempt. It arises first from the generalized fear of being rejected and separated from others, both counterparts of the basic need to affiliate and maintain social proximity. When I see the beggar on my street, by reading his shame and eventually dropping a coin into his pan, I do experience vicariously his shame and the painful feelings attached to it. I act accordingly to regulate this basic, painful feeling, as much as the beggar does by avoiding the gaze of others looking down at the pavement. The difference is just in form. As a well-off passerby, by dropping a coin, I just have the means to be more immediately proactive in my emotional regulation.

In dropping the coin into the pan of the beggar, I express an emotion of empathy. But this emotion is de facto just another derivative of shame, the basic self-conscious emotion that I experience vicariously. In the end, the beggar and I share the same basic fear. This is what we are basically communicating about from our different perspectives and social positions. If I drop a coin, I express empathy. If I ignore the beggar, I express contempt. In both cases, however, I deal with the basic fear of social rejection. I regulate my behavior and emotional expression accordingly, either by ignoring (contempt) or by being more proactive (empathy).

Once again, the corollary of the fear of social rejection and separation is attachment, hence affiliation and social fusion. These are two sides of the same coin, and empathy as an emotion is, as are pride and contempt, derivative of fears and tensions correlated to both separation and attachment. Separation and attachment (rejection and affiliation) are part of the same general phenomenon, each defined in the opposition of the other as in the Chinese yin and yang.

Although I have been insisting on separation, in my mind separation anxieties always express a correlative drive for social fusion. Separation and attachment are indeed totally interdependent. They form opposite poles at the heart of individuals' socialization as many theorists have proposed long before me.

However, my insistence on the anxieties and the basic fear associated with separation results from the fact that separation anxiety tends to have greater heuristic (explanatory) power in relation to self-consciousness. The rationale is that we are self-conscious primarily because we are afraid of being rejected. Then, and only as a consequence, we are afraid of not being able to maintain or create fusion with others. Following this basic premise, there is some precedence of social rejection over fusion as a basic psychological motive. The fear of rejection is comparatively more motivating than the drive to fuse with others. It all probably boils down to the issue of describing a bottle as either half-full or half-empty. The decision taints how one tells the story.

HUMAN SHAME AND EMBARRASSMENT

Most pet owners would concur that their companions do express emotions that they can readily interpret as shame or embarrassment. It is common to hear anecdotes of dogs behaving in unmistakable ways, with tail between their legs and shaking, sometime hours after they did something they have been punished for in the past.

The master reads mishaps in his dog's behavior that he eventually confirms: broken vase, torn sofa, or open food containers. These are real and quite striking cases of anticipation, namely, the anticipation of a punishment, at least in animals that have been bred and selected for their attunement to humans' ways of being and particular human tastes. Let us not forget that dogs, through careful breeding and training, have been for thousands of years human cultural artifacts. Their behaviors reflect what we are, and this is why dogs are the great companions they are. But can we call for the expression of shame or any derivative self-conscious emotions to account for such anecdotes? I doubt it. Clearly animals express attachment and separation anxieties, but not to the level humans do.

In his seminal book comparing the expression of the emotions in man and animals Darwin[4] viewed shyness (embarrassment) as a precursor of human blushing. He witnessed blushing in his son at around three years, and shyness months earlier, pointing to the fact that blushing causes the selective

---

[4] Darwin, C. (1872/1965), p. 329.

crimsoning of the face, precisely the region of the body that is most visible and attended by others. It is the face that is typically and desperately covered in bouts of embarrassment when feelings are exposed. Following Darwin, this is a unique outcome of human evolution. It is also the expression of a unique psychological process: the never-ending process of intersubjective negotiation by way of active self-presentation that is so pervasive and specific to humans.

Dogs and other animals might express anticipatory behaviors that only appear on the surface to be self-conscious, but that cannot be claimed to be metacognitive. In our example, the dog's behavior does not necessarily entail any representation of what others (i.e., the master) represent of the self; nor does it entail a concept of self. The dog shaking with its tail between its legs clearly anticipates punishment on the basis of stored associations between certain behaviors and their consequences. It does not entail, however, that the dog feels embarrassment and shame for what it has done, which would imply some higher-order metacognition, the comparison between the representation of own action and the represen- tation of these actions by others. In brief, the dog can be said to show remarkable anticipation, but not metacognitive, normative ability to con- struct shared concepts of good or bad behaviors.

In contrast, shame and its derivatives (pride, contempt, empathy) do entail normative and metacognitive ability. They are self-conscious emo- tions. As far as I know, dogs do not show embarrassment in front of mirrors; nor do they show any evidence of self-recognition. Young chil- dren clearly do so from the middle of the second year. Children see in the mirror not only themselves, but also what others see of them. This is presumably why they show embarrassment, typically trying to vanish from their reflection in the mirror for the reasons suggested earlier.

Embarrassment as a self-conscious emotion, which is a mild version of shame, rests on the metacognitive ability of construing and comparing one's own, versus others' representation of the self. It is a clear expression of higher-order metacognition and co-consciousness as discussed earlier. The expression of shame by the beggar on my street is metacognitive in nature because it entails that he represents what he is staging (shame) and what passersby will probably construe of his expressing shame. This stag- ing of shame is self-conscious in nature and carries social meaning. It expresses co-consciousness. The meaning that is shared in the staging of the shameful self is nothing but painful social rejection that is experienced by both the beggar and the passersby, whether the latter drop a coin into the pan, ignore it, or show contempt. The shared meaning is the pain of being separated from others. We can all relate to that.

7

The Roots of Guilt

I feel the ghosts breathing on my neck.
   Molina, Magnolia Electric Co. "What comes after the blues"

No one is immune to guilt. Sociopaths apart, it is a powerful emotional experience that shapes our lives. It is inseparable from the exacerbated preoccupation with reputation that is the cardinal feature of what it means to be human. But how does it come about in development and why? These are the questions of interest for this chapter. Guilt, as is shame, is the expression of the intricate set of representations one holds as to how others might construe and evaluate the self. It is from this set of representations of the self as perceived by others that arises the sense of social reputation and self-esteem, both fundamental in determining the perception of who we are.

At the origin of development, however, what we express are nonevaluative emotions or affects that are direct responses to environmental circumstances determined by events occurring within or without the body. We are born expressive, but not yet evaluative.

How do we develop from being primarily expressive to become obsessively evaluative, starting in the middle of the second year? How do we become, from this point on, so inclined to factor in others' views and values about us?

This developmental question is the Holy Grail of human self-consciousness, and I address it first. This will serve as a basis for a discussion of the differences between guilt and shame as evaluative, secondary emotions. This discussion presents guilt as another derivative of shame, once again rooted in the basic fear of separation and the need for affiliation.

PRIMACY OF NONEVALUATIVE EMOTIONS

Distinct emotions are expressed from birth on and even prior. Ultrasonic images of fetuses show them frowning in apparent pain, and newborns make faces. Caretakers read newborns' and young children's faces and other bodily movements as standing for particular feelings, the feelings of specific affective or mood experiences.

Newborns express pain when circumcised, disgust when tasting salty water or smelling acrid substances, distress in hunger, and pleasure after a good feed as they roll their eyes and smile away. We empathize with such affective experiences and feel for the young child who needs our care to survive. This vicarious affective experience is indeed the motivational core of the protracted care needed by the "exterogestation" of the human child who is born too soon.

The primary emotions displayed at birth develop rapidly. By two months, the expression of distress (crying) differentiates to express not only the overall negative affect of pain, but also, at times, distinct anger. By eight months, as we have seen in an earlier chapter, the child manifests further differentiation of negative affects with the expression of fear indexed by the developmental emergence of stranger anxiety.

On the positive side of the primary emotion spectrum, the expression of joy and interest develops from two months, a differentiation from the overall expression of pleasure that is evident at birth (i.e., reflex smiling of the newborn as expression of satiety).

By eight to nine months, infants express emotions that stand for more differentiated feelings in reference to increasingly specific affective experiences. All this starts from a biologically given set of positive (pleasurable) and negative (painful) affective experiences. However, it is not until the child shows signs of *objectifying oneself* that emotions become self-conscious per se, a radical developmental departure.

Up to the middle of the second year, if the expression of emotion becomes increasingly differentiated and readable in reference to specific affective experiences (e.g., hunger, pain, fear, discomfort), it does not yet imply any explicit metacognitive involvement. Emotions remain primary in the sense that they are not yet evaluative.

It is only by approximately fourteen months, or possibly even earlier (by eight months with the emergence of the fear of strangers), that the expression of emotions is linked to norms. Emotional expression then begins to imply some knowledge of standards, rules, or goals.[1] Emotions

---

[1] See Kagan, J. (1984). *The Nature of the Child.* New York: Basic Books.

develop to become what is usually described in the literature as secondary or *self-conscious.*[2]

The primary emotions expressed from birth do not imply any high-order, self-reflective representation. In some sense, they are analogous to what I described of the dog expressing apparent (and only apparent) embarrassment or shame in anticipation of punishment. Newborns' and young infants' emotions, up to approximately the end of the first year at the earliest, do not imply any explicit metacognitive ability, hence no consciousness, nor any co-consciousness.

When young infants cry, their pain is not objectified, not an object of contemplation yet. Likewise, young infants do not represent yet the vicarious experience of others listening to their crying. That does not prevent them from quickly learning to "instrument" their cry, recognizing that when they cry someone generally picks them up. Early on, infants are exquisite at learning to anticipate a particular contingent outcome. But such learning can be accounted for with theoretical parsimony by low-level operant conditioning. No data suggest that prior to nine months infants might already represent the empathy or shared experience of the person who eventually dispenses care.

Up to about nine months, it is all about the spatiotemporal contingency and learning of relative co-occurrence between one's own and others' behavior. Prior to this age, infants do not engage yet in any explicit, high-order metacognitive evaluation of their situation in relation to others.

The secondary, self-conscious emotion of shame and its derivatives (contempt, pride, empathy) emerge with self-objectification, when children begin to manifest an explicit, conceptual sense of the self.

From this idea, Michael Lewis[3] has generated a compelling developmental account regarding the emergence of secondary emotions. Lewis presents these emotions as implying the cognitive capacity of what he calls objective self-awareness. It is the equivalent of what I call *self-objectification*, namely, children's ability to construe themselves as objects of exploration and knowledge. This is particularly evident for Lewis when toddlers begin explicitly to recognize themselves in the mirror. Lewis proposes that from this point on, a first set of self-conscious (secondary) emotions emerge that

---

[2] See Lewis, M. (1992). *Shame: The Exposed Self.* New York: Free Press.
[3] Ibid.

he labels "exposed emotions." This set includes embarrassment, empathy, and envy. These emotions are self-conscious but, according to Lewis, *nonevaluative* still.

It is only by the middle of the second year, according to Lewis, that a new set of self-conscious emotions that are evaluative in nature emerge. This second set includes shame, pride, and guilt, emotions associated with the development of children's cognitive capacity to construe standards, rules, and goals. It is also, according to Lewis, the sign that children reach metacognitive levels, capable of knowing that they know and capable of feeling what they feel (mind state of consciousness according to our definition).

Some aspects of Lewis's account are quite different from the ideas I have proposed. On one hand, Lewis provides what amounts to a finer account of the developmental progression from primary to secondary (self-conscious) emotions by distinguishing a two-step progression in the latter between one and a half and two and a half years. On the other, Lewis does not construe shame as a generic emotional expression of social rejection from which all other self-conscious emotions derive, as I suggested in the preceding chapter.

The divergence in our respective accounts results from the fact that Lewis's approach is primarily cognitive. His account of emotional development is from the perspective of the individual child's growing cognitive capacity. In contrast, my focus is on the development of co-consciousness. Lewis adopts an "internalist" view that focuses on cognitive changes within the child and not on the development of active self-presentation and the intersubjective negotiation of the child with others.

My interest is in the development of basic motives leading children to have others in mind. I propose that the fear of rejection organizes the development of self-conscious emotions, and this premise influences the way one theorizes about emotional development.

On the whole, Lewis rightly acknowledges the growing metacognitive capacity required for self-conscious emotions to develop. Our views diverge on the meaning of shame, which I consider more generic, linked to the basic fear of social rejection from which all other self-conscious emotions would derive. Contrary to Lewis's assumption, I do not think that evaluative capacities emerge suddenly by two and a half years. Precursor expressions are evident long before, in particular by eight months, when infants begin to develop robust expression of separation and stranger anxieties. From this point on, they show some strong standard of affective comfort. This said, Michael Lewis rightly insists that by two and a half years children raise their evaluation to metacognitive levels that are incomparable. From then on, with no ambiguity, they begin to construe the impact they have on others. They begin actively to manage their public image, showing pride, empathy, or, on the contrary, ignoring others by contempt. They become self-conscious in a stricter sense.

In relation to pride, by two and a half years of age children begin to express positive affect such as joy when succeeding at a difficult task (e.g., stacking blocks to match a high tower). In contrast, such positive emotions vanish when succeeding at a much less challenging task. This differential expression of pride as a function of task difficulty indicates that children begin to set new standards for themselves. They express hubris depending on levels of self-achievement that, in their mind, justify self-flattery and congratulations.

Pride, like any other emotion, is public. It is to be seen by others, not just experienced in private. If not seen by others, pride cannot reflect its basic function, namely, the active underlying positive aspects of the self that *others should see*. Pride is among the clearest signs that children begin to engage in active self-branding and management. Such emotion entails, in addition to self-objectification, a sense of self-worth that should be perceived by others.

In relation to empathy and contempt, it is also by age two and a half that children begin to be newly proactive in helping others. If someone gets hurt, they will check on him and inquire about how he is doing.[4,5] This new proclivity, and the emergence of prosocial behavior, also give the child the opportunity to express the reverse, ignoring the misfortune of others and acting more antisocially.

Contempt is indeed the counterpart of the prosociality that emerges by the middle of the second year. The child will continue to cultivate and use his selective attention and self-presentation to others, particularly during school age, when social seduction and contempt seem to reach a climax, exploding by the teenage years.

It is interesting to note that the emotion of empathy, or shared feelings experienced by others, seems to rest on neurobiological mechanisms that are very primitive and possibly hardwired in our brain.

[4] Zahn-Waxler, C., Radke-Yarrow, M., Wagner, E., & Chapman, M. (1992). Development of concern for others. *Developmental Psychology* 28: 126–136.

[5] For a good review chapter, see Eisenberg, N., & Fabes, R. (1998). Prosocial development. In W. Damon ed., *Handbook of Child Psychology*, 5th ed., vol. 3; also sep. Eisenberg, N., ed. *Social, Emotional, and Personality Development*, pp. 710–778. New York: Wiley.

A few years ago, a group of Italian neuroscientists found brain cells, in the premotor cortex of monkeys, that respond equally to an action that is self-produced and to the same action performed by someone else. These cells fire when, for example, the monkey grabs a grape from the end of a stick, as well as when it sees someone else do the same thing.[6] Because of this functional (dual) property, these cells are called *mirror neurons* (see Chapter 9 for more discussion).

The discovery of mirror neurons is important because it suggests, way upstream of the empathy we see developing in the child by the second year, that there is a neural substrate that supports the bridging of self and others' experience.[7] The development of empathy and self-conscious emotions has deep evolutionary and biological origins that researchers keep trying to unveil. There is still a long way to go, however, until we will be able to relate what one observes at the level of the brain cell, and what we observe at the level of the developing child as a whole organism trying to gain intimacy and recognition from other individuals: others whom the child eventually perceives as persons, engaged in reciprocal exchanges and equally caught in the struggle for recognition.[8]

SHAME VERSUS GUILT

At the core of Freud's psychoanalytical theory there is, as you probably know, the concept of *repression*. In his second topic or second general interpretative grid of psychic life, Freud proposes a conception in which personality is shaped by the tensions among the Id, the Superego, and the Ego, three hypothetical psychic systems.

The Id represents the urge of libidinal pulsions that are erotic and sexual in essence. The Id is governed by the pleasure principle, the urgency of immediate gratification. It is the Id that, according to Freud, the infant expresses mainly early in life, progressively repressed by "dos and don'ts" that are internalized by the child in the development of the Superego. The Superego is the rule system that polices the Id and its libidinal urges for immediate gratification. The Ego or "public Me," in a nutshell, is the resulting, outward compromise between the clashing forces of the Id

[6] Rizzolatti, G., & Craighero, L. (2004). The mirror-neuron system. *Annual Review of Neuroscience* 27: 169–192.
[7] Preston, S. D., & deWaal, F. B. M. (2002). Empathy: Its ultimate and proximate bases. *Behavioral and Brain Sciences* 25: 1–72.
[8] Honneth, A. (1995). *The Struggle for Recognition: The Moral Grammar of Social Conflicts.* Cambridge, MA: MIT Press.

(urges and libidinal needs) and the Superego (rules and what is socially acceptable).

In simple words, the Ego is the compromiser, the "ambassador" *between the wants and the ought-to* of the individual. This theory entails tension and resulting repression that Freud sees as the principal source of anxieties that lead toward psychopathologies. Repressed urges for love and seduction lead to anguish, phobias, obsessions, or depression, all so-called neuroses. No one escapes neuroses. Although unpleasant and a source of tension, they typically do not jeopardize our adaptive ways in dealing with the world. They are part of our existence.

We can be conscious of our neuroses and to some extent control the oddity of their outcomes, the ways they affect our relations to others, with or without seeking the help of a therapist. Who can claim that he is not mildly obsessional about certain things? Checking three times whether the oven is turned off before leaving the house or obligated to engage in some superstitious rituals before doing certain things? All these are odd behaviors. We are compelled to perform them for unknown reasons; fully aware of their oddity we somehow accept them as the irrational part of our lives. Problems arise when they begin to get too much in our way, when, for example, we have to kneel in front of our mailbox in the middle of the street before picking up our mail or we feel compelled to take the toaster oven with us to work so we are sure that it is unplugged.

Rather than shame, *guilt* is a term that is more common in psycho-analytical theories to capture the experiential result of repressed urges, typically the sexual urges to seduce and consume love with unattainable objects. If urges cannot be satisfied according to the pleasure principle, then they have to be buried. But, as any therapist will tell you, to bury does not mean to cause to disappear. These urges are obligatory and manifest themselves in disguises, as in the two examples of odd obsessive behaviors given. We remain conscious of our odd behaviors, not knowing the exact reasons behind them. We mask them as best we can so as not to *embarrass ourselves*, avoiding superstitious dances in front of our judges.

In general, neurotic experiences result in *guilt*. Guilt in its most generic sense stands for the uncontrollable feeling of causing wrong and being wrong in relation to evaluating others. Guilt is a major paralyzing factor in our lives and a major source of mental ills. This is why it is the main object of psychoanalysis.

Much of the claimed success of therapies rests on the fact that there are healing and good feelings attached to getting rid of guilt. Lightness is gained in reconciliation with the sense of wrongdoing, whether by accepting it or debunking it. The representation of self as culprit is a major hindrance to flow in life. Typically, and in the broadest sense, psychotherapies try to help people in regaining their potentials for enthusiasm, curiosity, and the feeling of comfort with others, all basic propensities that alleviate social separation and that are obstructed by neurotic symptoms. This is the credo of therapists, the source of their success, and ultimately the source of their income.

Therapies work because guilt can be controlled. The same, however, does not apply to shame. If it is possible to work toward changing the paralyzing conception of self as a past, present, or future cause of ills in others, the typical source of guilt, it is much harder to cure shame. Here lies, in operational terms, the main albeit subtle difference between guilt and shame as self-conscious emotions.

Both shame and guilt are oriented toward how others perceive us, how others might form negative impressions and judgments that could lead to rejection and ostracism. However, at a psychological level, shame and guilt are associated with different mental constructs regarding what causes the ill feeling, the actual *locus of control* of such feelings.

In guilt, the locus is the self. Ills and wrongs are perceived and represented as being caused by and originating from within. In shame, the causes are construed as entering from "without," outside the individual. Typically, we experience shame as "befalling" us. It is inflicted by a situation we are placed in, not because we committed a specific act causing the situation.

Guilt, as opposed to shame, is often considered to be associated with regrets, regrets of having done wrong, typically to people or society as in the sense of criminal justice. Guilt is thus associated with potential repair, either by paying for wrongdoing or fixing some behaviors that might have caused some harm.

In contrast, shame captures a contrasting experience of the individual. It is more diffused and not necessarily reparable, despite active attempts at masking it. We can be ashamed of our poor origins, for example, and mask shame by living ostentatiously. We can be ashamed of the color of our skin and mask it by bleaching it. We can be ashamed of our physical appearance and mask it by applying makeup or wearing certain clothes. Behind shame, there is a psychology that has more to do with the feeling of a loss of power than with repair and redemption. In contrast to guilt, shame has to do specifically with the *loss of social power*.

"Shame is all that we would like to hide and that we cannot bury," says Levinas in his 1982 book *On Escape*.[9] This definition captures nicely the impotence, hence loss of power, attached to this emotion, as opposed to guilt, which seems more proactive and connotes more resources for damage repair. With the emotion of guilt comes a sense of *responsibility*. Shame connotes something inflicted or imposed upon the individual that she is not directly responsible for.

Let us take the example of a nude model posing for an artist. It is her profession and she is accustomed to undressing for the sake of displaying her body as a paid model. The artist might be a total stranger, as is the case in most live drawing classes, the model standing naked in front of a group of aspiring visual artists. The model might show some signs of being prudish and timid, but there is no shame per se in posing publicly naked in front of the class.

What would it take for the model to feel ashamed? If the model suddenly detects that one of the students, or the painter hiring her, is not actually painting anymore, as was the original agreement, but is lusting over her body, explicitly violating from this point on the original agreement with which she was hired as a model. She might then feel ashamed. In contrast, the lusting artist might feel guilty, not ashamed per se, as he is caught. He is not ashamed because the responsibility for the shameful situation for the model falls on him. He is guilty of causing shame to the model and has the possibility to fix it by apologizing or confessing.

Contrary to guilt, as discussed by Williams in *Shame and Necessity*,[10] what causes shame in relation to nudity is not only the potential of being seen at a disadvantage. It is also the fear of being admired or dismissed by the wrong people for the wrong reasons: to be perceived in unanticipated ways as in the case of the model catching the painter lusting over her instead of keeping his artistic eye.

Shame is inseparable from the general feeling of losing power over others' perception of the self. According to Williams, in contrast to guilt, shame is a narcissistic emotion par excellence, as it focuses on the integrity of the self, in terms of power in relation to others.

Both shame and guilt are emotions that betray feelings of being judged *negatively* by others. They permeate all aspects of our lives. They are the source of most self-conscious behaviors, including active self-presentation

---

[9] Lévinas, E. (2003). *On escape* (De l'évasion). Stanford, CA: Stanford University Press.
[10] Williams, B. A. O. (1993). *Shame and Necessity*. Berkeley: University of California Press.

and self-image management in terms of masking (e.g., covering up) and self-branding (e.g., bragging).

As we get old, we get particularly good at masking to prevent the humiliation and shame accompanying physical and cognitive deterioration. We become expert, often even desperate, at covering up the decline of our memory capacity as well as our physical appearance. We use more makeup and fancy clothes to cover our parchment skin, to the extent that we can afford such fancy decoys. My old hippie neighbor comforted me the other day as I was complaining of having a harder time remembering faces and names. She patted me on the back and kindly told me: "Nothing to worry about, dear. The mailbox is full." Her kind humor did not alleviate my confessed shame of losing social power.

It is fascinating to see how much intelligence is put into masking major handicaps that we are bound to suffer from, one day or another. We are actively avoiding the shame and social debasement that accompany aging, particularly in our Western industrialized culture. Elderly people show much sophistication and, actually, intelligence at hiding their lapses to avoid public (negative) exposure and the humiliation generated by physical and psychological deterioration. Not enough research is devoted to the talents devoted, particularly as we get old, to masking potential shame and to the maintenance of some *dignity* in the face of aging, a process that is not meant for "sissies," as claimed by some famous actor.

Much could be learned from the discreet and clever ways that old people deal with incontinence, denture problems, the application of thicker makeup, or the way they might hold their cane to raise their dignity above handicap. These are all complex stratagems to prevent shame and humiliation, and ultimately rejection.

Research typically emphasizes prevention and the description of what goes wrong with age. Once again, not enough attention is paid to the talent and intelligence that grow out of inescapable natural deterioration, even if slowed down by plastic surgery and preventive medicine. Motivated by the avoidance of shame and rejection, this is terrain for great psychological savvy. We could still learn a lot if we were paying more attention to it.

We like to claim that as we age we lose cognitive performance but gain experience and wisdom. It might be true, but not for those suffering from Alzheimer's disease and other forms of dementia. Aside from such debilitating diseases, horrendous cancers of the mind, whatever experience and wisdom might be gained in aging, most of it emerges from the struggle to avoid shame and humiliation.

Humiliation is the sister feeling of shame, the sense of being debased, devalued, and ultimately rejected by others. Interestingly, *humiliation* also has a "cousin" noun, which is *humility*. Humility captures the feeling that results from the own, voluntary (as opposed to inflicted) devaluation in relation to others. One decides to bow down or erase herself as an expression of humility, something that is highly valued in Asian cultures, for example. Humility as a self-conscious emotion is the contrary of pride. It corresponds to the voluntary deflation of the self in relation to others.

Humiliation is associated with shame because it is effortless, it befalls us, imposed from the outside. In contrast, humility is in essence more proactive and deliberate. One learns and eventually chooses to be humble. As for guilt, the cause of humility and its locus of control are primarily within the individual, not outside.

I have suggested that both shame and guilt arise from the general anxiety about being judged negatively by others (the impact of the *Superego* in Freud's theory). We see, however, that if they express the same general anxiety, they have different psychological meanings. These meanings continue to be debated in existing theories of emotions. For example, William considers guilt as containing more inherent virtue (i.e., allocentrism as opposed to egocentrism) compared to shame. But we have seen that shame is more often than not experienced vicariously. It is often mixed with some empathy, thus has some connotation of allocentrism. Therefore, it does not seem reasonable to contrast shame as more egocentric (narcissistic) than guilt since shame is often experienced by proxy.

For example, we feel shame for people who are being humiliated. Or we feel ashamed by proxy when close associates endorse racist attitudes or any other behaviors that are for us screamingly incorrect. Shame, as much as guilt, can pertain to specific features of others' behaviors that we feel can rub off on us and affect our public reputation. As an example of the ongoing debate on the psychological meanings of self-conscious emotions, Michael Lewis proposes an alternative, more cognitive view on shame and guilt. He considers guilt, and not shame, as the focus on a specific action of the self that led to a failure. The debate goes on.

SUMMARY

In this chapter, I have discussed self-conscious emotions from a more developmental perspective. I first contrasted the primary emotions infants express from birth and even prior. Once again, I traced down the ontogenetic origins of the self-conscious emotion of shame to major psychological transitions at two months, but particularly by nine months, and by the middle of the second year. I then proposed a simple vocabulary to define emotions, as opposed to affects and feelings, concepts that are too often confounded, if not confusing, in existing literature on emotional development. I considered that self-conscious emotions were public expressions of the generalized feeling of being judged and potentially rejected by others. In this context, shame is considered as the generic secondary (self-conscious) emotion from which all the others might be derived (i.e., pride, contempt, and empathy). Shame and its derivatives are evaluative and depend on the construction of standards and rules that are perceived by the individual as governing others' view on the self. They all imply, at minimum, the ability of self-objectification, namely, the ability to contemplate the self as an object from within the own body, but also from without, by adopting others' perspectives.

Self-conscious emotions rest on the ability to juggle first-, second-, and third-person perspectives on the self. Once again, I insisted that this juggling and integration of perspectives take place in the context of a generalized fear of social rejection. In the end, I contrasted shame and guilt. Each corresponds to a variety of psychological processes underlying self-consciousness. Shame and guilt reveal different ways we express the basic fear of being socially left out and ultimately ostracized by the judgment of others. In their differences, shame and guilt are revealing of the variety of fearful reasons for having others in mind.

8

Giving and Sharing

Do ut des. (I give for you to give.)

Human ways of sharing form a central issue of human self-consciousness. It is a major expression of the human propensity to have others in mind. The question of interest in this chapter is, Why do we share the way we do?

Here I develop the idea that the way humans share is linked to their particular ability to reflect upon themselves, upon their situation, and in relation to others. Our unique, sophisticated ways of sharing and transacting with others are inseparable from the fact that we are a self-conscious species.

EXTERNAL MEMORY OF EXCHANGES

Humans have evolved unique social ways and, as no other species, spend much of their time accounting for exchanges. They are constantly tallying what is owed to whom. We calculate, project, and expect from others on the basis of past transactions. In the life of our species, all social exchanges are accounted for, and little is gratuitous in the long run.

Writing, which can be considered the greatest of all human inventions, emerged in modern human evolution less than 10,000 years ago, presumably as part of the tallying of exchanges. There is a consensus among prehistorians that writing as a symbolic system evolved under the pressure of keeping track of agricultural and other surplus good *exchanges*. Writing, as a cultural artifact, served primarily as an external memory of exchanges and transactions among individuals or groups of individuals. What we know of Oriental antiquity, particularly the ancient history of Sumerian civilizations in the Middle Eastern region of Mesopotamia, is that writing as a system appears to have coevolved with the emergence of the first known urban concentrations along the rivers Tigris and Euphrates. Writing, as a cultural invention, is a major, most reliable expression of modern humans' unique creativity and psychological sophistication. It might have been a major factor in bootstrapping recent human evolution, contributing in a major way to the ratchet effect of technological discoveries of the past seven thousand years, which exploded exponentially in the past few centuries, and particularly in the last few decades.

It is not uncommon to hear the argument that language, rather than writing as a symbolic system, is what demarcates humans from nonhuman primate species. This argument, however, is hotly debated and often contested by researchers suggesting rudiments of symbolic aptitudes in close relatives like common chimpanzees and bonobos.[1] Furthermore, we should not forget that prior to the evolution of modern humans (*Homo sapiens sapiens*) many other human species preceded and even coexisted. For example – and I will return to this striking fact – *Homo neanderthalis*, a distinct human species, did coexist in the same region of Northern Europe with our modern Cro-Magnon species for over thirty thousand years before becoming extinct some thirty thousand years ago. They seem to have shared sophisticated symbolic abilities with modern humans, hence presumably were able to speak, or at least to do more than to communicate as any other animals do. Archaeological digs demonstrate that *Homo neanderthalis* buried their dead in systematic ways and wore bodily adornments. All these are signs of sophisticated self-representation and self-consciousness.

GIFT SYSTEM

Ethnology and anthropology are modern scientific disciplines that focus on the comparative account of the ways modern humans live. These disciplines blossomed barely a century ago to become major departments in most universities around the world today. There were important forays during the great discoveries of the eighteenth century with the well-documented voyages of great explorers like the British Captain James Cook and the French Louis de Bougainville. But ethnology, and eventually anthropology, became academic disciplines only by the beginning of the last century.

---

[1] Savage-Rumbaugh, E. S. (1994). *Kanzi: The Ape at the Brink of the Human Mind.* New York: Wiley.

Early anthropologists documented stories and myths around totemic figures transmitted down from generation to generation via tales and other rituals within the oral tradition of these small primitive societies. Note once again that no writing systems existed yet within these oral yet highly symbolic cultures. Literacy was eventually introduced to these small societies by missionaries and other colonial forces as late as the eighteenth or even the nineteenth century in regions of Oceania (i.e., Polynesia, Melanesia, and Micronesia), Africa, and South America, where much of early ethnographic and anthropological fieldwork was conducted.

The first anthropological field studies took place in regions chosen for their isolation, a warrant of cultural traditions that have been alive unspoiled with other Western traditions over long periods, virgin of other cultures' influences for sometimes thousands of years: Early ethnographers and anthropologists took advantage of this virginity and preservation to seize some basics about human culture: what it is made of, what functions it might serve, how it stabilizes, and eventually how it can abruptly change under what appear to be minor perturbations, including the visit of strangers studying them, despite the best intentions of tact and respect.

Early anthropological works are invaluable in their account of a life that might resemble the life evolved by our modern human ancestors when it first emerged some 120,000 years ago. The study of modern humans is based on the latest, constantly revised fossil discoveries, from which physical anthropologists try to reconstruct human evolution.

Pioneer anthropologists such as Bronislaw Malinowski, Marcel Mauss, Claude Levi-Strauss, Franz Boas, and Ruth Benedict, to cite the most famous, all recognized something that appears to be pervasive, if not universal among what they called "primitive" or "archaic" small human societies. They all showed the inescapable importance of group-rallying *totems*. Across very varied cultures from all over the world, with little to no contact with other cultures, thus no possible contamination, small societies have evolved highly complex ways of symbolic group identification with some striking similarities. Universally, human primitive cultures rest on symbolic elaboration and incorporation of the surroundings, with particular emphasis on animals on which survival depends.

Such symbolic elaboration as totems serves the larger function of asserting group belonging. It regulates social life via rituals that mark the passage of time. It shapes group memories and gives meaning to regular events like birth, puberty, marriage, or death. Early ethnographies of primitive cultures from all over the world point to great varieties of rituals and collective tales synchronizing the lives of individuals within their group, ultimately serving the basic function of supporting group cohesiveness.

Early fieldwork pointed to one particular aspect of social exchanges shared by most archaic societies: the cultivation of gift giving and complex systems of reciprocation. The ethnography of small archaic societies over the world showed that most of these societies that evolved in total independence have in common an analogous cultivation of social reciprocation via *gift giving and receiving*. Early cultural anthropology theories interpreted, rightly so, that the universality of such phenomena across isolated archaic societies demonstrates a core principle regulating human group living.

Tribes still living at the beginning of the twentieth century in ways that resembled those of our Neolithic (Stone Age) ancestors organized their lives primarily around gifts and sacrifices: receiving gifts, giving gifts, and reciprocating for gifts. Gifts were given for the sole purpose of asserting social ties; offerings and sacrifices were performed for the sole purpose of taming magical powers. Fieldwork of early anthropologists and ethnographers, as well as the tales of encounters with native populations by the great discoverers who preceded them (e.g., Cook, de Bougainville), all seem to revolve around the cultivation of gifts and exchanges.

But what does it all have to do with self-consciousness? In the broadest sense, gift giving, receiving, and reciprocation *objectify* and make public, for the record, the relation linking the self to others. They present this relation for contemplation and assessment. More importantly, in the dynamic of social transactions, gift giving and receiving objectify the social worth of the self via reciprocation. If one gives to eventually receive, the value of the gift reflects the perception and representation of the receiver by the donor, and vice versa.

Gift giving specifies both self and others. Via reciprocation and exchanges, gift giving contributes to the development of a co-consciousness of self and others. It contributes to the construction of shared values. Gift giving and receiving can be thus construed as a major process by which we assess each other as persons, as well as the degree of our alliances. Although striking, it is not surprising that this process is universal and so pervasive across cultures. It is a trademark of our self-conscious species.

Bronislaw Malinowski was among the first anthropologists with Marcel Mauss[2] to reflect upon the act of giving: why it is so prominent in most

---

[2] Mauss, M. (1952/1967). *The Gift: Forms and Functions of Exchange in Archaic Societies.* New York: W. W. Norton.

archaic cultures, how it evolved into complex symbolic systems, and what it all means in human culture in general. Malinowski[3] suggests that the act of giving rests primarily on the basic trust that all obligations are scrupulously fulfilled. Instances when they might not be fulfilled place any human in an intolerable situation: "The slightest negligence in filling an obligation (i.e., the obligation to reciprocate) attracts disgrace" (Malinowski, 1932, pp. 31–32). On the basis of minute observations among Melanesian islanders (Trobriand Islands, located southeast of Papua New Guinea), Malinowski insists that human transactions and sharing imply more than a mere dualism between donor and receiver or any protagonists of an exchange. Human transactions in most cases imply internal *symmetry* in terms of reciprocity ("Do ut des" principle).

Malinowski sees reciprocity in services and goods as the cornerstone of any primitive community. He concludes that without this principle, the community would not exist. What is interesting is that cultural practices seem to have evolved to emphasize reciprocity, particularly the trust that links individuals in a community. In the culture of gift, there is at the core the implicit idea that in the long run all obligations and debts among individuals will balance out. As a matter of fact, in these small societies, gift giving creates social debts. In the context of an immutable trust of reciprocity, gift giving is therefore some insurance of future return, often greater. Hence, gifts become not only markers of the intersubjective values linking individuals, but also memory traces of their relationships that frame communal existence and reinforce social ties in the long term.

In a sense, gifts, in the context of an implicit rule of reciprocity, are a precursor of writing as a system, a cultural and shared memory system to tally exchanges and to ensure equity among transacting individuals in a group. In the process of giving and receiving, the gift becomes the memory of a debt expected to be repaid. That does not mean, however, that the gift system can be reduced to utilitarian or pure economic purposes.

Gifts are not like modern money. They do not measure directly the values of physical goods and services as money does, in its most generic, modern sense. Gifts are highly symbolic of *personal assessments*, hence closely linked to the process of self-consciousness and co-consciousness.

Behind gift giving and receiving there is always an attempt to assess how one relates to others. Gift giving and receiving are thus inseparable from

---

[3] Malinowski, B. (1932). *Argonauts of the Western Pacific: An Account of Native Enterprise and Adventure in the Archipelagoes of Melanesian New Guinea.* London: Routledge & Sons.

attempts at repairing, maintaining, or fostering new representations about the self.

In the ritualized gift exchanges of most small traditional societies, the things exchanged have no direct economic value. Rather, they carry complex psychological values. As mentioned by Godbout[4] in his *The World of the Gift* (L'esprit du don, in French): "Primitive money does not measure the value of things; it measures first the value of people" (p. 165 of the French edition, translated by the author). I would add that gifts, as opposed to money, primarily measure the value of the self in relation to others. Note, however, that money can be transformed and given in the spirit of a Gift. But it is then diverted from its modern, economic function. It becomes *self-conscious* in the sense discussed in this book.

Gifts, as a primitive form of money in small traditional societies, exist in parallel to money in the modern sense. The two are often confounded in rituals such as funeral, marriage, or birth celebrations. Money, as a highly symbolic gift, can be given to the bride's family in the case of a marriage or to the widow in the case of a funeral. Note that it is only when money becomes independent of any personal value that it can serve its modern economic functions, which are transpersonal and abstract. Money can then only serve the functions of measuring the value of goods and services, allowing their circulation, and allowing the payment of material debts.[5]

Money becomes modern when its value is independent of who owns it now or who owned it in the past. In contrast, the value of primitive money and, in particular gifts, depends on its former and current owners. Its value varies, depending on whether it participated in other past donation rituals or belonged to other more or less prestigious individuals within the group. It is in this sense that gifts as primitive money can carry memory traces of past transactions, particularly if they are reused in later donations: "In nonliterate (oral) societies, gifts as primitive money support collective memory" (Godbout, ibid., p. 166, translated from French by the author).

A remarkable example of primitive money is the famous *stone money* used on the island of Yap in Micronesia. Huge doughnut-shaped stones,

[4] Godbout, J. (1998). *The World of the Gift*. Montreal: McGill–Queen's University Press.
[5] For further detailed discussion from a historical perspective, see Polanyi, K. (1957). *The Great Transformation.* Boston: Beacon Press.

sometimes weighing a few tons, were used for gifts and payment of debts in land transactions and other rituals. These stones were carved out of one particular quarry in the island of Palau, a few hundred miles east of Yap, and transported perilously on fragile wooden outrigger canoes to their destination. Once given, these heavy gifts were laid to rest and sunk against the house or on the land of the addressee. When you travel on this island today, you can still see these huge stones lying there on display. Part of the landscape, like abstract repetitive sculptures, they are memories of past gifts and transactions and are a constant reminder of indestructible interpersonal ties among the Yapees. Each token of Yap stone money is a unique gift, recognizable only by its invariant doughnut shape. The value to the stone money is symbolic more than economic. Its treacherous journey from Palau on frail canoes and the great weight of the stones are symbolic or conceptual measures of the social ties among the Yap people. It represents essentially dedication, effort, and work as compensation for a debt that is more social and affective than economic.

On the island of Western Samoa, where traditional Polynesian culture is still very much alive, much of social life is regulated by ritualized ceremonies that are systematically accompanied by extensive gift giving and receiving protocols. Food, animals, money, and fine mats are donated in colorful ceremonies, often with the perennial drinking of kava, a mildly intoxicating root-based drink, poured into a coconut shell and passed around according to strict rules. These are scenes often seen in Samoa, at funerals, birth celebrations, weddings, national holidays, and other political and artistic gatherings. In fact, analogous scenes with slight variations are pervasive all through the vast region of the Pacific: from Easter Island all through Polynesia, as well as all over the vast region of Melanesia and up north in the hundreds of Micronesian atolls that stretch between the island of Hawaii and the island of Palau near the Philippines.

I had the opportunity to travel in these regions and witnessed, as well as participated in, traditional gift giving and receiving ceremonies. Despite regional variations, these ceremonies all have in common the general attempt to stage an absolute lack of hesitation in giving and receiving. The donors make all kinds of choreographic and staging efforts to *overwhelm* the recipient(s), the latter either bowing in submission to such effort or sometimes witnessing passively, as if feigning indifference.

In Western Samoa, it is striking to see mountains of gifts presented one by one to the addressee in ceremonies that can last hours. Often the gifts have no other function than being gifts, like fine mats that circulate in reciprocation from ceremony to ceremony and that are a major daily labor of women who are constantly weaving new ones, all year long. A large fine mat can take a year or more to weave. The finer and larger it is, the more dedication value it has as a gift. When presented, one at a time during the ceremony, it is not simply handed to the overwhelmed addressee(s). It is *rushed* and sometimes even *thrown* on a rising pile that lies in front of them. This choreography is unmistakably meant to convey the absence of any hesitation on the part of the donor, the absence of any second thoughts and regrets on his or her part in the act of giving. In other words, there is an absolute dedication expressed in the act of donation.

Marcel Mauss, in his seminal book on gift and donation systems, describes different forms of the same general effort in cultures as varied as the famous potlatch of northwestern American tribes studied by Franz Boas and the Kula of the Melanesian islanders studied by Malinowski. In potlatch, a sometimes extremely agonistic form of gift giving, donors go so far as to destroy goods, instead of giving them, in an apparent act of indifference to receiving back from others. Mauss writes, regarding pot-latch: "In some instances, the point is not even to give and give back, but to destroy so to give the impression to the recipient that you are not even interested in getting something back. Houses and thousand of blankets are burned, the most expensive copper pieces are destroyed, all that in order to crush, to flatten his rival" (Mauss, 1952/1967, pp. 201–202 of the French edition, translated by the author). In the less dramatic Kula, or circles, linking partners of neighbor islands in Melanesia, there are alternation and reversibility in gift giving and receiving.

As in Samoa and other South Pacific islands, such specific "precious" goods as archaic money are presented as gifts, circulating across ceremonies from donors to recipients, and vice versa. Once again, aside from the size and quality of the goods, their intrinsic value varies proportionally to the number of partners they have already transited with. Malinowski points that with such gifts as archaic money, there is a radical dissociation between symbolic and economic or utilitarian value.

In the Kula, described by Malinowski, there is strict application of the "Do ut des" principle by which no gift is actually gratuitous. Malinowski describes instances when islanders organize some kind of gift hunting expeditions to other islands, loaded with bait gifts, to oblige partners of the Kula to reciprocate with better gifts. In return, the other party, with the guarantee that such an obligation will be reciprocated, organizes the same kind of expedition some time later. That is the circularity of the Melanesian Kula, cultural artifacts that confer cohesion, welding solid mutual feelings among these remote island societies. In all instances, gift ceremonies are highly symbolic of interpersonal ties and dispositions. They provide an opportunity to stage *feelings* toward others.

Gift exchanges in archaic and small traditional societies are fundamentally different from bartering or any other tit-for-tat, term-to-term economic exchanges. In his analysis, Marcel Mauss makes the point that in all archaic systems of gift rituals there is at the core the notion of honor and credit. In general, the one receiving a gift should not reciprocate immediately, but later, some time as late as possible.

Mauss makes the intriguing point that a delay in the necessity to reciprocate raises the transaction above mere economic bartering, above mere permutations of goods, without any proportional increase of the debt in return. As stated by Godbout, "To reciprocate immediately would signify that we try to slip away from the weight of the debt, that we worry about not being able to repay, that we try to escape the obligation, and that we turn down the establishment of a social tie, afraid not to be generous enough in return." Once again, we see that gift giving and receiving constitutes a privileged cultural vehicle for the expression of very complex feelings toward others, hence a privileged cultural tool for self-presentation that evolved in archaic human systems all over the world.

Interestingly and as a case in point, in the native Canaque language of New Caledonia in Melanesia, the same word stands for *debt* and *life*. This indicates the high social meaning of such rituals that cannot be reduced to utilitarian economic transactions as in immediate bartering or good exchanges.

At a more general theory level, there are different views as to why gifts and reciprocity seem to be a central, seemingly universal feature in small human societies of contrasting cultural traditions. Despite the fact that these traditions sometimes evolved in very different environments – from the dense tropical forest of the Amazon, to the American Northwest and the remote islands of the South Pacific – there is indeed a necessity in gift systems that reveals something unique about human ways of relating to each other. No other species evolved a complex culture of reciprocity and gift exchanges. This is part, I think, of the unique ability of humans to be self-conscious: to construct metarepresentations of self in relation to others.

Marcel Mauss starts his essay on gifts asking the basic question "In primitive or archaic types of society, what is the principle whereby the gift received has to be repaid? What force is there in the thing given which compels the recipient to make a return?" (Mauss, 1952/1967, p. 1). This question is the why of the obligation to reciprocate that appears to be the common denominator among small human societies. As suggested, it would be trivial to answer this question from an economic standpoint: the expression of reciprocity in gift exchanges typically has highly symbolic rather than utilitarian status; the bartering and market exchanges of goods happen in parallel with ritualized gift systems. Gift systems are marginal to market exchanges, yet essential to social cohesiveness. They give individuals within a group the opportunity to situate themselves in relation to others, to construct memories, ties, and social trust.

Claude Levi-Strauss, in his structuralist approach, suggests that gift systems and reciprocity might have evolved from basic functional necessities, namely, the necessity of incest prohibition for the survival of the species (i.e., what would be the elementary structure of kinship according to Levi-Strauss). Levi-Strauss[6] suggests that originally, the necessary enforcement of a prohibition to engage in sexual intercourse with relatives probably constrained the establishment of exchange systems based on reciprocity, in particular the exchange of women between families and clans. This necessity would be a basic evolutionary push toward sharing and reciprocation cultivated in human societies as a rule. For Levi-Strauss this rule might have originated in the trade of women.

In contrast, for Marcel Mauss, who, as does Malinowski, confines his interpretation of gift systems to less formal and more psychological processes, giving a gift is much more than obeying a law that has been selected under evolutionary pressure. For him, "To present something to someone is to present something of the self." Mauss continues, "One must give back to others what in reality is part of his own nature and substance" (Mauss, 1952/1967, p. 160). Accordingly, and in resonance with the ideas proposed in this book, self-consciousness and co-consciousness about the self are deeply involved in any gift system still practiced all over the world, in small-scale traditional societies as well as in postindustrial urban cultures. Gift giving and receiving remain a universal process by which individuals measure their worth in relation to others and reinforce their social ties.

TRUST AND PROMISE

Aside from promoting social cohesiveness, gift giving and receiving, as well as the creation of social debts, provide ground for metarepresentations of

---

[6] Lévi-Strauss, C. (1987). *Introduction to the Work of Marcel Mauss.* London: Routledge & Kegan Paul.

self in relation to others. A basic function of gift and debt systems is to provide ground for probing degress of reciprocity, hence the sense of how we are *valued* by others.

It is primarily through the experience of reciprocity, or lack thereof, that one develops trust, or alternatively distrust, in others. Trust, however, is an elusive concept. It is laced with various meanings that philosophers have debated for centuries.

As for any concepts that are difficult to grasp fully, it is helpful to go back to the dictionary and look for the etymological meaning of the term. It gives conceptual ground and prevents basic semantic misunderstandings. The French word for trust is *confiance*. It derives from the Latin word *confidentia* which means literally "faith with" (*con*, with; *fiance*, faith). *Confidentia*, in turn, stands for the English word *confidence* that is synonymous with *trust*. The literal meaning of *trust* is therefore the sense of shared values with others. When we trust someone, we share a value with this person.

When handed change in a transaction, for example, I typically *trust* that the money given back to me is of the right amount and is not fake. Trust, therefore, captures the promise of basic value agreement and understanding. It pertains to things that exist outside the individual like paintings, banknotes, or bread. But it also pertains prominently, if not primarily, to the self and its value in relation to others.

When one is robbed or cheated, a *promise* has been broken, whether this promise was implicit or explicit. Trust and confidence are destroyed, or at least need to be renegotiated. In this process, there are a disruption of how one relates to others and the necessity to reconfigure one's own situation and value in relation to others. This reconfiguration typically translates into new actions. For example, after being ripped off a few times, I will not lend the key of my apartment to a stranger anymore, or now the terms of my sales to customers are only cash on delivery: "No if, no but, no credit," as you sometimes read in bars. In reading such signs, we figure out the story of betrayal behind them. But more deeply, the betrayal affects self-worth in relation to others, either positively or negatively, depending on the circumstances, since we are not always victims, but sometimes beneficiaries, building up confidence and trust. We gain, as well as lose, confidence in others as we move on in our social transactions. One way or another, the name of the social game is a constant process of renegotiation that situates the self in relation to others.

Gift and reciprocation systems seem to revolve around the establishment and the probing of trust among individuals within and between social groups. Giving, receiving, and reciprocating gifts have the funda-mental function of consolidating and specifying the faith in shared values among individuals and groups of individuals. Through gifts and recip-rocation, alliances can be probed, created, maintained, reinforced, and eventually undone. It is an instrument, sometimes a highly symbolic instrument, of endless negotiation between self and others, between in-group and out-group individuals.

But what does it mean to be allied with someone or a group of indi-viduals? What does it mean to trust and to be confident of others? These are difficult, fundamental questions that I do not intend to resolve here. However, here are a few ideas on the issue.

The first idea is that if one of the most basic functions of sharing is to establish shared values that can be trusted among individuals and groups of individuals, such an establishment is *dynamic*. Shared values are never established once and for all. Rather, they are the product of constant negotiations. The circulation of gifts in the Kula, described by Malinowski, as in many other small traditional societies, shows that the human gift system is open and never closed. It is an ongoing process within certain constraints dictated by history and tradition of the particular culture where it takes place. The obligatory circulation of gifts dictated by the basic principle of symmetry and reciprocation makes the gift system a constant negotiation. In other words, the values that are expressed in the process of sharing and reciprocation, whether gift exchanges or the sharing of personal experiences, are constantly reassessed.

From this constant, ongoing reassessment, trust and confidence, as well as promises, emerge as the sedimentation or by-product. Each exchange reinforces, maintains, or puts into question the relative trust in values we share with others. The human gift and reciprocation system never reaches absolute balance, never comes to total closure. There are always gaps and discrepancies that keep it going, sometimes from generation to gen-eration, as in small traditional societies. As individuals or as groups, we are constantly probing our place in relation to others, adjusting for any dis-crepancies and changes, chasing after an elusive balance. Monitoring discrepancies in reciprocation is the rule, not the exception.

Via gifts and exchanges, one gauges the value of the self in relation to others. One is also given the unique opportunity to establish trust and promise, two human values that are co-constructed in the context of reciprocal exchanges. From constantly gauging the value of self in relation to others derive psychological phenomena that tend to dominate much of our social and affective life, for better but mostly for worse.

ENVY AND JEALOUSY

In the permanent gauging of self in relation to others envy and jealousy, two highly invasive expressions of self-other discrepancies, occur. These two affective phenomena lead individuals and groups toward passionate, uncontrollable, and often irrational acts. By all accounts, both are sources of great suffering. Envy and jealousy are the maladies of love and desire. They are, once again, maladies that derive from the basic need to affiliate and the counterpart of this basic need, the fear of being socially rejected.

Envy and jealousy both arise in the realization of discrepancies between self and others. In envy, one realizes that others have something that he or she does not have. Envious acts are oriented toward either gaining what is perceived as lacking to the self or sabotaging what the other has to reestablish balance. Jealousy, in contrast to envy, typically pertains to the realization that one is deprived of something he or she once possessed and had control of. Jealousy is about the experience of an unwilling loss of control over a loved one. It is also among the most straightforward expressions of the experience of being rejected by others.

As we know, jealous acts can reach high levels of irrationality. Jealousy can become uncontrollable for the rejected individual who falls into vicious, self-feeding rumination on obsessions leading to delusion and physical violence in some cases. Acts of jealousy are typically more violent than envious acts. They are more desperate, not just oriented toward gaining what is perceived as lacking to the self. They are attempts at *regaining* something once possessed, now lost or perceived as being lost. Jealous acts are expressions of deep fear and desperation in the face of such loss, which is essentially a loss of ascendance over someone. The experience of such loss corresponds to the sense of losing ties or connection with the other, in other words, the experience of losing agency and social power.

Following the argument of this book, the experience of a loss of social power falls into the rejection matrix and translates into fear. The resulting pain in both the jealous individual and the person who is the object of jealousy is commensurate with the fear of the loss of social agency, hence the fear of rejection.

Worth noting is the fact that the English word *envy* translates in French as *envie*, which is a contraction of the preposition *en* (in) and the noun *vie* (life). Thus in French, *envy* stands semantically for being in life (*en vie*), that is, alive or *living*.

In general, etymologically, the word *envy* finds its root in the Latin verb *videre*, "to see," but also "to know," "to perceive." There is a sense of voyeurism attached to the etymology of the word *envy*. To be envious is indeed to see in others what is lacking in the self, what is not possessed by me. From a group perspective, it is a threat to social cohesiveness. It is divisive as envious individuals compete with each other rather than collaborate. This explains the strong etiquette evolved in most societies across cultures that controls envy. For example, uniforms are promoted to eliminate ostentatious differences that could foster envy, a threat to group cohesiveness. But social codes tend universally to control envy because it is a threat shared by all individuals, a threat to their possession, what has been acquired and is experienced as owned by the individual.

Envy is a threat for the envious but also for the envied, as captured by Virginia Woolf with all her wit and talent in her novel *Mrs. Dalloway*[7] in the following portrayal of the servant in the voice of the Master:

> For Miss Kilman would do anything for the Russians, starved herself for the Austrians, but in private inflicted positive torture, so insensitive was she, dressed in a green mackintosh coat. Year in year out she wore that coat; she perspired; she was never in the room five minutes without making you feel her superiority, your inferiority; how poor she was; how rich you were; how she lived in a slum without a cushion or a bed or a rug or whatever it might be, all her soul rusted with that grievance sticking in it, her dismissal from school during the War – poor embittered unfortunate creature! For it was not her one hated but the idea of her, which undoubtedly had gathered in to itself a great deal that was not Miss Kilman; had become one of those specters with which one battles in the night; one of those specters who stand astride us and suck up half our life-blood, dominators and tyrants; for no doubt with another throw of the dice, had the black been uppermost and not the white, she would have loved Miss Kilman! But not in this world. No. (Virginia Woolf, *Mrs. Dalloway*)

Here, in this passage, Wolff captures the resentment of the envied of being put in this situation of being the privileged, the dominant, the Master by the servant. The guilt and unease associated with envy do indeed go both ways, affecting the envious, as well as the envied. Envy is a global social threat.

To be an object of envy is to be an object of covetousness or desire, in other words, an object of robbery. It is threatening. In Switzerland, for example, a rich country whose culture is for the most part deeply rooted in

[7] Woolf, V. (1925). *Mrs. Dalloway*. New York: Harcourt, Brace and Company.

Protestant Puritanism, the tradition is not to display wealth, particularly old aristocratic money. The rich work hard at hiding their material difference. Conventions help them to melt with the populace, those who are potentially envious because they have less and might want more equal shares. Rich individuals in Switzerland and elsewhere can work hard at playing down their wealth, living relatively simply while sitting on immense wealth. If they indulge in ostentation, it is in foreign lands where they might build lavish houses, like respectable people expressing their lust in the privacy of bordellos. They tend to wear the same clothes as less wealthy people and share the same leisure activities. Any ostentatious sign of wealth is typically sanctioned as vulgar, the expression of "nouveaux riches," not of classy, old, and aristocratic wealth. To maintain and transmit wealth across generations, cultural habits have evolved to control envy. But the exact reverse is also true.

It appears that another cultural device to control envy is to be overly ostentatious, to drive in ridiculously stretched limos and to wear oversized jewelry with price tags still attached to them. Displaying wealth and power differences so lavishly, like "show biz" stars or eccentric businessmen (the Donald Trump kind), is another way to control envy by overplaying it. Part of the implicit logic behind such public display is to overwhelm others, not unlike what Boas described in the potlatch ritual of Native Americans. What is publicly projected in wealth ostentation is overwhelming power, too great even to be envied.

The hidden point, aside from the enjoyment of getting much social attention, is not to promote desire in others, but to generate awe instead. The logic would be that social awe prevents envious acts that are, by definition, threats to the privileged. This is the opposite strategy from that of the wealthy Swiss as portrayed previously. In history, however, ostentatious wealth did not prevent lavish landowners and monarchs from being toppled by envious, angry crowds of have-nots.

Regardless of cultural attempts at controlling envy, it remains a major engine of social changes. Arguably, envy is, in some cases, a source of social progress as it leads to greater social equality and broader wealth distribution. As we will see next, the control of envy is an intrinsic part of the complex process of sharing we have evolved as a species, a process that involves negotiation instead of coercion, more subtle ways of having others in mind.

What envy and jealousy have in common, regardless of whether we accept the definition and contrast I have proposed, is a comparison of the self to others.

Ancient Greek philosophers discussed envy as self-reproach, the reproach of not possessing what others have (Hesiod in Theogeny).[8] In this sense, and interestingly, envy is closely linked to guilt as discussed in the preceding chapter, a reproach to the self for having done something that could have been done differently to prevent harm (I feel guilty because I cheated on an exam I could have studied for).

At some level, envy and guilt involve the sense of responsibility. Aristotle points to the fact that we tend to envy those who are close to us, live in our vicinity, and are of comparable age as well as social status. In other words, we tend to envy those in whom we can recognize ourselves: "Envy pertains to the idea that we have of ourselves, what makes our difference, our identity; it touches us at our very core" (Moessinger, 2000, p. 112, translated by the author from French).[9]

Self-other comparison is what fundamentally underlies both envy and jealousy as psychological phenomena. But what is upstream of the expression of such phenomena? It is important to consider this question since envy and jealousy are arguably among building blocks of what it means to be human (see the recurrence of their reenactment in tragedies, comedies, and other classic myths and tales across cultures). Here I propose that what we see upstream is the sense of *ownership and entitlement*, other inescapable psychological phenomena that we need to touch upon in the context of this discussion.

Following Hesiod's idea, in envying others, we tend to reproach ourselves that we do not own something we *should* have. We are frustrated by the incapacity to own the same thing. Accordingly, to envy is to mourn our own impotency at getting what we could have. In other words, associated with envy is the experience of one's disempowerment. Likewise, in jealousy, the experience of loss or of losing an object of love and devotion, there is the experience of losing something we felt we owned because we had control over it. Thus psychologically, inseparable from both envy and jealousy is the sense of *entitlement and ownership*. But what are they, where do they come from, and what do they imply from a psychological viewpoint?

THE SENSE OF ENTITLEMENT AND OWNERSHIP

At the core of jealousy, in the tragic sense, the control over a loved one is lost to some rival that is real or can be imaginary. In many instances of

---

[8] See Moessinger, P. (2000a). *The Paradox of Social Order: Linking Psychology and Sociology*. New York: Aldine de Gruyter; Moessinger, P. (2000b). *Le jeu de l'identité*. Paris: Presses Universitaires de France.

[9] Moessinger, P. (2000a), p. 112.

jealousy-related drama, a delusion of rivalry is involved, as if the jealous objectifies causes of his or her ordeal in another individual. Such objectification serves the purpose of imposing some coherence on the chaos of irrational thoughts and feelings, the dreadful pain associated with jealous experience. It is a desperate rationalization of rejection, whether real or fantasized.

Jealousy is the disease of love, a disease we all share, in various forms and to various degrees. In common language, it is synonymous with the compulsive loss of good judgment of others. The compulsive irrationality associated with jealousy is recognized in codes of law across cultures. Such codes tend to stipulate extenuating circumstance for crimes done under its spell. Crimes linked to jealousy (i.e., rejection and loss of relational control), also labeled crimes of passion, call for more tolerance and lenience because of their impulsive and irresistible nature. They leave less room for malignant premeditation, therefore, are less punishable. It is easy for us, as expressed in justice, to empathize with and show compassion (literally share passion) for individuals who are diseased by the debilitating effects of social rejection.

Passion and wrath aside, jealousy entails a sense of possession, the possession of another entity that is differentiated from the self but that one feels *entitled* to own. In a generic sense, possession is the experience of assimilation to the self of things or persons that exist in independence of the own body. This process is in essence symbolic but can become embodied when the object of possession becomes a natural extension of the body as in the case of a tool (e.g., stilts, tennis racket, glasses, jewelry, hammer). The same applies to envy, which consists in a claim of ownership of something that is missing from the self and needs to be incorporated or self-appropriated.

Incorporation and self-appropriation are central, highly complex, and not well understood psychological processes. They entail *incorporation*, literally, the assimilation into the body (embodiment) of external things, whether material (a nice home, the beautiful body of another, or a car), or immaterial (an idea or an idyllic model). In a sense, the process is analogous to the metabolizing of food by the body, which incorporates and processes energy for its survival. Such a process generalizes to immaterial things like objects of love and fantasies about people.

In possession, at a psychological level, external things tend to be assimilated and end up fusing with the self. In a way, jealousy is the fear or the actual experience of the loss of something that belonged to the self, the wrenching of someone's integral part.

Mundane examples of possession as a process abound, most of the time expressed at an unconscious and implicit level of awareness. For example, it appears that many people invest a lot in their cars, both materially and emotionally. They groom them as they groom their own body. Cars, like many other artifacts of possession and in most instances are an extension of the self. People can recognize themselves in such a material thing, which they carefully choose and groom. Like shoes and ties, cars are a nontrivial extension of one's own body by which personality and social "aura" are projected to the public eye. They are experienced as such, notwithstanding the fact that, in the case of a car, they facilitate self-propelled locomotion. They also promote social affiliation by the public display of presumed status and reputation.

In general, we are very much aware of what we wear and what we drive, projecting what we like to think we are into material things for the world to see. We seek affiliation and self-affirmation in the things we choose to own and claim as possessions. Ultimately, we search for others' evaluative approval that we are worth affiliating with, capturing their attention by all possible means of seduction, even if not so obvious. There is no social innocence in most things that we own and that we wear, all geared toward influencing our affiliation with selected others, a constant imaginary target audience.

I would argue that much of the possession game is to seduce others, or at least gain recognition from those we select to maintain social closeness with, gaining reputation and social ascendance over them. Possessions, the ways we possess and how we display or carry them, are instrumental in our constant attempt at controlling what people see of us. We incorporate all of our possessions as part of "Me," in William James's sense, "Me" as a conceptual and constructed notion of self that is projected into the public eye for evaluation.

Once we purchase something, we own it, not only on paper, but also as a property, something that is "mine," literally metabolized or incorporated into the self. It is interesting to note that the word *property* is derived from the Latin word *proprius*, which stands for "what cannot be shared with others." In this sense, with the choice and eventual acquisition of a thing, it becomes my own, part of my embodied self.

The choice to own one thing over another is never socially innocent, always deliberate in relation to the impression it will have on the mind of others. Often with the false veneer of innocence, there are comparison, intention, seduction, and struggle for social ascendance; a deliberate effort toward social affiliation and recognition. The calculation of our public projection is endemic in our lives, including what we own or try to *appropriate* (in-corporate) as self.

A simple model could account for the origins of a sense of ownership and entitlement in relation to people and things. There are at least three basic psychological ingredients underlying the irrepressible tendency to appropriate as *ours* and to feel entitled to things that do exist in independence of us, be they people or material things like cars, houses, clothes, or land.

The first ingredient is a sense of self, in particular a sense of self as *differentiated* from objects and other people. The idea is simple: in order to incorporate something, the necessary prerequisite is to have something that is from the outside. In other words, ownership and entitlement imply, at the most basic level, a differentiation between self and world: what pertains to the body, and what does not.

The second necessary ingredient is the propensity to *objectify* things and people as differentiated entities, to perceive them as objects of contemplation and exploration. It pertains to the ability of the individual to project, or to *eject,* feelings and affects outward, things that exist independently of them. Contrary to the Freudian meaning of projection as a defense mechanism, *projection* is understood here as the propensity to eject outward and to create objects of thoughts, contemplation, and desire. It is the conscious process by which subjective (self) experience is objectified, projected into an object that is physically external to the body: a feeling of love objectified in a person, a feeling of desire objectified in a physical object, be it a house, a boat, or a good meal. It is a process associated with the conscious mind state as discussed in an earlier chapter.

But self-world differentiation and projection are not yet sufficient to explain the sense of ownership and entitlement we are so inclined to experience. In addition, and this is the third ingredient, there is the necessity to *identify* with the thing differentiated and objectified. Identification is the process of self-recognition in entities that exist outside the own body, entities that are differentiated and objectified. In the process, one recognizes his own subjective experience (feelings, affects, emotions) in the external object of desire and contemplation.

Following this model, ownership and entitlement would rest on the combination of these three basic ingredients. The model can be summarized in a simple equation:

$$Ownership = Differentiation + Projection + Identification$$

This simple model will be useful in the discussion of the next chapter regarding how such a sense develops, particularly the ways by which children develop the very human ability to relinquish ownership via sharing and *negotiation* as opposed to coercion.

HOMO NEGOTIATUS

To live in society is to split resources, whether space, food, sexual partners, or caregivers. As has any other social animal, humans have the propensity to split or share primarily via coercion, where the stronger gets the lion's share. However, as a species, humans also evolved alternative ways of splitting resources via trades or *exchanges*, and in particular via the explicit process of negotiation and agreement reaching. These ways, at least to the extent that they are actually implemented, are arguably unique to our species.

Coercion is, at bottom, determined by the selfish law imposed by the most powerful. However, that does not make such forceful sharing simple. In a coercive context, power struggle, power enforcement, and assertion can be highly complex, as is well documented, particularly in our close primate relatives (e.g., chimpanzees). But suffice to say that no other species evolved the human way of negotiating to reach explicit, mutual agreement in sharing and trading.

When bartering at a market, sellers and buyers go back and forth in offering and counteroffering values in the exchange of goods. It is active matchmaking, hence active coregulation. The agreement reached allows the transfer of ownership, a reciprocal give and take. The process of negotiation is the process leading to mutual agreements, hence the establishment of explicit shared values. But this process does not apply only to the economic context or active trading of gifts and physical goods. It also applies to feelings, emotions, and the network of affects that link self to others.

The sense of shared experience (intersubjectivity) and relative social affiliation arises from a constant negotiation of the self with others. Social experience is indeed the constant probing and readjustment of what is mutually projected and identified between me and others with whom I transact. We project images of ourselves, monitoring and probing how others respond to them, constantly adjusting to unavoidable gaps between what we project from within and what is reflected back to us from without.

In this image trade, there is ongoing, never-ending mutual transaction. The sense of shared experience or intersubjectivity is thus a process of constant negotiation with agreements that are never reached, except in delusion, as, for example, in instances of extreme narcissism when individuals do not perceive any gaps in self-other image exchanges.

As mentioned, the process of negotiation is the process leading to some mutual agreement on values, values that are shared. In economics, such values are represented in terms of prices or bartering chips. In affective terms, they are represented and expressed in less quantifiable terms such as gifts or reciprocal feelings. But the underlying process of constant negotiation is analogous. In the marketplace, prices and values are constantly readjusted depending on the law of supply and demand. Likewise, in the affective realm, feelings and representations are constantly probed for confirmation and revision in interpersonal exchanges. In this realm, feelings and representations are constantly readjusted in terms of intersubjectivity: the elusive, dynamic sense of shared experience with others. This process is systematic, not haphazard.

In the economic world, values and prices are always fluctuating, and hard to predict. This difficulty is the bread and butter of millions of venture capitalists betting on the future of prices, making all kinds of predictions based on various theories and analyses. All these wishful speculations have only one common denominator: they are never totally accurate and are always in need of revision. Likewise, the value we perceive of ourselves in relation to others is made of constant revision and probing in interpersonal exchanges, an equivalent to the economic marketplace except that, rather than being the place for exchanges of material goods or stocks, it is an affective marketplace where the sense of self-worth and social belongingness is permanently probed and revised.

It is the affective marketplace where the social situation of the individual is assessed, where first- and third-person perspectives about the self are meeting. Representations from these perspectives are unstable, always corevised. They meet as the economic forces of supply and demand of any marketplace do. Marketplaces are always the hot spots in any human society, places where things are happening and hopping, even in the most dormant regions of the world. Likewise, in the affective domain, most things happen when dispute and seduction between self and others happen. Individuals become alive when active sharing via negotiation takes place, whether it pertains to physical goods or feelings. Analogous trading and negotiating processes occur in the economic and affective domains. In fact, we could argue that the exchange of physical goods is never detached from affectivity and emotions, never detached from feelings.

Needless to say impulsivity, superstition, and other intuitive shortcuts underlie most economic decisions as much as they feed interpersonal exchanges via seductive and other impulsive, passionate moves.

There is a lot of irrationality involved in both the economic and the affective marketplace, both having much room for ghostly fears and unreasonable hopes. Gambling is a case in point where emotions and seemingly rational strategies share the same bed. Multiple studies show that we tend to base economic decisions more on superstition and other broad similarity judgments than on careful reasoning about probability outcomes.[10] For example, research shows that investment, betting, and other gambling decisions are influenced by gains rather than losses. When winning, we tend to bet more, even though logically, the probability of future gains or decreases. Gamblers, as do lovers, tend to base their bets on wishful thinking and superstition rather than the systematic consideration of all possible outcomes. Intuition and wishful thinking dominate economic decisions in the same broad way that delusion and uncertainty determine intersubjectivity. In both domains, typical discrepancies between expectations and outcomes call for constant adjustments and negotiations.

FAIRNESS AND PERFECT SHARING

The word *utopia* is from Greek and means the "nowhere place." Egalitarianism is the utopia of politics, the "nowhere place" of democratic ideals. The common denominator of all political programs in modern democratic societies, from Left to Right and arguably with more or less honesty and success, is the easing of differences among citizens. In these societies, no political programs would disagree that the ultimate goal is to foster progress toward a place where each citizen would have a fairer share of the common good. Each group and denomination has its bill of rights. From communism to fascism and all the intermediates, modern political systems and ideologies pretend to promote what they view as increased fairness in sharing, each with their own priority on what needs to be equally distributed and how it should be fairly shared. Each program has its own rationale of what is fair and what is less fair. Regardless of our political horizon, we all have a sense of what is fair, or at least what is unfair or fairer. But what is it, and how could we all agree on what is fair sharing?

In absolute terms, fairness is the sharing of something with no resulting envy or jealousy in any of the sharers. Fairness is thus what surrounds

---

[10] See, for example, Kahneman, D., & Tversky, A., eds. (2000). *Choices, Values, and Frames.* Cambridge: Cambridge University Press.

perfect sharing. Perfect sharing is socially optimal. It exists "if there is no other way to share that would give a bigger share to a participant, and other shares to others that are at least as big" (Moessinger, 2000, p. 102, translated from French by the author).

Finding formal ways to create perfect sharing has preoccupied not only philosophers and political scientists pushing for some brand of egalitarian ideology, but also mathematicians, economists, and historical philosophers.[11] Ancient formulations of perfect sharing can be found in Greek mythology and the Old Testament. It is exemplified in the way Hesiod recounts how Zeus and Prometheus shared meat or how Abraham and Lot shared Israel: one divides into what he thinks are two equal parts, *and the other chooses*. It is a clever way to prevent envy in the protagonists, particularly if they are "optimizers" or "self-maximizers," both equally motivated to get as much as they can.

This perfect procedure of sharing excludes the problem of envy. It does not, however, exclude the issue of guilt or seduction. The procedure is perfect in the context of envy suppression where both sharers are optimizers. But in reality, the context of human sharing is much more complex.

More often than not, it entails seduction, reciprocity, debt creation, and long-term interpersonal plans, hence potential guilt (see the chapter on shame). If I share a pizza with you, it is not always to get as many slices as I can while you do the same. It might be that my pleasure resides in giving you more and eventually sacrificing my appetite for yours. Most people do that for their child or their lover.

In fact, we are not mere short-term optimizers in our interpersonal exchanges. On the contrary, we are inveterate seducers. We like to create affective debts with others, project gratuitous gestures, and are sensitive to the sacrifice of others as a sign of affective engagement toward the self. We tend to use and display sacrifices to build durable prestige and social fame to further affiliation with others.

Seduction, as a human attribute, is in many ways the opposite of a short-term, self-maximizing, and utilitarian rationale. It is also far from being guided by the utopian idea of fairness. Sacrifice contradicts the idea of fairness; it is self-inflicted unfairness favoring others. Seduction and the effort to maintain closeness with others often lead to self-sacrifice that

---

[11] Austin, A. K. (1982). Sharing a cake. *Mathematical Gazette* 66: 212–213; Steinhaus, H. (1948). The problem of fair division. *Econometrica* 16: 101–104; Lowry, S. T. (1987). *The Archeology of Economic Ideas: The Classical Greek Tradition*. Durham, NC: Duke University Press; Moessinger, P. (2000).

overrides the concern about equal sharing. It overrides the tendency toward self-maximizing.

The creation of rules promoting equality in sharing such as "I divide; you choose" does show concern for others. However, seductive sacrifices are much more potent to communicate care for others. To show care, love, or concern toward others; to increase closeness and intimacy, there is nothing like the display of an explicit overriding of one's own needs to serve the other, the display of "costly sacrifice."

The demonstration of selflessness is a more powerful gesture than the deliberate attempt at reaching elusive fairness. As a matter of fact, in most cultures, etiquette dictates that to choose less is more polite. Etiquette typically provides ready-made gestures and staging of the self all pertaining to self-sacrifice, the opposite of selfish and self-maximizing behaviors. We are told not to eat first, not to sit first, to let the other go first, and to give our seat on the bus to elderly people and pregnant women.

Perfect procedures, which lead to perfect sharing and the suppression of envy in the sharers, have been invented by mathematicians and other intellectuals to split something in two, three, four, and even more procedures formally recognized as producing "even shares" among protagonists. However, these cleaver procedures can apply only to objects that are homogeneous, not spread out in multiple distinct pieces. They can apply to homogeneous objects like a pizza or a piece of land. However, they cannot be applied to a collection of heterogeneous objects, the collection of an estate to be shared among inheritors and that would include cars, apartments, paintings, or furniture. The sharing of such an estate would require negotiation and can never be perfect, never eliminating the potential for envy and guilt. The best it could reach is "satisfaction" among the sharers, an agreement that could never be perfect and absolute, always open for discussion and dispute, always open for further negotiation.

Satisfaction, rather than perfect agreement in sharing, is the kind of agreement one can hope to reach in the sharing of experience with others. Contrary to perfect sharing, negotiation is always involved when it comes to intersubjective exchanges. It is never closed, always open, never complete and settled.

Negotiation in sharing is at the core of social cohesiveness. It is the process by which envy is tentatively controlled and jealousy tamed. This process is also responsible for regulating open-ended interpersonal relationships. Sharing, giving, and negotiation are at the heart of human fragile social peace.

These are the mechanisms humans evolved to resolve and avoid disputes, disputes that have to do with the fear of losing what one feels entitled to own, what one experiences as integral and constitutive parts of the self in relation to others. The next chapter addresses the question of how the sense of ownership and entitlement, as well as the propensity to share, come about in development. By adopting a developmental perspective, the goal is to explore further the psychological nature of these phenomena, in particular the concern for others.

9

Origins of Owning and Sharing

"Mine!"
                A child, twenty-one months

Humans evolved to become *Homo negotiatus*, a species in which social behavior revolves primarily around the tallying of exchanges, the co-construction and constant reassessment of shared values. We spend our time assessing and adjusting our consensus about the values of things with other people. But more importantly, once again, we are constantly gauging the degree of our affiliation with others, our social proximity and social impact on others, fighting off the basic fear of rejection.

Children grow to become such creatures, deeply immersed in the negotiation of values about things, including the value of the self in relation to others. This chapter is concerned with how children come to give and share in reciprocal exchanges, in what psychological context they become concerned about others by either sympathizing or empathizing with them.

First, I consider the human sense of ownership and entitlement as a necessary condition. I ask, Where does the sense of ownership come from? What are the first manifestations of an apparent sense of entitlement in the child, and how does it come about? I then turn to the developmental emergence of empathy as opposed to sympathy toward others, active sharing and negotiation, ultimately questioning what might lead children to relinquish property with others in mind.

FIRST CLAIM OF OWNERSHIP

Unmistakable first signs of possessiveness are expressed early on in relation to the mother or any primary caretakers, anybody who is familiar to the young child. Pediatricians, psychiatrists, and psychoanalysts like René Spitz, John Bowlby, Donald Winnicott, and Melanie Klein emphasize the emergence and importance of an *object relation* in the first months following birth. These authors notice and try to account for the fact that very early on infants not only develop self-world differentiation (some kind of dualism), but also *project* their affectivity into people and things that furnish their environment. In short, infants do manifest an early propensity to project feelings and emotions into objects and people they progressively perceive as distinct from themselves.

At the origins of psychological development, there is a primal tension between the progressive realization of infants that they are agents in a world that exists independently of the self, and the need to maintain contact and fusion with what is furnishing this world. The child's survival depends on such contact maintenance, which, in turn, depends on the propensity of the child to project feelings and emotions.

If young children were merely developing cold knowledge of an ecological self, coming to the cognitive realization that they are a differentiated, situated, and agent entity in the world, there would be no possible attachment, and without attachment young children would die. Stated bluntly, without attachment and object relations, infants would not survive. They would not survive because they would lack the basic propensity or drive to maintain proximity with the resources they depend upon. As already discussed in a preceding chapter, following the seminal work of John Bowlby, humans, as have most avian and mammalian species, have evolved complex attachment systems that contribute to the survival of their young. Attachment of the young to a primary caretaker, usually the mother, is indeed crucial to ensure necessary food and protection, with its inherent counterpart: the fear of separation.

The affective root of such fear is in the formation of an object relation with selected individuals, eventually physical things as substitutes for such individuals. Early on, particular people but also particular objects are invested not only as physical things existing in independence of the self, but also as affective objects that are invested to become *extensions of the self*, the warrants of social proximity.

The affective investment in things and people as extension of the self is a central psychological phenomenon, if not the most central. It is at the root of the sense of entitlement and ownership that is so central to the organization of the human psyche. But what might be the mechanisms that the sense of ownership rests upon and when can we say that it first manifests itself in development?

The first question is complex but it suffices to say here that infants are endowed with mechanisms evolved by the species as a phylogenetic adaptation to humans' premature birth, the mixed altricial (dependent on others) and precocial (autonomous from others) states human infants are characteristically born in.[1] Attachment and the early propensity of children to form object relations are part of such mechanisms. There is biological readiness for infants to invest affectively in others and form such relations. It is therefore undeniable that infants do not have to construct from scratch their capacity for affective investment in others. By extension, ultimately, they do not have to construct their basic capacity to invest feelings and emotions in physical things as a substitute for people, as, for example, the substitute artificial mothers in Harlow's famous experiments that demonstrate infant monkeys' specific psychological need for attachment, independent of feeding need.

Infants are biologically prepared to form attachments; the motivational mechanisms underlying object investment are in place from birth. If not at birth already, such an investment is definitely evident, for example, in the greeting social smile of infants by the second month as they begin to engage in their first reciprocal exchanges with others. As proposed earlier, such exchanges would correspond to the actual psychological birth of the infant.[2]

Although infants appear to be born equipped to invest affectively in others and in physical things, their biological preparedness does not account for the emergence of entitlement and ownership per se. The capacity for attachment and affective investment in an object relation are a necessary, yet not sufficient ingredient for the sense of ownership and entitlement that becomes explicit within months after birth. For example, the capacity for affective investment and projection into things and the establishment of an object relation are necessary ingredients or primitives for the child to say, "Mine!" The possessive word *mine*, typically uttered over and over again from the end of the second year, means that it is not yours. It marks the emergence of a new affirmation of the self in relation to others. But how does this explicit self-other boundary come about, what might be the function of such a claim, and what does it mean psychologically for the child?

The claim of ownership derives from the capacity to invest affectively in things perceived as distinct from the self, yet experienced as belonging to

[1] Gould, S. J. (1977). *Ontogeny and Phylogeny*. Cambridge, MA: Harvard University Press.
[2] See also for further discussion: Rochat, P. (2007). Intentional action arises from early reciprocal exchanges. *Acta Psychologica* 124: 1, 8–25.

the self. This, in fact, forms a profound paradox. On one hand, there is the realization that something is distinct from the self, in particular the own body. It is differentiated from the self, yet experienced as part of it, experienced as being "incorporated." Here lies the paradox and to bypass it and eventually live with it, the child is in need of others. The sense of ownership and entitlement is determined by the presence and existence of others (i.e., their potential envy, jealousy, desire, or covetousness for the same thing), and the paradox can only be resolved in relation to them.

Without others, there would be no need to claim ownership, no need to experience objects as differentiated yet incorporated in the self. The paradox is bypassed once the child eventually realizes that such incorporation gives him or her *social power*, the power of controlling social proximity by relinquishing claimed ownership, either by giving or by trading. Comes a point in development when children realize and implement the fact that by owning, one actually gains privileged control in the drive to affiliate with others. One comes to realize that owning gives the power to negotiate, to introduce claimed ownership into a space of negotiation with others.

This paradox and its resolution are thus social in origin, coming from a need to delimit and assert the self in relation to others. Its resolution via sharing will serve the child to gain further control in the maintenance of proximity with others. Here, it is necessary to repeat that without others there would be no self, psychologically as well as conceptually. The self can exist only in relation to others (no-self entities), as a figure can exist only in relation to a ground. If there is no ground, there is no form, in the same way that without others, there is no self. It is as simple as that. The self is revealed in differentiation from others, but also in negotiation with others via reciprocal exchanges. The origins of ownership need to be considered within this logic.

In short, the claim of ownership is an emotionally based appropriation of things that are assimilated to the self. It delimits and defines the self in relation to others. If this appropriation is the necessary basis for any claim of ownership, an important ingredient is still missing to become the kind of ownership that can be negotiated in reciprocal exchanges. It takes more than a claim of ownership for the child to become *Homo negotiatus*. Children need to grasp the meaning of this claim from the perspective of others. Only then will they eventually discover that much control over social proximity can be gained by relinquishing such a claim. They can also sooner or later start to work on their reputation and make a decisive step in the process of their enculturation.

ORIGINS OF OWNERSHIP AND SHARING

The claim that "it is mine" is an affective stamp communicated to others. It sets some clear rules, including that "it is not yours." It might be sharable but requires negotiation. It sets a particular social atmosphere with an overtone of competition. Parents across cultures, in order to prevent conflicts and fights, tend, more or less successfully, to enforce sharing, to ensure cohesiveness within the family. However, this process of enculturation begins much earlier than the second birthday when children begin to use the possessive *mine*. It starts at birth and particularly by nine months in the context of nonverbal triadic exchanges (i.e., joint attention).

The counterpart of the intensive care required by the human young is intense fusion during the first weeks of life. As discussed in an earlier chapter, early human bonding is particularly intense before the emergence of independent locomotion that gives radically new freedom to the child. Human life starts with intensive care and is nurtured by formidable parental attention, as well as emotional resonance and affective sharing of unmatched sophistication in the mammalian order.

No other species spends so much time deliberately sharing affects with their progenies in face-to-face mirroring and other protoconversation. This is observed across highly contrasted cultures and socioeconomic circumstances. The intense emotional resonance and affective sharing set the stage of child development, namely, the necessary movement toward autonomy, as children must somehow snap out of the great emotional and affective dependence that is the primal mark of their interpersonal world. It is a necessary move toward greater affective autonomy and social control.

In healthy development, I see three main steps in this movement toward affective autonomy and control, all unfolding within the first nine months (see later discussion). Note that this proposal overlaps and integrates ideas of existing theories put forth by more eloquent others long before me, in particular Erik Erikson, Donald Winnicott, and John Bowlby. All insisted already that at the core of infant and child development, there is a tension between proximity maintenance and exploration, between comfort and adventure.

Let me reiterate that, on one hand, the child enjoys and depends on the care received from others. On the other, he needs to exhaust all possibilities for action outside this dependency. This is a core conflict that sparks a whole dynamic in development, whether cognitive, social, emotional, or affective as discussed here. This existential dilemma young children start to grapple with during the first months will never really leave them in their journey through life and relationships. It is a *constitutive dilemma* of our psyche. The question for them will always be how to expand outside the primal bind without jeopardizing it, how to leave a secure base in order to explore beyond, without taking the risk of losing it? The sense of entitlement and ownership finds its roots probably in the management of such risk. It is when first encountering and trying to resolve this fundamental dilemma that infants begin to expand their own physical body, literally *incorporating* discrete entities as parts of themselves, as I will try to show next.

Early on, and particularly by the end of the first year (approximately nine months), infants begin to bind to preferred toys, dolls, pacifier, or blanket. They cling to them and protest when threatened with separation from them or actually losing them. They start to claim exclusive ownership of and implicit entitlement to such objects of predilection. This claim becomes more than an incorporation, quickly also serving the purpose of sharing with others, a privileged way to control others' attention to the self.

Once again, the idea is that with object appropriation and sharing, the child gains social control. From nine months on, infants use the appropriation of objects to capture and maintain the attention of the other. They learn by necessity the logic that in order to receive attention one needs to give reasons for such attention. But at this stage, it is still nonverbal and not yet very convoluted, pretty straightforward as shown in the photo of a child trying to capture the attention of an adult by presenting his toy (see Figure 6). Quickly, infants realize that by owning, they create currency for exchanges and social proximity.

The following is an account of *three main steps* in healthy development that lead infants toward autonomy and social control. I use these steps to exemplify the sense of ownership as I see it emerging early in life.

Step 1 (Birth to Two Months)

As pointed out by Freud and his followers – Karl Abraham in particular – oral activities dominate the life of the newborn. Without any stretch of the imagination, and even if one is reluctant to endorse psychoanalytical concepts and theory, it is obvious to anybody observing a neonate in a wakeful state that all behavior seems to revolve around the mouth. Aside from breathing, newborns cry, move their hands to the mouth, and suck

FIGURE 6. Social control and power gained by owning. A year-old child uses an object of possession to capture and control the attention of an adult. The child expresses secondary intersubjectivity (shared experience with someone about an object), but also a budding mastery of the social "sharing" power gained by claiming possession over things.

everything that has contact with their lips and tongue, even with their cheeks, as they orient and suck systematically toward any tactile stimulation (rooting response).

I conducted multiple experimental studies early in my career that demonstrate the sophistication of oral behavior at birth and in the course of the first six months of life. Young infants use their mouth not only to feed, but also to explore and gain perceptual information about physical objects in the world that exist independently of them but on which they can act.[3] Feeding is clearly at the outset the dominant function of oral activity. From this dominant function derive all the others, from perception, to eroticism, or any other libidinal expressions stressed by Freud and his followers in

---

[3] For a review of this research see Rochat, P., & Senders, S. J. (1991). Active touch in infancy: Action systems in development. In M. J. Weiss & P. R. Zelazo, eds., *Infant Attention: Biological Contraints and the Influence of Experience*, 412–442. Norwood, NJ: Ablex; as well as Rochat, P. (2001a). *The Infant's World*. Cambridge, MA: Harvard University Press.

trying to capture the affective meaning of such activity, in particular the role of oral pleasures at the origins of psychic life and its development.

Infants are equipped from birth, and even prior, with sophisticated sucking competencies. Even fetuses during the last trimester of gestation are shown, via ultrasonic recording, to move fingers and thumb to the mouth for sucking. Their sucking is strong: it is not uncommon to see self-inflicted blisters on arms and hands of neonates produced by sustained sucking in the womb. Newborn sucking is organized, flexible, and selective. They reject objects from their mouth that are eccentric relative to the shape and texture of the biological nipple. Sucking is also typically strong, if not voracious, hence the overwhelming feeling that the whole body of the infant seems geared toward oral contact and the ingestion of food as a source of basic pleasure and appeasement. In some old research, for example, we have shown that newborns put their hand at the mouth as part of the engagement of the feeding system, coming to rest when in oral contact with something they can suck on, and in particular a substance laced with sucrose.[4]

The assimilation of outside things inside the body is therefore a primal experience for which infants are well prepared and equipped. In addition, it is highly reinforced via a complex network of neurochemistry that gives intense pleasure to the child, of the same kind we enjoy while exercising. This neurochemistry is endogenous and triggered by the ingestion of sweet food that is known to engage the endorphin (opioid) system phenomenally associated with pain reduction and intense pleasure.

When not ingesting food, but sucking nonnutritive objects such as hands or thumb, young infants do experience reversible or temporary incorporation via the mouth that is not only well organized but also the locus of rich intermodal perceptions including pressure, temperature, taste, texture, as well as the proprioception of tongue, jaw, and lip movements. We can speculate that such perceptions can serve the infant to explore the process of *incorporation*, putting things in and out of the mouth, for example, things that belong to the self already (e.g., hands and fingers) and things that do not (e.g., nipple, food, pacifier).

---

[4] See Rochat, P. (1987). Mouthing and grasping in neonates: Evidence for the early detection of what hard or soft substances afford for action. *Infant Behavior and Development* 10: 435–449; Rochat, P., Blass, E. M., & Hoffmeyer. L. B. (1988). Oropharyngeal control of hand-mouth coordination in newborn infants. *Developmental Psychology* 24(4): 459–463; Blass, E. M., Fillion, T. J., Hoffmeyer, L. B., Metzger, M. A., & Rochat, P. (1989). Sensorimotor and motivational determinants of hand-mouth coordination in 1–3-day-old human infants. *Developmental Psychology* 25(6): 963–975.

Be reminded that newborns do show discrimination between double touch and single touch, between a tactile stimulation of their mouth or cheeks that originates from their own hand and one from someone else's hand.[5] It is therefore reasonable to consider that infants have the means to explore what they own, and what they do not; what is incorporated or added to the self, and what is not.

Because of their established sophistication at discriminating with their mouth, it is also reasonable to think that they would quickly detect what is inside or outside their mouth, what is incorporated and what is separated from the mouth. The first step toward the development of a sense of ownership is probably the perceptual discrimination of what is captured or released by the mouth, the incorporation of something that is or is not part of the own body (own hand vs. a pacifier).

Beyond two months, from the time infants begin to reach for and grasp objects systematically (approximately four months), they first tend to do so with a consecutive transport to the mouth. Eventually, by six months, they spend more time simply looking and fingering objects they grasp.[6] Yet, from this time on, infants often engage in the circular game of grasping and dropping objects to the ground from their high chair, for example. This deliberate "dispossession" of the object, often food, is a primal game. It provokes social responses, be they picking up or cleaning up, from attentive others. In this common scenario, the object in the child's possession becomes instrumental in causing social events (i.e., adult's response) via dispossession, leading eventually to repossession. This script is not unlike the oral transaction with objects observed in younger infants over the first two months, except that the social aspect is not clearly involved yet.

Step 2 (Three to Nine Months Approximately)

One of the most robust phenomena in all infant studies is the fact that between two and nine months, the average duration of visual attention to faces decreases markedly. This attention also loses inertia.

In the multiple experiments on object and people exploration in the first months of life conducted at our lab, we systematically find that two-month-olds are very enticed by and prefer to look at people rather than objects, even

---

[5] Rochat, P., & Hespos, S. J. (1997). Differential rooting response by neonates: Evidence of an early sense of self. *Early Development and Parenting* 6(3–4): 105–112.

[6] Rochat, P. (1989). Object manipulation and exploration in 2- to 5-month old infants. *Developmental Psychology* 25: 871–884.

attractive toys. Also, they tend to sustain longer engagement in face-to-face interaction with a joyful adult. By four to six months, however, matters change. They get bored much faster with a joyful, enticing person, and, in general, they prefer new objects to new people. From four months, infants develop a new infatuation with objects, showing more fleeting attention to people and to their emotional scaffolding in play. They show increased agency and apparent understanding of the physical environment, becoming less stimulus bound (increased adoption of a contemplative and active exploration stance toward things in the world).

Because of marked progress in postural control and motor skills, infants also explore what objects afford for novel actions. They are enticed to explore newly acquired effects they can produce on objects. At a cognitive level, it is also the time when infants begin to manifest core physical knowledge and anticipation regarding objects and their behaviors. Multiple clever experiments demonstrate that at least by four months, infants begin to have a strong sense of object permanence and understand that objects cannot be in two places at the same time; that objects occupy space, are substantial, subject to resistance from other objects.[7] Infants from this point on, live, act, and think in reference to an increasingly objectified world they gain control over.

With this second step, infants learn to possess objects in action and volition. Beyond two months, infants gain both physical and mental control over objects, and to some extent over people's reactions. Via increased planning, agency, and anticipation, one could say that infants gain a greater sense of *authorship* (command) of their actions, but also of their perceptual experience. This is marked progress compared to newborns' oral experience of objects introduced into and out of the mouth. This progress is primarily in the control of the experience with objects, an experience that arises from more deliberate actions under the control of multiple modalities, including vision.

If there is an increased sense of authorship at this point of development, infants do not yet manifest a sense of ownership of objects proper. As I will suggest next, this latter sense requires *sharing*. The origins of the sense of ownership are triadic. Claims of ownership become explicit at around nine months in a third and last developmental step. In my view, this third developmental step opens the door for the expression of entitlement and is the beginning of a sense of property.

---

[7] For a review on infant object perception and conception, see Rochat, P. (2001a), pp. 81–136.

Step 3 (Nine Months and Up)

If by four to six months infants' attention to people tends to become shorter and show less inertia, giving room for the solo exploration of objects, this trend tends to change dramatically by nine months. From this point on, children try to include and refer to others in their forays into the world, as part of first triadic competencies manifested in well-documented joint attention and social referencing.

As illustrated in Figure 6, they present interesting objects to others in an attempt at capturing and controlling others' attention. For example, they begin to check back and forth whether others are jointly attending to the object they are infatuated with, or they enjoy having caregivers mimicking them as they are being fed, from time to time moving the spoon to their mouth. In general, infants begin to show their first proclivity for sharing their perceptual experience of objects with others (secondary intersubjectivity).

This is significant progress over the rather egocentric second step discussed prior. It points to the willingness of the child to be *co-conscious* in his or her exploration. This third step sets the stage for the emergence of a sense of ownership and entitlement proper, a sense that is by definition social.

From being "Mine," the experience of object in action and manipulation becomes *"Ours."* This is such a decisive developmental step that some (e.g., Michael Tomasello) do not shy away from describing it as "the nine-month miracle." It is indeed some kind of a miracle to the extent that when this shared attention space comes online, it opens up for the child not only a brand new arena for social-cognitive development, including word learning and language,[8] but also the possibility to specify further who she is in relation to others, in particular what is hers.

The claim of property over things is an assertion of the self that cannot emerge outside possibilities for sharing. Again, with no sharing possibilities, there is no reason to claim ownership, and there are no grounds for the manifestation of entitlement, no reasons for the child to develop a property sense. This third step marks the emergence of such possibilities in the construction of a sharing space where objects are introduced into this space for joint attention.

Aside from the sharing of attention, evidence supporting the idea that the sense of ownership and entitlement proper finds its first expression by nine

---

[8] Tomasello, M. (1999). *Cultural Origins of Human Cognition.* Cambridge, MA: Harvard University Press; Bruner, J. S. (1983). *Child's Talk.* New York: W. W. Norton.

months is the fact that it is also, coincidentally, the age by which infants are typically reported to show renewed wariness in the face of strangers. They begin to have a strong inclination toward selective proximity to people, particularly an intense "clinginess" to the primary caretaker. Note, however, that selective attachment can take various forms, sometimes disorganized or reactive forms that, from the outside, are somehow contrary to clinginess (so-called disorganized or ambivalent expressions of attachment).

But on the whole, attachment research shows that by nine months infants begin to express selective closeness and seek protection from primary caretakers. They become explicitly possessive of their mother in the presence of a stranger or another child, what Spitz coined the "eight month anxiety."[9]

AFFECTIVE BINDING AND TRANSITIONAL OBJECT

Donald Winnicott[10] provides a complex analysis of the emergence of what he calls "the transitional object," starting at approximately nine months of age. With the transitional object, whether a blanket, a doll, or any other suckable, huggable, and transportable physical object, infants suddenly devote particular closeness and demonstrate a need to cling to them. It is the new expression of a strong affective investment or projection, the binding of affects into a physical object (affective binding).

The young child uses such affective binding, in part, to cope with temporary separation from the mother or any primary caretaker. For Winnicott, by the end of the first year the child finds in such objects of devotion a way to cope with separation anxiety, a comforting external entity that becomes a substitute companion of their forays away from the secure base of the mother.

At the origins, transitional objects are an affective means, created by children, to allow them to behave with independence and to explore the world outside the primary sphere of fusion with the mother. Literally, they help them to make this transition away from the mother's secure sphere.

Transitional objects are the primitive objects of possession as substitution, some kind of a reincarnation of the mother. The comfort of the mother is transferred and projected into the object that now functions for the child as substitute to cope with temporary separation. The child's

---

[9] Spitz, R. A. (1965). *The First Year of Life: A Psychoanalytic Study of Normal and Deviant Development of Object Relations.* New York: Basic Books.

[10] See, for example, Winnicott, D. W. (1989). *Psycho-Analytic Explorations.* Cambridge, MA: Harvard University Press.

possession of the mother is transferred to this particular object that becomes transitional.

Transitional objects are, by definition, objects that have value, particularly high *affective value*. They contrast with any other toys or physical things that the child encounters and plays with in that they are affectively invested, hence incorporated to the self. Children become attached to them as if these objects become part of themselves. This prefigures the sense of entitlement and ownership that becomes generalized to other objects by the end of the second year, when children start to use possessive pronouns and adjectives to communicate what is "theirs" and "not yours."

The infatuation and obsession associated with transitional objects are, to some extent, commensurate with the emotion and affect the child projects onto them. These objects are endowed with new meanings. From being distinct physical toys with particular affordances, they become objects of comfort, endowed with an affective affordance that is created by the child. Objects are transformed into "fetish" standing for comfort and security.

Fetishism is not a strong word to describe the phenomenon. *Infantile fetishism* might be more accurate. Think of the numerous anecdotes of weird rituals young children tend to develop in relation to their transitional object, be it a pacifier, a doll, a pillow, or a blanket: the need to wash it once a day with lavender soap (my requirement as a child) or, on the contrary, to leave it dirty and decomposing. In the latter case, it is as if the child sensed that cleaning or repairing the object would remove its comforting power, would take away its effectiveness and somehow remove its affective "soul." It would literally denature it, probably causing a double separation anxiety for the child (i.e., the anxiety of losing both the mother and her substitute).

We can draw an analogy between the constitution of transitional objects early in life and the mild forms of *fetishism* commonly found in adults. As adults, we have the propensity to invest emotionally a single element of a whole person or of a whole complex experience. The French psychologist Alfred Binet, at the turn of the twentieth century, was the first to dare to talk about and pay attention to the phenomenon of fetishism.[11] Binet, who ironically is very well known for his invention with his colleague Simon of intellectual quotient testing (famous Binet-Simon IQ test), was the first to describe, explore, and name the phenomenon in an article and a book entitled *Fetishism in Love Life*.

In his article and book, Binet defines *fetishism* as the phenomenon by which specific body parts tend to become particularly potent sexual

---

[11] Binet, A. Le Fétichisme dans l'amour. *Revue philosophique* 24(1887): 143–167, 252–277.

arousers, be they breasts, feet, eyes, hands, mouth, big toes, or backside. Some people obsess over high-heel shoes, over stamps, or over old cars. For Binet, fetishism is the appropriation of these objects or body parts by association with particular arousing states, whatever they might be: the experience of intense comfort, security, or sexual arousal. The fetish object, so invested, becomes an intrinsic part of the individual's own private affective life, associated with strong affective and emotional tones.

What is astutely described by Binet could be paradigmatic of how in general we bind affective values to objects that become highly symbolic and potent as standing for complex affective states. Eventually, fetishism and the binding of affective values onto objects will not only serve the self as they do with infants in their coping with separation anxiety. Sooner or later, in self-presentation, objects that are appropriated, literally incorporated to the self, will stand in the mind of the individual for the affective states they can cause in others. Thinking of cars and clothes as common objects of infatuation, this infatuation is linked to what we think we project to the outside. More often than not, we become selectively attached to things with others in mind.

Fetishism is our trademark as lovers, but also as shoppers and hoarders. Most of us collect and accumulate useless things. The reasons for such a propensity do not lie in the individual. They are not to be found in individual psychology because they are social. Fetishism is a social phenomenon arising in part from social competition and fear, but also from the generalized craving for social closeness and approval from others – paradoxically the need for potential exchanges. This is paradoxical because in hoarding, for example, one does not share. Sharing remains a remote possibility, typically never fulfilled. Despite this appearance, I would submit that sharing is at the core of hoarding, like any other form of fetishism, but in a deviant way. It is socially motivated, despite the fact that obsessive accumulation and the control of things seem primarily selfish. But the more selfish an act is, the more validating of others. It explicitly recognizes others as a threat. Why be selfish if nobody cares? Selfishness implies others, as it is defined, and it exists only in relation to them.

The constitution of the transitional object early in development is a primary form of fetishism. As adults, we keep building transitional objects to cope with our obsessions of separation, our craving for social proximity and affiliation. The need for physical fusion is obviously what sexual fetishism expresses, even in its most deviant forms. In reality, at a functional and even cognitive level, it is no more deviant than the infant's obsession with the corner of her blanket that has to have a certain smell and a particular flexibility for finger rubbing and manipulation in order to allow her sleep. As suggested by Winnicott, the transitional object is what the child constructs, and uses, to cope with separation.

The mechanism underlying the constitution of transitional objects is what makes sharing possible. This mechanism is the projection of affects and emotions into discrete physical entities that are separated from the own body, yet incorporated as part of the self. These objects become an integral part of the embodied self: they literally become the child's *own*. In this phenomenon, I suggest, we find the roots of the property sense and, by extension, the roots of sharing. It allows for the child to become *Homo negotiatus*.

As suggested by Winnicott in his *Playing and Reality*,[12] young children must abandon and eventually let go of the possessiveness toward the transitional object as a first offering to negotiate something valued and recognized as such by others. This offering marks the decisive entry of the child into human culture.

EMPATHY AND SYMPATHY

In this discussion on the developmental origins of owning and sharing, it is necessary to return to empathy as an emotion that corresponds to the sharing of feelings with others. It is the emotion of sharing "par excellence." We need to discuss empathy in the context of emerging sharing and negotiation, beyond its relation to shame, as discussed in Chapter 6.

How does empathy as an emotion by which we share feelings with others emerge in development? This development participates in the development of how children own and share objects, a major development that sets us apart as a species, a species inclined to negotiate and collaborate with each other.[13]

The construction of a sharing space by nine months and the corollary emergence of a sense of ownership and entitlement are indeed a cardinal change. As suggested already in many places, it opens the door to participation in language and complex symbolic development that starts in the second year. Here I propose that it also opens the door to further development in sharing, particularly the development of *empathic feelings* in the child. We will see later in the chapter that this is evident when considering the development of *active sharing* or distributive justice in the child. These processes entail much more than the *passive sharing* of emotional resonance or contagion.

---

[12] Winnicott, D. W. (1982). *Playing and Reality*. London/New York: Tavistock.
[13] For further discussion see Rochat, P. (2005). Humans evolved to become *Homo Negotiatus . . . the rest followed*. *Behavioral and Brain Sciences* 28(5): 714–715; also Rochat, P. (2006). What does it mean to be human? *Journal of Anthropological Psychology* 17: 100–107.

The term *empathy* derives from the German *einfühlung* (feeling for or with), itself derived from the Greek *em* (in) and *pathos* (suffering), meaning literally "in suffering" with or for others. The word captures the vicarious experience of feelings, thoughts, and attitude of others, which gets under one's skin and into one's mind, sharing their experience, for good or for ill. It is arguably among the most important psychological concepts.

Empathy stands for what bridges subjective experiences among people, whether good or bad. It is what underlies prosocial behavior and self-sacrifice. It is typically understood as the phenomenon that is at the origin of what makes us good and sensitive toward others, as opposed to just evil and insensitive self-maximizers.

The term *sympathy*, in turn, is from the Greek *sym* and *pathos*, meaning literally "suffering together." It also captures a vicarious experience. However, compared to *empathy*, *sympathy* captures a broader, more passive sense of vicarious experience. If empathy implies some perspective taking, or mechanisms of *getting into the shoes of others*, sympathy does not.

As we all know, empathy and sympathy are real phenomena that shape our existence. However, for many years, hardcore behavioral scientists were reluctant to deal with such phenomena, as important as they might be, considering them too soft, conceptually too slippery and too broad to be experimentally tested. They were left to the speculation of philosophers and group therapists.

For the past ten years, however, the issue of empathy has gained the limelight in cutting-edge science with the discovery of *mirror neuron systems* in the brain of monkeys by a team of neuroscientists in Parma, Italy.

Studying the neural mechanisms involved in eye-hand coordination and manual actions in monkeys, the Parma scientists (Giacomo Rizzolatti, Vittorio Gallese, Luciano Fadiga, and colleagues) were recording single cell responses in a specific area of the monkey's motor cortex (F5, to be precise). Cell responses were recorded as the animal reached, grasped, and eventually transported to the mouth a piece of food presented on a pick or on a tray. The single cell recording device was connected to a loudspeaker so that each time the monkey's neuron or group of neurons fired, it emitted a loud rustling static sound to alert the experimenters during testing.

One day, some of the Parma scientists[14] had a lunch break, a picnic at the lab in the presence of the monkey attached to the recording apparatus. As one of the scientists sitting across from the monkey put his sandwich at his

---

[14] This anecdote is based on personal communication with Luciano Fadiga in May 2005 in Paris.

mouth, the recorded cell(s) of the monkey started to fire, the same cell(s) that discharged minutes before as the monkey itself was producing the analogous intentional action. The monkey demonstrated that there exists in the brain a population of cells that fire equally when producing a specific action and when the same action is seen performed by someone else.

It is in this rather mundane, serendipitous circumstance that Rizzolatti and his Parma team made a stunning discovery that is currently inspiring a huge wave of research in laboratories all over the world.[15] With this happy accident, they discovered that unique neurobiological systems (mirror systems) are involved in controlling specific actions that are either self-produced or performed by another individual. Evidence is now pouring in to the cognitive and affective neuroscience literature demonstrating the existence of similar mirror systems in humans.

What the Parma team discovered is that the brain discriminates among and controls functional actions, somehow independently of whether they are self-performed or performed by another individual. The brain of the monkey, and by extension our brain, is sensitive to a grammar of action that is represented for the self as agent as well as for others as agent. One can see immediately that this discovery provides some physiological grounding to the broad issue of how we bridge and relate our subjective experience of acting and feeling to the subjective experience of others who are acting and feeling in the same way. The Parma discovery opened the possibility that indeed there might be a neurobiological underpinning to intersubjectivity.

One of the promises of the discovery is that mirror cell systems are the key to explain at a neurobiological level what underlies the rich and complex vicarious experience of empathy. Researchers are now rushing to conclude that the Parma team found the neurological substrate for empathy, giving new credentials and greater scientific status to the issue.[16]

---

[15] It is quite fascinating how breakthrough discoveries are often accidental and the result of happy accidents like the one described regarding mirror neurons. A similar story is the one of Hubel and Wiesel, who in the 1950s discovered that some nervous cell columns in the visual cortex of the cat were specialized to respond to horizontal or vertical features of the environment. They made the discovery one day because one of the transparent pieces of glass supporting an old-fashioned slide had a vertical crack. The cat's brain was responding to the accidental crack in the glass, not the intended image. Hubel and Wiesel received the Nobel Prize in the early 1970s for their serendipitous discovery! Nice demonstration that it pays to take accidental, odd phenomena seriously and to make the effort to figure out why they happen.

[16] See, for example, Prestons, S. D., & de Waal, F. B. M. (2002). Empathy: Its ultimate and proximate bases. *Behavioral and Brian Sciences* 25: 1–72.

With the discovery of mirror systems in the brain, it is as if empathy received its stamp of approval from the scientific community, in particular the reputable brain science community. This stamp of approval is particularly important in today's new culture of "substantiating" or naturalizing (biologizing, anchoring in the natural sciences) well-known, complex psychological phenomena such as the bridging of mental experiences among people. But brain accounts have their limitations and cannot capture all the subtleties and experiential complexity of phenomena like empathy, or even sympathy. Beyond the individual brain, these phenomena are embodied in social exchanges and negotiation, as well as in a culturally rich environment. They need psychological analyses going far beyond groups of neurons firing in an individual brain.

The difference between sympathy and empathy at the etymological level corresponds to an important psychological distinction. *Sympathy* refers more to a passive contagion of emotions and affects between self and others. We feel and express sympathy to victims because we are somehow contaminated by their suffering, in automatic resonance with their miseries. It does not mean, however, that we do so by getting into the shoes of victims and by trying to *simulate*, literally to reenact in our head, what the experience of the victims might be. Sympathy can be based on mere emotional resonance. It corresponds to the gut feeling one might base on a smile, a word, or a gesture.

Sympathy is as direct as a reflex. Likewise, we might feel immediate antipathy toward someone that is based on a particular gesture or expression. Experiencing such a gut feeling does not require any perspective taking or simulation of others by getting into their shoes and under their skin. It is an immediate experience not unlike the direct contagion expressed by newborns when hearing other infants cry in their nursery. They automatically join the chorus.

In contrast, empathy captures a more *active way of sharing* that entails perspective taking, metarepresentation, and evaluation, in other words, higher-order cognitive processes. It is a conscious phenomenon, following the distinction proposed earlier, finding support with current affective neuroscience research.[17]

Empathy, in contrast to sympathy, is a *self-conscious emotion* proper. It is evaluative in essence, and as an active sharing of feelings, it entails the three ingredients discussed in the preceding chapter regarding entitlement

---

[17] Decety, J., & Jackson, P. L. (2006). A social-neuroscience perspective on empathy. *Current Directions in Pschological Science* 15(2): 54–58.

FIGURE 7. Various levels of empathic feelings. It is impossible to experience positive "happy" feelings while contemplating this photograph. However, there are different levels of "participating" feelings that can be associated with this experience, from the direct perception of a sad facial expression to the emotional resonance of pain, empathic feelings leading to action, or meta-cognitive attempts at figuring out what this picture might actually be showing: is it a Tutsi mother in mourning for her killed child?

and ownership. Empathy entails *self-other differentiation*, the *projection* of feelings, and *identification* with the other person.

To illustrate this point, I would like to review different ways of experiencing and making sense of the poignant picture of the crying lady in Figure 7. It is indeed difficult to be indifferent to such a dramatic expression. It is unmistakably powerful because of the tragic content it calls to mind. We would all agree that the photograph in Figure 7 is anything but funny. But what exactly is its tragic content?

There are different ways of experiencing the tragic power contained in this image, only one qualifying as *empathic* per se. Let us consider in turn the different possible readings of this image.

A first, literal reading of the photograph, based on the surface characteristics of the picture, is to see a woman crying. In this reading, there is no attempt at figuring what it means beyond what is directly perceived: a crying face.

A second, less literal reading of the photograph is to see a "sad" woman. There, the tears and the expression of the lady are now perceived as standing for some affective state of the mind. Such a step entails some matching of emotions between self and others, some emotional resonance between first- and third-person perspectives. However, this resonance does not have to be active and could be based on automatic, passive mirror mechanisms as discussed prior. Sympathy rather than empathy is involved at this level of reading.

A third genuinely empathic way to read the picture is to add to its meaning the reasons behind the state of her mind. For example, it could be a lady mourning her child, who was killed by some rebels on a rampage. The construal of such complex context in the reading of the photograph leads eventually to empathy proper, via active simulation and perspective taking, in other words, getting into the shoes, under the skin, and into the mind of this person. This empathic response entails active reconstitution of her circumstances.

One *empathizes* only by virtually taking the place of the other, by being "perspectival." Such higher-order representational processes add to mirror systems and other direct, sympathetic, and low-level mechanisms of emotional resonance. Empathy entails the combination of differentiation, projection, and identification that underlies *active* as opposed to passive sharing.

An important caveat to this combination is that it might give the false idea that with empathy we actually gain access to what the other person feels. But the question is, How much do we actually perceive and experience of the other's feelings? This is a crucial question that we tend to overlook assuming that empathy constitutes an equivalence of feelings in the empathizer and the empathized. In fact, it is absurd. No one will be able to experience with the same authenticity the feelings of the other. The reason is simple if we consider that all of our present experience of the world is tainted with what we lived prior; with our idiosyncratic learning, habits, and affinities; with our life story that is unique and our own. This is a realm to which no one but the person involved has access, corresponding to what philosophers call the authority of first-person perspective. Empathy, however, does actively bridge our experience with others'. There is an alignment of feelings, but this alignment is always an approximation, never an identity of experience.

Empathy is an active approximation by simulation that includes the metarepresentation of others' mental state. It leads to a certain alignment of feelings but not to an absolute equivalence of experience. It is an active sharing by approximation and by *negotiation* with others in intersubjective exchanges, not a perfect sharing based on absolute vicarious experience. Absolute vicarious experience is a unicorn, a fancy.

To illustrate further the development of active sharing in a more concrete, economic context, I turn now to a research we recently conducted in the United States as well as in various regions of the world including Peru, Brazil, China, and Fiji, where children develop in strikingly different physical, economic, and cultural circumstances. We studied the development in these children of the ability to share desirable objects with others.

ACTIVE SHARING IN DEVELOPMENT AND ACROSS CULTURES

There are different ways of possessing objects, and there are different ways of relinquishing possession of them. It is evident that someone who refuses to let go of a valuable object cannot be compared to someone who presents the same object for giving, sharing, or bartering. The former resembles the behavior of a dog fetching a ball and not wanting to let go of it. The latter resembles more what my baker does when selling me bread, a reciprocal exchange. Both are antonymic expressions of active sharing. One corresponds to active refusal, the other to reciprocal exchange.

Children's development reflects the tension between these contradictory poles: either to keep it all for themselves or to let go and enter negotiation with others. This topic is what I would like to discuss now, in terms of existing research and recent findings on the development of object sharing in young children of various cultures.

In a previous section, I discussed the idea of objects as transitional, the affective constituents of such objects. Following Winnicott, transitional objects are objects of devotion, invested with high affective value, and used by the young child to cope with separation. I proposed that the mechanism of affective projection onto physical things that are differentiated from the body, as well as transportable (a blanket, a doll, a pillowcase), could be what is at the origin of the sense of ownership in the young child, the sense that "it is mine."

Since the sense of ownership is a necessary condition for relinquishing (one cannot relinquish something that is not primarily owned, or at least feels owned), the mechanisms underlying the constitution of transitional objects could also be what make sharing possible. However, as mentioned, once they are invested and owned, there are multiple ways of sharing objects. Each reveals different levels of the self's and others' understanding. I consider now how these levels seem to emerge in the chronology of development.

There is a developmental trend from a reluctance to share, to subtle, reciprocal exchanges. This developmental trend is associated with an increased feeling for as well as understanding by the child of others' mental states.

By their second birthday, as infants start to claim explicit ownership and invest affects in objects of devotion, they do so by first manifesting unmistakable exclusivity in their possession, a blunt reluctance to exchange. They show overwhelming egocentrism. When the child begins to say, "Mine!" she does not only imply that "it is not yours." She also expresses an explicit statement of defensive exclusivity, a reluctance even to contemplate sharing, an unmistakable claim that she wants to keep it for herself.

In recent cross-cultural observations,[18] we found that this "egocentric" or "egotistic" trend is universal. We observe it in children of the same age, from all over the world, growing up in highly contrasting physical, social, economic, and cultural environments. It happens in children living in rich or poor neighborhoods and in cultures fostering radically different values regarding private property. We observe this trend in children from small, highly collectivist villages of rural Peru and from small isolated fishing communities in Fiji. It also occurs among children growing up in violent and lawless as well as affluent neighborhoods of Rio de Janeiro; unschooled kids begging and living on the streets of Recife in Brazil; as well as young children attending a Communist Party–controlled preschool in Shanghai, China; and middle-class North American children of Atlanta.

These observations are based on a simple, standard procedure we used and were able to apply in all cultures, despite the language and other cultural barriers. This procedure consisted simply in asking children to

---

[18] Rochat, P., Dias, M. D. G., Guo, L., MacGillivray, T., Passos-Ferreira, C., Winning A., & Berg, B. (2009, in press). Fairness in distributive justice by 3- and 5-year-olds across 7 cultures. *Journal of Cross-Cultural Psychology*.

share a collection of candies or desirable objects between them and an experimenter, or between two dolls. Children agreed that these objects were valuable or highly desirable. The number of objects the child was asked to share was never more than seven, so presumably children could discriminate the divided quantity by simply looking at it rather than having to count each of the two resulting collections. Counting could be a problem for some children, particularly if they are unschooled and unsupervised by adults. So, the children we tested could check, compare, and monitor the quantities they actively shared by either looking (so-called subitizing, or discrimination process without counting) or counting, if they were inclined to do so and could.

In all instances, the candies were poured onto a central plate and then the child was instructed to share. The task was for the child to distribute the candies between the two treasure boxes ("piggy banks") of the recipients. Note that in this procedure, the child is the agent of the distribution and ultimately is the one responsible for the relative value of each property at the end of the game.

We tested children between the ages of three and five years, ages at which sharing games are easily played, understood, and enjoyed by the child. Furthermore, as already mentioned, children by this age use possessives like *mine* that have more than a protodeclarative meaning. By using these possessives, they do more than point at and request objects; it is a claim of ownership.[19] As already mentioned, when children say, "Mine!" by their second birthday they do mean that the thing in question is "mine, not yours!" They are explicitly demonstrating a genuine sense of property and ownership that resembles adults'.

In the research, we chose three years as the youngest age, assuming that property and sharing could be reliably tested in this kind of standardized game. Existing research published in the literature on the topic provides very little information on sharing at such a young age and particularly on early sharing in a cross-cultural perspective.

Children were asked to share either *even* ($N = 6$) or *odd* ($N = 7$) numbers of candies in a succession of conditions. These conditions affected whether equity in sharing was possible or impossible to achieve. In some instances, all candies were identical. In others, one or two in the collection were "special" candies. A special candy was bigger, shinier, and more colorful, particularly desirable for all recipients.

[19] Tomasello, M. (1998). One child's early talk about possession. In J. Newman, ed., *The Linguistics of Giving*. Amsterdam: John Benjamins.

After a short preliminary discussion, both child and experimenter agreed that those "special" candies were indeed more desirable than the others. In each condition, we recorded the way the child shared, by simply counting how many ended up in each treasure box. We also recorded where the special candies ended up when they were part of an odd-numbered collection that rendered equity in sharing impossible. For the sake of simplicity, I will just summarize the results, extracting some of the main findings.

In general, we found that across cultures, between three and five years, there is a robust developmental trend toward more equity in sharing. In conditions where the child was one of the two recipients, three-year-olds tended to distribute overwhelmingly more candies to themselves, whether equity was possible or not. By five years, however, this trend was still evident but significantly tamed. Children continued to favor themselves and be selfish but markedly less. Interestingly, this trend was the same across all cultures but lower in children growing up in small rural and collective communities (i.e., Peru and Fiji in our sample). In development, there is thus a universal drift in active sharing from massive to reduced selfishness between three and five years of age, a trend that is moderated by the cultural environment of the child. Despite the significance of cultural factors, the trend toward increased altruism/prosociality in sharing is remarkably robust from the time children begin to be explicit in claiming ownership.

Culture appears to play a role in the developmental pace at which the child becomes inclined to share with greater equity, but the general trend is present regardless of marked variations.

In China, children were tested in a preschool that primarily emphasized group activities and sharing. Children always play, sing, and learn as members of a group, rarely as individuals isolated from the group. Such attempts are much less frequent in middle-class North American children like those we tested in Atlanta. In Fiji or in Peru, children lived in small, close-knit communities where public and shared properties dominate ostentatious private ownership. When they exist, preschools in these regions are known to emphasize synchronized group activities in children.[20]

The stability of this developmental trend is particularly striking when considering the three groups of Brazilian children. The groups grow up in

---

[20] In reference to the island of Samoa in Polynesia, see Odden, H., & Rochat, P. (2004). Observational learning and enculturation. *Educational and Child Development* 21(2): 39–50.

highly contrasting economic and cultural circumstances within the same national borders. A group of children lived in the poor and insecure environment of a favela in Rio de Janeiro, an environment dominated by young drug lords who terrorize and dictate law and order. Another group was composed of privileged children, of the same age, from an affluent private preschool situated just a few miles away from the favela. The third group of Brazilian children was composed of three- and five-year-old unschooled street kids from the city of Recife, a few hundred miles northeast of Rio. These children spent their days unsupervised by adults, begging on the street, collecting refuse, and typically spending the night with an extended family member living in precarious, unsanitary slums, sometimes close to public dumps.

One could easily presume that the drive to own, and not to share, in the young children of the favela, and particularly the street kids of Recife, might be different from that of the privileged children of Rio. Our research shows that it is not. All of these children demonstrate the same developmental trend toward a significant decrease in selfishness and increase in more equitable sharing between three and five years. But why is that?

Young children develop to become more equitable in their sharing, regardless of their economic and cultural circumstances, because they enter the culture of their species (*Homo negotiatus*), a culture that is fundamentally based on reciprocal exchanges. Hoarding and coercion are antithetical to this culture. If it exists, it is an anomaly, due to particularly stressful circumstances (war, disaster, rebellion, madness). It is not cardinal to the culture of *Homo negotiatus*, as it is for other animal species that did not evolve to have others in mind in social exchanges and sharing of resources.

We construct equity as well as agree on values by an active process of approximation and mutual monitoring. This process takes form within reciprocal exchanges. We do so by negotiation and ultimately by caring about reputation and our relative proximity to others. What happens between three and five years, is marked progress in this process that channels children away from greed and immediate gratification. The product of this development is the emergence of a moral space in which children begin to care about reputation (as discussed in the conclusion of the book).

Children between three and five years develop an understanding that they are potentially liable and that they are building a history of transactions with others. Needless to say, parents and educators foster this development in all cultures, but this fostering is essentially the enforcement of the basic rules of *reciprocity*, the constitutive elements of human exchanges. Children are channeled to adapt to these rules they depend on to maintain proximity with others. From this, they begin to build a moral space in relation to others, a moral space that is essentially based on the basic rules of reciprocity. It is a moral space that is constantly in the making, constantly revised, and in which equity is endlessly approximated by way of negotiation. Following the argument of the book, it is in the context of reciprocity as a principle and equity as an ongoing negotiation that children become self-conscious.

EQUITY IN SHARING

No concept is more difficult and elusive than the concept of equity, namely, the notion of a natural justice in the appreciation of each other's rights. This is puzzling when considering that the meaning of equity is, de facto, the cornerstone of any moral or judicial system. The elusiveness of equity as a concept also explains the marked variations of its interpretation across individuals, ages, and cultures.

Equity implies that some rightful justice can be reached when sharing. But the question is, of course, What is rightful justice? Equity as a concept presupposes some equivalence among things, actions, or services that are shared or exchanged (literally that have the same or *matched values*). The main function of justice as an institution is to provide regulation of such equivalence, useful in cases of conflict but also in setting up rules among individuals within a group, from family to society and even culture at large.

As we know, however, the rules of equity and justice vary greatly in their interpretation among individuals and across cultures. For example, in France and in other European countries, the law stipulates that the organs of an individual do not belong to him or her once he or she is dead.[21] It means that by default, once dead, French citizens lose the ownership of their own body. It now belongs to the state, which, through its public and health services, has the exclusive prerogative to dispose of and donate organs as needed by others. Historically, this default law exists in the mind of French lawmakers to foster public solidarity among citizens.

An inverted rationale prevails in the culture and justice system of the United States, where individuals are considered legal owners of their own organs beyond their death. They, and only they, can relinquish their body for donation after accidental death. Many Americans or U.S. residents like me

---

[21] Godbout, J. (1998), p. 103. *The World of the Gift*. Montreal: McGill-Queen's University Press.

carry at all times an official document that allows such relinquishing. Sadly, some individuals in poor countries go as far as selling their own organs while alive for export to rich countries, one of their kidneys, for example.

Underlying this traffic of donor organs is the rationale that individuals own what is inside their body. But this is not a universal belief. Another example of marked cultural variation is the anecdotal evidence that in small Polynesian communities I frequently visit, if one leaves his shoes in front of his hut to go to sleep, chances are that the shoes will not be there the next morning. They tend to vanish not because they are stolen, but because someone in the community needed them to go about his or her business. In Polynesian and Melanesian cultures as in most small societies all over the world, there is a collective sense of ownership that can be incomprehensible and irritating to Westerners. The sense of exclusivity, property, and justice is indeed determined by the cultural circumstances of the individual.

From a more formal, epistemological standpoint, equity in sharing is also rather elusive and not easily reached, always approximated at best. In his *Sociological Studies* published in 1965, Piaget notes: "The balance (equilibrium) of exchange is determined by the conditions of equality... But it is clear that such a balance is rarely attained" (pp. 51–52, author's translation from French).[22]

It is true that what typically concludes an exchange and is considered agreeable to all parties in terms of value equivalence is always a shaky balance. If starving, we buy bread by necessity, even if the price is outrageous, and the same for cigarettes for someone addicted to nicotine. Ticket scalpers in front of stadiums and concert halls make a living out of it. We buy a house at a certain price because it "feels" right, not only because of other recent sales of comparable size buildings in the same neighborhood.

In any exchanges, urges, gut feelings, and intuitions play a major role. When bartering two stones for a fruit, who says that it is an equitable exchange? When donating a gift, who determines what is appropriate? All these issues are settled among the protagonists in reciprocal exchanges and in *negotiations* that are most revealing of human psychology. Such exchanges and negotiations give meaning to the social life that all individuals ultimately strive for. They are the human ways of expressing basic affiliation needs.

By being recorded and not forgotten, exchanges also provide continuity in the quest toward social proximity and reputation. As already mentioned, a gift donated now is somehow commensurate with and reflects past

[22] Piaget, J. (1965/1995). *Sociological Studies*. London: Routledge.

exchanges. It also predicts future transactions in the context of reciprocity. Each transaction adds to a history of past exchanges, this history determining future transactions. The finding that children become more equitable, or less selfish, in their sharing of candies demonstrates that they develop to become increasingly attuned to the long-term consequences of their actions. They become moral to maintain their reputation and the future of their relative proximity with others. Recorded history of past exchanges does indeed provide continuity to current interpersonal exchanges. More importantly, it provides an opportunity to gauge our own situation and reputation in relation to others constantly.

It is through the process of reciprocal exchanges and negotiation that one builds trust and reputation in relation to others. Children are quick to learn it from the time they say "Mine!," as the sense of ownership is the necessary prerequisite for the construction of an intersubjective sense of value. If the intersubjective sense of value pertains to objects, it pertains also, more meaningfully, to the value of the self in relation to others.

NEGOTIATION AS SOURCE OF SELF-CONSCIOUSNESS

Negotiation is what happens when we bargain with others, whether ideas, feelings, or objects. It is the process that captures most exhaustively what human transactions are all about. It is also in this process that self-consciousness emerges and becomes consolidated. I will argue that it is by becoming *Homo negotiatus* that children become self-conscious. My idea is that self-consciousness is the by-product of negotiation.

The sense of equity and trust is socially constructed, constantly put to test in *negotiation*, always revised on the basis of new transactions with others. This is what I view as the major source of self-consciousness. It is a permanent process of complex interpersonal readjustments, especially when values are not externally prescribed via explicit rule systems or due procedures.

Likewise, however, even in cases of externalized law and juridical systems, rules and regulations are constantly revised in their application on the basis of precedents and the history of past cases. This is what jurisprudence is about. Ethics and the philosophy of laws are not fixed but change over time to accommodate new circumstances and new cases. This is done without putting into question some basic constitutive rules, that, for example, everybody is innocent until found guilty or that the same juridical rights are given to all citizens. The interpretation and application of these constitutive rules are part of a constant negotiation in and out of the courtroom.

In all cultures there is pressure on individuals to abide by certain rules of equity or equivalence that are externally prescribed via cultural institutions. Justice as the symbol of balance among individuals is used to protect equity rules and to give some guidelines in the reestablishment of lost equity.

When we think of it, what we do all day is to try to find agreement with others, to compromise, or not to compromise on all matters, whether affective, intellectual, or material. We are constantly trying to come to closure with some deals so we can open new ones. In this process of negotiation, we form knowledge about others as much as we form knowledge about who we are in relation to others. Self-consciousness is primarily a by-product of this process.

Negotiation is the major proving ground by which we weigh ourselves in relation to others. It is also, ultimately, how we calculate how much we weigh in the mind of others, how much relative social proximity and how much recognition we have in the eyes of others. The way people respond to our bargain tells us how important we are to them. Inversely, the way we respond to and deal with others tells *them* how important they are to us. The point is that negotiation is a permanent game of reciprocal evaluation between self and others. But how does it come about in development? At what point in development do we become *Homo negotiatus?*

Negotiation in ontogeny finds its roots in the first reciprocal exchanges between infant and caretaker starting at the middle of the second month after full-term birth. As already described, this is indexed by the emergence of socially elicited smiling in protoconversation with others (so-called primary intersubjectivity).

In this new face-to-face communicative context, the child engages in a give and take of affects that implies a turn taking format that is the prerequisite format of negotiation. In bartering and in protoconversation alike, one makes a bid and the other takes it or turns it down. The mother smiles, and the child can respond either a smile or a frown; he can look toward or look away. There is fundamentally an alternation of bids among the protagonists in the exchange. Furthermore, there is continuity in the exchange as it unfolds, in the same way that there is continuity in bartering and negotiation. Even in protoconversations between a mother and her infant, a history unfolds, in the sense that prior bids will determine future bids.

In such affective protoconversation that emerges by two months, we find the primal form of the negotiation frame. It is from this alternating and reciprocal frame that infants develop to become *Homo negotiatus.* The difficult questions are then, How do they develop, and what happens next?

Infants are born *from* and are immersed *in Homo negotiatus* culture, but they are not born *Homo negotiatus*. The alternating and reciprocal frame of protoconversation is encouraged and provided by attuned and responding caretakers. However, this is not sufficient. To become *Homo negotiatus*, infants need to develop on their own initiative, pushed by something that originates in them.

Once again, my idea is that this something is the experience of a basic dilemma, a constitutive tension between the propensity to explore and roam about the environment and the urge to maintain proximity with others. I have already discussed this constitutive tension in an earlier section. We have seen that by nine months, infants are channeled to resolve this basic dilemma by including others in their roaming and exploration of the environment. Infants by this age work hard at incorporating the attention and gaze of others in their forays. They do all they can to captivate others and include their gaze in their exploration. They begin to solicit social attention to themselves and to what they are trying to achieve. This is the true beginning of negotiation as well as the true source of self-consciousness.

In their attempt at resolving their basic dilemma, infants are eventually *constrained* or channeled to objectify themselves in the gaze of others. They are constrained toward self-objectification as they have to make themselves noticed and to present themselves to others as object of attention and intention. This is indeed the beginning of self-objectification, hence of self-consciousness.

Note that this triadic objectification of the self could not occur if others, in particular adults, were not themselves attuned to the attention and intention of the child. Self-objectification can only develop in a community of already intentional and self-conscious individuals. Comparative research shows that nonhuman animals, even close primate relatives, do not engage in joint attention and intentional exchanges, at least to the levels humans do. This is obviously a prerequisite condition for the development discussed here that is unique to *Homo negotiatus*.

In this fundamental process of social attention getting in order to resolve the constitutive tension between proximity seeking and exploration, infants are discovering the *social power* potentially attached to objects. With the intermediary of objects, infants learn to control the attention of others, capturing this attention to themselves, the experiential warrant of their social proximity and intimacy (see Figure 6).

Children discover that objects are the means by which they can control their sense of social inclusion and recognition, the means by which they ultimately can fulfill their basic affiliation need. They discover that by owning, they can use what they own in a space of exchange and negotia-tion, gaining further control of others' attention. They also gain further leverage in promoting themselves and gauging their own social worth.

There is clearly a deep incentive to own and claim property as it allows children to negotiate and accessorily to gain social leverage and control of their own situation in relation to others. By two, children understand explicitly the social power and leverage attached to property, and this is the long-term outcome of early reciprocal exchanges emerging by two months. The motivational background of this development is, once again, the basic need to affiliate and maintain proximity with others.

In summary, I have argued that negotiation is the main process by which we co-construct what we are as persons. This process develops early but gets a new life by the second birthday when children become explicit in *claiming property*. They discover social power in introducing what objects they claim as theirs and they feel entitled to negotiation space. Interest-ingly, it is also at this age that they begin to manifest an explicit *conceptual awareness* regarding who they are, an objectified sense of self as "me" when, for example, they identify themselves in the mirror.

By this age also (two to three years), we have seen that children begin to *identify* themselves with others. They are able to consider themselves as differ-entiated, yet similar to others, as in the case of their expression of empathy that is more than simple emotional contagion. The idea proposed here is that all these capacities coalesce by the end of the second year, the time when the child begins to claim property and becomes *Homo negotiatus* proper. All these capacities correspond to the constitutive elements of negotiation, the basic process by which the self is co-constructed in relation to others.

NEGOTIATION AND THEORIES OF MIND

If negotiation is a privileged proving ground of what we are in relation to others, it is also, as mentioned already, a privileged source of knowledge about others, namely, the construal of what is on the mind of others, in relation to the self but also in relation to the world at large. Negotiation is a privileged source of what other cognitive psychologists call *theories of mind,* or, more appropriately, I think, what is sometimes also called *folk* or *people psychology.*

People psychology revolves around the understanding of the thoughts, emotions, beliefs, desires, and intentions that underlie other people's actions. Accordingly, we are constantly conjecturing about and factoring what is on the mind of others in order to predict and figure out their behavior, but also their decisions and valuations. It is also by this constant conjecturing that we probe how others relate to us, always trying to determine our place in the mind of others. We do indeed conjecture about others not only for what they are as sentient, psychological entities, but also for what they reflect of our own worth.

The point I would like to make here is that driven by our insatiable needs for social proximity and affiliation, we primarily try to figure out others in order to figure out ourselves, in particular what we are in relation to them. This is part of an ongoing negotiation or active sharing process that starts very early in development.

There are many studies on the developmental origins of theories of mind, revolving around the question of what children understand and conceptualize of what people have in mind (hence, the label *theories of mind*). For example, many research documents how children come to construe others as having beliefs that can be either the same as or on the contrary different from their own, to determine that someone might have a false belief about something the child knows is not true. In the developmental and comparative literature, the ability to construe the false belief of others is considered as the acid test for the existence of theories of mind.

In the classic false belief task first proposed by Wimmer and Perner,[23] children witness, with two adults, a desirable object (candy) being hidden under one of two or three cups. Once it is hidden, one of the experimenters leaves the room on whatever pretext (e.g., phone call), telling the child that she will be right back. Once alone, the second experimenter invites the child to play a trick on the absent experimenter by moving the object under another cup, thus changing the hiding location. The experimenter then asks the child to predict where the other experimenter will eventually search for the hidden candy upon returning.

Much existing research indicates that it is only by five years that the child predicts that the experimenter will look for the object where she saw it being hidden. By this age, children figure out that someone else can have false beliefs about the state of things in the world, beliefs that are different from their own. By three years of age, in contrast, children do not predict that the experimenter will look for the object at its old location, not construing the false belief. Rather, they are assimilating the belief of the experimenter to their own, that is, the new changed location of the candy.

---

[23] Wimmer, H., & Perner, J. (1983). Beliefs about beliefs: Representation and constraining function of wrong beliefs in young children's understanding of deception. *Cognition* 13(1): 103–128.

At such a young age, children have a hard time decoupling and inhibiting their own beliefs when considering others'. They generalize and assimilate from their own, egocentric perspective. In a recent study, we confirmed that this developmental transition has a universal character. We found remarkable developmental synchrony between three- and five-year-old children growing up in five highly contrasting cultural contexts: Canada, Samoa, Thailand, India, and Peru.[24] In all cultures, 80 percent of three-year-olds failed the false belief task as 80 percent of five-year-olds passed it. This is a clearly universal developmental trend.

So, between three and five years, children develop a sophisticated understanding of what is on the mind of others, construing the representations held by others that guide their behavior and determine their worldview: what they hold as being either true or false, desirable or undesirable, realistic or unrealistic. One can assume that when children begin to construe others in this way, going beyond the surface information of their behavior and inferring mental states, they also have more sophisticated ways of construing themselves as sentient individuals.

We have seen in a previous chapter that by three years children do begin to manifest self-conscious emotions, including shame and its derivative, empathy. This development appears to prefigure the development of theories of mind applied to others, although both entail sophistication in metarepresentation. In a sense, self-conscious (secondary) emotions such as shame or empathy do express metarepresentational abilities, but first primarily oriented toward the self. Theories of mind research, in particular the false belief test, suggest that within a few months of developmental time, these metarepresentational abilities are generalized to the construal of others. If that is the case, the question is, What makes this development possible?

In the developing theories of mind literature, there are two opposite schools of thought. One school proposes a view of children as little scientists who develop theories about what is in the mind of others. They generate hypotheses regarding mental states that they confirm or reject on the basis of what they observe "objectively" in others.

Another school proposes a view of children as simulators of what is going on in the mind of others by getting into their shoes, metaphorically speaking. Children build expectations and construe the psychology of others by adopting the perspective of others and by living vicariously and

[24] Callaghan, T., Rochat, P., Lillard, A., Claux, M. L., Odden, H., Itakura, S., Tapanya, S., & Singh, S. (2005). Synchrony in the onset of mental-state reasoning: Evidence from five cultures. *Psychological Science* 16(5): 378–384.

"subjectively" through the eyes of others. Children as simulators engage in the imaginary reenactment of others' acts, thoughts, and emotions, matching them to their own. The latter interpretation presumes, to some extent, the developmental precedence of self-knowledge to which the simulation of others would ultimately be compared for the elaboration of folk psychology and theories of mind. This latter view fits better the evidence that metacognitive self-conscious emotions appear to precede in development the passing of theories of mind tests such as the false belief task.

The simulation theory seems to prevail, but probably both approaches identify processes that play a role in driving the development of children's construal of others, the inference of their mental states. However, there is something lacking in both theory-theory and simulation views. None of them takes into consideration the fact that children develop an understanding of others primarily to get a better grasp of themselves, in particular their situation and who they are in relation to others, how much intimacy and impact they have on people surrounding them and with whom they are constantly *negotiating*.

What is lacking in both theory-theory and simulation theories is the interpersonal content of so-called theories of mind, a misnomer as the term subtracts the interpersonal and, ultimately, affective dimension of children's efforts to construe the mental states of others. The process of negotiation is a better descriptor of what drives the developmental emergence of theories of mind as it takes into consideration the interpersonal dimension that such emergence involves.

It is likely that theories of mind are actually a spinoff of the insatiable drive children have to reach agreement and closure with surrounding others, constantly engaging in emotional trading and bargaining, for better or for worse. Children are constrained to engage with others, to share resources but also primarily to obtain from others in order to survive. This affective as well as material game is set from the outset but changes dramatically in the course of early development.

Negotiation is essentially a conversation that with development is increasingly initiated by the child in the form of bargaining.[25] The child

---

[25] It is interesting to note that the Latin root of the noun *negotiation* or the verb *to negotiate* is from a contraction of *neg*, meaning "not," and *otium*, meaning "leisure." Thus, negotiation has the original meaning of the antithesis of leisure, in other words, of time free of the demands of work. This original meaning of the term is rather counterintuitive as we spend most of our time, whether at work or in leisure, seeking agreement and closure with others. This is an endless game that pervades all of our lives. It is as part of this quest that interpersonal values are established, the values of actions and gestures that specify the degree of our affiliation and intimacy with others. Theories of mind take their roots in this process, not the reverse.

acts to push against and explore the limits of the *"no,"* as Spitz claimed many years ago. The toddler runs to cliffs, cars, and treacherous places, probing how they will be chased by presumably pursuing adults to be picked up and saved. They explore the limits at which others will intervene by either helping or hindering their action.

Children act primarily to probe their social world, to probe how much people care about them and how much intimacy they are capable of generating and controlling in others. This is the main game most evident by the second year but already budding by the second month. It is a game that never leaves us as grown-ups.

Interpersonal needs (intimacy and affiliation) have precedence over the development of theories of mind. They determine them, and this is particularly evident when considering the development of active sharing and distributive justice. This development constrains children to construe the mental states of others, to figure out their desires, their beliefs, and value systems. Children develop such a capacity as a requirement for negotiation and active sharing. In fact, children develop theories of mind in the context of learning the rules of constant negotiation and active sharing with others. They channel the child toward the construal of others' mental states, not the reverse.

We collected some data for three- and five-year-old children, before and after they succeed in the false belief task described, about their ability to negotiate. We observed that children at three years of age who do not pass the false belief task show little flexibility and understanding of reciprocity in negotiating a barter deal with an adult experimenter.

In our little experiment, the child was given a large collection of small stickers that he could take home if he wished. The experimenter gave himself a smaller collection of stickers that were much bigger and brighter. Both child and experimenter agreed that the experimenter's stickers were much nicer. The experimenter then asked the child whether he or she wanted a sticker from her nicer collection. Of course, all children agreed and the experimenter asked, "What would you give me for one of my stickers?"

Children were invited to barter stickers from their collection. Following the child's offer and according to a strict experimental procedure, the experimenter systematically refused any first or second barter deal, eventually accepting it by the third. We were interested to see the extent to which children tended to modify their bid to barter following the refusal by the experimenter. In other words, we were interested in the relative flexibility of the child in the negotiation process.

Results showed that by three years, when children still failed to construe false belief in others, they also failed to modify their barter offering appropriately to revive the negotiation with the experimenter. Typically, three-year-olds repeatedly offered the sticker that was rejected by the experimenter, demonstrating rigidity or fixedness in their response.

In contrast, by five years of age, when the majority of children pass the false belief test, children do demonstrate much more flexibility and appropriate negotiation adjustment by increasing their offer following the experimenter's refusal.

Our observations clearly indicate that the development of negotiation skills parallels, and possibly could cause, the development of theories of mind as measured by the false belief task. Although we do not have supporting data yet, negotiation, as a trademark of the human environment to which children must adapt, could form the facilitating context in which theories of mind come to life.

Negotiation as a reciprocal social adjustment process would call for some construal of others' mental state. Children grow to become *Homo negotiatus*, and the rest follows, including theories of mind.[26] What I propose is that negotiation precedes and constrains progress in the construal of what others have on their mind, particularly the construal of what they represent about us: the representation of *who we are* through the eyes of others. The next chapter focuses on this representation by discussing the social construction of personal identity.

[26] Rochat, P. (2005), pp. 714–715.

10

Social Construction of Identity

There is no truth in you,
There is no truth in me,
It is between.
From "Truth Serum," a song written and performed by Smog

Descartes's *cogito* ("I think, therefore I am") is tainted with circularity. Descartes claims his existence, but this claim presupposes an "I" as an a priori. It does not exhaust the question of self-consciousness. When he claims *cogito, ergo sum* – "I think, therefore I am" – one is left with the question, Who is talking to whom? Who is the "I"? In general, what do we perceive and what do we represent as "I"? These are the basic, unanswered questions of self-consciousness.

The issue is profound, and it is hard not to fall into Descartes's circularity trap when dealing with the issue of self-consciousness. How can we talk about ourselves and try to specify who we are when such talk presupposes us as talkers? It is as impossible as trying to construe one's own death when immersed in life, as impossible as construing oneself deaf and mute when talking and listening. How could we construe ourselves as nothing since our thoughts require that we are something? How could we construe ourselves as nobody since this reflection implies us as thinkers and feelers? Arguably, this is a contradiction in terms and an impossible quest.

However, in this chapter, I propose that there is a piece that is fundamentally missing in the quest of who we are in the Cartesian tradition. This piece is formed by others we have in mind. Accordingly, and in contradistinction to Descartes's internalist view and tradition, the issue of self-consciousness is *not* a private matter and cannot be construed independently of how one relates to others. In this sense, I will argue that the question "Who am I?" is ill formed, leading inescapably to the circularity and infinite regress suffered by Descartes in his meditation. The way out of the circularity trap, is to include others in the question of self-consciousness by asking, Who are we and *for whom*? The addition of the others, that is, the added social dimension in the second part of the question (for whom?), changes the approach.

I will argue that this addition renders the issue of self-consciousness more dynamic and takes us out of the circularity trap. It is also a better approximation of what constitutes the conscious experience of our identity. This experience is not private to the extent that we always have *others in mind* as we try to construe who we are.

The aim of this chapter is to show that the consciousness of who we are is not a fixed entity. It is constantly changing and revised as a function of our encounters with others, driven by the need to affiliate and get social recognition.

CONUNDRUM ABOUT SELF-CONSCIOUSNESS

If I am conscious or "aware" of myself, the question is, What am I aware of? Who am I, feeling, thinking, and being in the world? Where are my boundaries? What delimits and determines I versus thou? In less phenomenological and more conceptual terms, the question is, What constitutes a person and what is the nature of our identity in the midst of constant changes and fatal, inescapable disappearance in physical death? What is the sum of invariants that we call the *self*, and are these invariants the same in both first- and third-person perspectives? These questions form the conundrum about self-consciousness.

The eighteenth-century Scottish philosopher Hume claims that when he looks inside himself in search of a self, he finds only perceptions and nothing else. From this he concludes that there is no such thing as a self, only perceptions. Hume proposes that if there is such a thing as a self, a person, or an identity, it exists only as a reconstruction, the figment of our imagination. In other words, if we talk about ourselves as selves, it is only within a fictive narrative frame. But is the self merely the product of our imagination, or does it stand for something distinct and real?

I certainly will not solve these perennial philosophical questions here. However, I wish to make two general claims that I consider essential in any discussion of self-consciousness, in particular how we construe who we are with others in mind (who are we and for whom?), the topic of this book.

The first claim is that it is essential to distinguish a construal of the self from an experiential or first-person perspective and a construal of the self from a formal or conventional third-person perspective. For example, there is an irreconcilable difference between the construal of myself as an embodied experience (e.g., Hume in search of himself or Descartes meditating about his own existence) and the conventional construal of myself as perceived by others (e.g., me as defined by my passport, my age, or my social status as a Ph.D., an artist, or a bank teller). The first is phenomenal and the second is conventional or public. The former is fleeting and changing, constantly reformulated, as the latter is socially calibrated and tentatively fixed by conventions and cultural institutions. These construals of the self are fundamentally different and too often confounded. I propose that they interact to produce the elusive sense of who we are.

The second claim is that the self, the person, and self-identity, all are in essence *dynamic*, not static entities. They are no fixed "things" whether construed from a first- or third-person perspective. Ultimately, the elusive sense of who we are is socially constructed. It is an ever-changing approximation and the product, once again, of a constant negotiation with others. The explicit sense of self is indeed a social construction.

DYNAMIC RE-PRESENTATIONS AND APPROXIMATIONS

To make sense of the world is literally to figure it out, to map it out as we do the Earth that we project on a globe or on a map. This is true of anything we think or talk about, anything that is explicit in our mind, including the self. We create meanings by acts of *re-presentations*, conveying to others or to ourselves simulations of what real things *might* be, not what they are.

Thinking is, in essence, the business of mental approximation, the mental approximation of what things in the world *might* be. Approximations are also what we convey to others in terms of ideas or meanings, as well as to ourselves, in private dialogs. With reflection and learning, these approximations can gain accuracy, or at least capture more of reality's complexity. But these approximations need to be constantly revised, always renegotiated within our internal thought dialogs and explicit interactions with others. The same applies for the construal of self-identity and the knowledge of who we are. Both participate in analogous acts of dynamic re-presentation and approximation but always *with others in mind*.

Our mouths are full of personal pronouns. We utter them almost as readily as linguistic fillers such as today's endemic use of *like* as a descriptive shortcut, a secular epidemic reflecting our hypervisual culture. But personal pronouns are no fillers, not just reducible to communication stutters. They do stand for a specific entity in our mind. The question is, What is this entity? I will propose that it is something dynamic and constantly changing, not a well-delimited and stable entity. It is an ongoing, fluctuating social construction.

When we utter or write *I, me, he,* or *she,* what are we hoping to convey? This question is far from being trivial. It pertains, no less, to the classical philosophical issue of what constitutes a person and its identity. This is an ongoing, classic puzzler for philosophers. Pages after pages have been written on the issue from the time of ancient Greece, and particularly since Descartes. No philosopher or psychologist can escape the issue, and the more you dare think about what constitutes a person and its identity, the more unsettling it gets. It reveals how complex the issue actually is and how much is taken for granted. It also shows how rigid our worldview can be.

The etymology of the word *person* is from the Etruscan word *persona* standing for "theater mask." It is interesting to note that from its semantic root up, the meaning of *person* is inseparable from some staging of the self or self-presentation (i.e., the social mask), terms Erving Goffman aptly coined in his seminal 1959 book *The Presentation of Self in Everyday Life.* From a pure semantic perspective, linked to the concept of person is the idea of staging, presentation, or display, a central aspect of self-consciousness as discussed in this book.

In today's vernacular, the word *person* refers to an individual in particular: "an individual of the human species" (*Le Petit Robert de la langue française*). Beyond the original meaning of *mask,* in its common use today the word *person* serves the purpose of designating people as individuated entities, as wholes that are distinct from other wholes, in particular other people and things in the world.

As in a game of infinite regress, the definition of a person as an individual still begs the question of what might constitute such an individuated whole. Is it the physical body as delineated by the envelope of its skin? Or is it a psychological profile pertaining to a particular temperament, a great sense of humor, or a mental clumsiness? Obviously, in our mind, it is a mix, and here, the problem becomes quite thorny.

How do we represent what serves as the basis for individuating *someone* (including myself) from others? Where does one individual end and another begin? What are the invariants from which a sense of permanence can be constructed despite the major developmental changes and transformations each individual goes through during the life span? What constitutes identity as the elusive invariant representation of the person as an individuated entity in the world?

DR./MR. JEKYLL-HYDE

Dr. Jekyll and Mr. Hyde, a novel written over a century ago, is emblematic of all of these thorny questions. The great Robert Louis Stevenson wrote it reportedly in six days, on a cocaine binge. The anecdotal fact that this story was reportedly written in a drug high is interesting because this graceful tale does revolve around the issue of altered states of consciousness.

As a quick reminder, Dr. Jekyll is a distinguished and well-respected scientist living in London's gentile society of the late nineteenth century. Dr. Jekyll is a gentleman scientist conducting mysterious research and experiments in a secluded laboratory room at his mansion. Jekyll, the story goes, concocted some chemical mixture that he swallows, altering his person, both physically and psychologically. For reasons that are unclear, driven by his curiosity, Dr. Jekyll becomes addicted in becoming Mr. Hyde, a ruthless individual roaming the streets at night and terrorizing citizens.

Dr. Jekyll swallows the concoction to become his most conceivable opposite, except for gender: Mr. Hyde, a dreadful criminal roaming the dark streets of London in search for loners he beats and terrifies, if not kills. At dawn, following his nocturnal terror expeditions, Mr. Hyde goes back to the mansion, just in time to reenter the gentle life, body, and soul of Dr. Jekyll. What Stevenson's tale suggests is profound. It suggests that what underlies a person are paradox and multiplicity, not singularity.

As persons, we have the ability to switch hats and transform ourselves according to circumstances, without any kind of drug induction. We are the kings and queens of dissociation, able to juggle fronts as no other species can. As Dr. Jekyll does, we even cultivate dissociation for reasons deemed appropriate. Dr. Jekyll becomes Mr. Hyde as he is conducting personal, respectable, yet secretive research, trying mind-altering drugs on himself.

Stevenson's novel reminds us that in all of us as persons, there is always an opposite, something in many ways radically different, always ready to manifest itself depending on life's circumstances.

It is not uncommon to hear stories, increasingly it seems nowadays, of some well-respected and pious priest who turns out to be a predator lusting after young boys. It is striking that more often than

not, horrendous criminals tend to be portrayed by friends and neigh-
bors as likable, quiet, unassuming individuals; good fathers, good
mothers, or good fellows. How is it possible that social predators, serial
killers, and dictators come across so differently to their intimate circles?
How can we account for such discrepancy and dissociation in the
representation of who these persons are, particularly considering that
these representations are as real as they are partial? Who could deny
one or the other? For example, it is difficult not to experience unease
and chills when looking at the non-imaginative, yet careful little landscape paintings Adolph Hitler created as a failed art student before he
started his dictatorial career. One wonders, How could a man like this be
capable of paying attention and showing some degree of sensibility to
light and color? Not exactly what belongs to the incarnation of evil.

Stevenson's novel, aside from being a literary gem, is seminal in what it
conveys regarding human nature: the paradox and duplicity of what a
person is as a whole. It dwells on the idea that a person is not merely
the individuated thing of the dictionary's definition. Closer inspection
shows that despite the obvious invariants we hold onto, a person by
definition is not singular, but rather multiple and constantly changing,
sometimes in the most contradictory ways, as in the tale of Dr. Jekyll and
Mr. Hyde.

Stevenson had the premonition of some basic concepts introduced a
few decades later by Freud, who posits that opposite forces shape what we
become as a person (the Ego). As his second topic, Freud proposes that the
Ego (the person) is the result of a compromise between the deep force of
immediate pleasure gratification (the Id), and the force of social conformity, the need to adjust to society's norms and values (the Superego).
Among many other things, Mr. Hyde and Dr. Jekyll represent these clashing forces that contrast with and define each other. These dual forces also
find balance in each other by mutually canceling their potential excesses.
But they are not just a source of stability and certainly not a source of
stagnation. They also need to be conceived as a source of constant pro-
ductivity and changes in the dialectic of their opposition,

Stevenson's tale is a tale about the inseparability of the multiple forces
that sum up who we are as persons. We, as persons, are not *a* thing, despite
what we might be representing and referring to in our use of personal
pronouns. Rather, we are the expression of a changing process that
emerges from multiple, interacting, and often highly contradictory forces.

What is interesting is that from an outside perspective, such as that of
the two friends who are the actual narrators of Robert Louis Stevenson's

story and who reveal the case of Dr. Jekyll and Mr. Hyde, what is apparent and at the heart of the dilemma is that both Jekyll and Hyde as persons might be fusing into one singular elusive self, although they are individuated persons from the outside. For the two friends, as outside spectators of the phenomenon, this is inconceivable. The dual reality of Dr. Jekyll/Hyde eludes the two friends, and this is what makes Stevenson's tale a mystery. However, what eludes the two observers might not be so mysterious from within the protagonist's singular body, the individual who experiences in succession the transformation from Jekyll to Hyde, and vice versa. The essence of what this person is from a first-person perspective – and this is my main point – is actually this transformation, a transformation that eludes the two friends with their third-person perspective. In Stevenson's tale, the two friends witness either Dr. Jekyll *or* Mr. Hyde, not the actual transformation from one to the other. This is the source of the mystery, but not for the person who is experiencing the transformation.

The identity of Dr. Jekyll/Hyde as a person can only be revealed in the transformation, not the product entities or selves that either preceded or followed the transformation. By analogy, the caterpillar and the butterfly are clearly individuated entities if, and only if, the process of metamorphosis is not factored in. In reality, they are individuated entities yet of the same transforming creature. The identity of this creature is thus neither to be found in the caterpillar nor in the butterfly, but in *both*. The identity is in their transformation or metamorphosis, the passage from one entity to the other. In other words, it is *in between*.

The caterpillar-butterfly example is limited as it occurs only one way; there is no reversed movement where butterflies return to their caterpillar state. In contrast, the transformation of our identity is recurrent and goes multiple ways, as we will see.

Likewise, individuated products of identity transformation are the only things witnessed by the two friends in Stevenson's story. The puzzler for them is how Dr. Jekyll and Mr. Hyde could in fact be the same and unique person. How might that be possible? Ask the friends as they stumble upon curious clues in their suspenseful inquiry. The question of multiple identities within a single man is at the core of Stevenson's famous mystery tale.

From a "within" (embodied) perspective, there might be no clear individuation between Dr. Jekyll *and* Mr. Hyde, one by day, the other by night. There is instead a *Dr./Mr. Jekyll-Hyde* that is defined by the process of its transformation at dusk and dawn. The main protagonist of Stevenson's story is in fact a self or person who is *neither* Dr. Jekyll *nor* Mr. Hyde, but rather the transforming process from one role to the other.

CHANGES AND INVARIANT FEATURES

What we experience as ourselves from "within" is different from what others experience of us from "without." I will argue here that from the perspective of our embodied experience, what we can identify as ourselves is essentially the constant transformation process that leads us from one social role to another, in our quest for control, affiliation, and intimacy with others. The argument is that self-identity is emergent from the dynamic process of constant role adoption and active self-presentation in response to changing social circumstances and social encounters.

Following this argument, the representation or conceptualization of who we are rests on *invariant features* that emerge from recurrent changes due to social circumstances and encounters. What we represent as self is not a static collection of personal traits, nor an elusive core self that would be stable as a built-in quality. The essence of self-identity is, on the contrary, dynamic. It rests on, and is shaped by, social exchanges, self-presentation, and the adaptation to others with the ultimate goal of control, affiliation, and intimacy. The idea is that the self, as an objectified entity (i.e., "self-consciousness"), is nothing but the sum of invariant features that emerges from changes in social encounters, and it is constantly reformulated. Here goes my social-constructionist argument: self-identity is constantly changing, constantly revised and renegotiated in the context of new social encounters. This is what the personal pronoun *I* refers to at an explicit, conceptual level.

What we identify as ourselves from within our own bodies (the embodied self) is of an unmatched complexity compared to whatever can be identified of us from without, namely, by others from their own bodies. I will expand on this as we progress through the chapter, but first we need to address the classic issue of what constitutes personal identity: what we perceive as self and that we represent as personhood.

WHAT IS A PERSON?

One can see a classic polarity of views in Western philosophy regarding the ontological or essential nature of what might constitute a "person" and "personal identity."[1] There is, on one hand, the view that a person exists as an objectified thing to be perceived, remembered, and thought about. I will

---

[1] See for example, the excellent volume edited by John Perry: Perry, J. (1975). *Personal Identity*. Berkeley: University of California Press.

call this view the "person as real thing view." On the other hand, there is the view that the idea of person is an illusion; it does not exist as a thing. One could call this view the "person as an illusory thing." As already mentioned, the most famous proponent of this last view is the Scottish empiricist (phenomenist) David Hume (1711–1776). Here is what he writes on the topic in his *Treatise of Human Nature* (1739):

> There are some philosophers, who imagine we are every moment intimately conscious of what we call our *self*; that we feel its existence and its continuance in existence; and are certain, beyond the evidence of a demonstration, both of its perfect identity and simplicity. . . . But self or person is not any one impression, but that to which our several impressions and ideas are supposed to have a reference. If any impression gives rise to the idea of self, that impression must continue invariably the same, through the whole course of our lives; since self is supposed to exist after that matter. But there is no impression constant and invariable. (Hume, *Treatise of Human Nature*, section 6, part IV, book I)

For Hume, what we observe are perceptions, and perceptions are always changing, as well as highly diverse, resulting from various sensory modes bombarding us at different points in time. So, he asks, how could someone have a notion of himself as a stable entity if this notion is based primarily on a bundle of fast changing perceptual impressions from multiple channels? How could personal identity as a unitary, stable notion arise from impressions that lack both stability and identity? For Hume, the idea of self and personal identity is false because our impressions from which ideas arise are fleeting and never identical. Therefore, one singular idea of self as identity can only be an illusion, not a real thing.

In opposition to Hume's "person as an illusory thing" view, philosophers such as René Descartes (1596–1650), John Locke (1632–1704), and Immanuel Kant (1724–1804) defend a "person as real thing view," within very contrasting philosophical systems.

Descartes, in his metaphysical meditations, identifies a first person that thinks and therefore is a conscious, identifiable entity rising above the physical realities of the body. For him, the person exists as a stable conscious entity. It is a thing that can be observed and captured, reflected upon, as in his meditations. Descartes's idealism is in exact opposition to Hume's skeptical view on the self as knowable, and therefore an existing object.

In contrast, the British philosopher John Locke, whose life overlapped with Descartes's, had very different views on the origins of knowledge.

Rather than as innate, Locke viewed knowledge as originating from experience. He is indeed considered the father of empiricism, the philosophical school that emphasizes the role of environmental pressure and experience rather than instincts and innate ideas in knowing the world, including the self. However, Locke and Descartes share the view that the self as identity exists; they share what I call the "person as real thing view." The following is an excerpt of John Locke's writing on identity and diversity taken from his opus, "Essay Concerning Human Understanding" (second edition, 1694):

> We must consider what person stands for; which, I think, is a thinking intelligent being, that has reason and reflection, and can consider itself as itself, the same thinking thing, in different times and places; which it does only by that consciousness which is inseparable from thinking, and as it seems to me, essential to it: it being impossible for any one to perceive without perceiving that he does perceive. When we see, hear, smell taste, feel, meditate, or will anything, we know that we do so. Thus it is always as to our present sensations and perceptions: and by this every one is to himself that which he calls self; it not being considered, in this case, whether the same self be continued in the same or diverse substances. For, since consciousness always accompanies thinking, and it is that which makes every one to be that he calls self, and thereby distinguishes himself from all other thinking things: in this alone consists *personal identity* [italic added], i.e., the sameness of a rational being; and as far as this consciousness can be extended backwards to any past action or thought, so far reaches the identity of that person; it is the same self now it was then; and it is by the same self with this present one that now reflects on it, that that action was done. (section 9 of the chapter "Of Identity and Diversity")

As for Descartes, in Locke's view the self is a stable object of thought, hence of consciousness. It is a thing that one can reflect upon and conceive as a notion that exists beyond the here and now of perceptual experience. The self is real as it can be re-presented as a knowable, invariant entity that we project in thought, backward and forward in time.

Immanuel Kant (1724–1804), another famous proponent of the "person as real thing view," writes in his essay "Anthropology from a Pragmatic Point of View": "To possess an 'I' in its representation: this power elevates man infinitely above all other beings on earth. By that he is a person; and thanks to the unity of consciousness in all its changes that can fall upon it, it is a singular and same person" (book 1, section 1: On the Faculty of Knowing, on Self-Knowledge, translation from French by the author).

Here again, for humans, at least according to Kant, the self is a knowable entity, stable in the unity of a consciousness that rises above the chaos of the perceptual impressions alluded to by Hume.

What I will propose now is that both the "person as real thing" view and the "person as an illusory thing" view have serious flaws. They both focus primarily on the content of what might constitute a person (whether it is thoughts, consciousness, re-presentations, or perceptions). However, they do not capture the *process* by which one might grasp what the self might be from either an embodied (within) or a disembodied (without) perspective. What I mean here by *embodied* and *disembodied* views are views from *within* the individual looking and reflecting on itself, or doing so indirectly from *without*, based on the construing and inferring of the "gaze" of others on the self (others as social mirror reflecting who we might be).

In relation to the idea of the irreconcilable gap between these views discussed earlier, this distinction is primordial, a distinction not clearly made by most philosophers, as far as my reading indicates.

PERSONHOOD AS A PROCESS RATHER THAN A PRODUCT

Hume's view of the "person as an illusory thing" is compelling to the extent that in many ways, trying to capture what the self might be is like hammering mercury: it is slippery and multifaceted. Yet to deny that our personhood is perceived and recognized by us, as well as by others, as invariant entity despite changes, is not tenable as it overlooks phenomena that are obviously real. We do recognize ourselves as well as others in mirrors and photographs sometimes taken years ago and in very different circumstances (naked on the beach or bundled up skiing up in the mountain years later). We are able to recognize our, as well as others', faces, gaits, styles in writing, singing, tastes, ideas, ways of maintaining eye contact, or shaking hands almost throughout the life span. It is undeniable that there are personal constants underlying what we experience as stable identities. We typically do not experience miraculous metamorphoses of the person across contexts and over developmental time. We are attuned to stories in which personal pronouns stand for an entity that remains a constant feature despite major changes and transformations. It is more than an illusion: the sense of personhood is arguably based on real invariant detection and conceptualization over time and experience.

Thus, at a conceptual and identification level, Hume's view of the "person as an illusory thing" is too radical and untenable. However, it cannot be dismissed quickly because it emphasizes something that Descartes's, Locke's, and Kant's views of the "person as real thing" tend to overlook. It emphasizes the fact that the self, if ever captured, is not static, but made of changes, actually *revealed* in changes.

In the essentialist view of "person as a real thing," there is the underlying assumption that personal identity is one unitary consciousness (see the quotation by Kant). The emphasis is on the coherence of the self as it is represented, not its underlying chaos and diversity. It emphasizes the singularity of the person as a stable, unified entity. The flaw of the "person as a real thing" view is that it does not capture the fact that the self is constantly wearing multiple hats, its invariance only revealed in changes or role transitions. As a concept, personal identity is indeed constantly renegotiated, reassessed, and, more importantly, reframed in relation to others and social circumstances.

As a day goes by, an individual might be behind her desk in a business suit striking deals with important clients, feeding her children, riding a horse, solving sibling conflicts, caring for her mother, volunteering at a day care center, fighting with her husband, courting her lover, or praying to God. As for Dr. Jekyll/Hyde, personal identity is mainly what emerges from the dynamic process of social role changes. It cannot be referred to as one or the other (e.g., Dr. Jekyll *or* Mr. Hyde). It is "in between," as suggested by the excerpt of Smog's song heading the chapter. It is revealed in neither, but *in the transition*.

CLOUDY SELF

The cloud that I see in the sky is not a thing in itself, despite the fact that it can be individuated and explicitly labeled or pointed to. In physical reality, the cloud I see in the sky is nothing but the trace of an ongoing dynamic phenomenon, the condensation of a humid airmass caused by atmospheric temperature changes. If that is true, the essence of a cloud is not a *thing* in itself, not a well-defined and stabilized thing, as by nature it is constantly changing. The same applies to self-identity. One could freeze the phenomenon by taking a picture of a cloud and making it look like a coherent static whole, but that would be an illusion, as suggested by Hume.

We cannot "thingify" a cloud as much as we cannot "thingify" the self because what defines both is change. To render them static is to denature them. It is to remove from their definition what is constitutive of them, overlooking their essence. In the same way, and by analogy, we denature the self by objectifying it as something static. But most philosophers and cognitive scientists keep ignoring this crucial dynamic component of the self.

That does not mean that the self is an unfathomable entity that cannot be conceptualized and identified. The self is knowable, but, by analogy to a meteorological phenomenon, it is a "cloudy" concept: an entity that is revealed by the dynamic of its constant changes. These changes are what we perceive of ourselves from within our body as well as from without by the way people respond to us and reciprocate with us. This is a core aspect of the process by which we perceive and represent who we are.

The problem of self-identity is rendered particularly complex by the fact that our cloudy self is *doubly* cloudy. It is cloudy because it is the product of changes, constantly modified depending on our roles and the context formed by particular social encounters and situations. It is also cloudy because self-identity is ultimately based on the tentative integration of two perspectives that are incommensurable: the first- and third-person perspectives on the self (see the six theoretical propositions outlined in Chapter 2).

By the second year of life, we have seen in earlier chapters that the authority of first-person perspective on the self (i.e, the embodied sense of self in perception and action) is increasingly blurred by the tentative integration of the evaluative gaze of others (third-person perspective on the self, the sense and construal of what others perceive of "me"). From this point on, the sense of self becomes triadic and intersubjective, adding "cloudiness" to what constitutes self-identity. It relies on the cues and construal of others' view of the self, not just on the authority of first-person perspective.[2]

I have suggested that the integration of first- and third-person perspectives on the self in the attempt at reconciling them is a never-ending process. This process is, in the view proposed here, at the core of self-identity, the product of a social as opposed to a private construction.

In the next section, I try to render this dynamic view more alive and explicit by reconstructing a clinical case that was reported to me and that I view as a good illustration of the dynamic dimension (i.e., contextual and interpersonal) that would constitute primarily the notion of who we are,

---

[2] The persistence in development of the sole authority of embodied first-person perspective can actually be very detrimental. This seems particularly evident in the case of people suffering from eating disorders (e.g., bulimia or anorexia nervosa). In such instances, the person develops a distorted embodied perception of the self. The authority of first-person perspective becomes dictatorial, associated with social alienation and delusional self-identity, particularly grossly transformed body image despite clear contradictory social clues from attentive and caring others. Intersubjective clues are not properly integrated in the constitution of self-identity.

this of course if we assume that, contrary to Hume, there is something to be grasped and that we are not just dealing with a mirage.

My point is that what constitutes the notion of identity emerges primarily from the experience of contrasting social engagements and exchanges across interpersonal domains, be they professional, familial, or more intimate. Each domain calls for the wearing of different psychological "hats" and different self-presentations. They are the multiple domains of intimacy we create in relation to others and through which we are all constantly transiting.

I chose this particular clinical example because it illustrates such transiting and represents a good thought problem regarding the psychological nature of personal identity: what constitutes the notion of self-identity. I would like to illustrate with this example that this notion is primarily constructed in the dynamic of social exchanges. It is revealed in the constant transition across domains of intimacy and represents the dynamic source of self-identity as a unitary, invariant notion (i.e., a conceptual sense of who we are as individuated persons).

The case demonstrates, by negation, the importance of transition in the determination of personhood and illustrates that when this transition is prevented or vanishes, in dream or in reality, the experience of personhood collapses.

A HEART MADE OF ABUNDANCE

John[3] is a happily married man with two young children. But he also has mistresses whom he loves and enjoys. Furthermore, from time to time, on his own and secretly, he takes pleasure trips to a large city nearby for wild nights in gay bars and same-sex public bath spots.

Who is John? Which one of his various contexts captures best the essence of what he might be as a person? Is John as a person better captured by the role he plays as father? Husband? Lover? Or is it John the explorer of new pleasures? It appears that it is none of these roles taken separately as illustrated by one of John's dreams.

One night, as John was sleeping in the conjugal bed, he woke up by his wife's side, breathing fast and heavily, soaked in cold sweat. He felt that he

---

[3] Note that John, his life, and his dream are broadly reconstructed, a masked synthesis of a report by a close psychotherapist friend. For obvious ethical reasons, the name and precise situations are transformed. The person depicted is an amalgam of the real case report. However, the general script and theme are faithful to the actual case observation as it was reported to me.

was dying, and so thought his wife, who had never witnessed her husband in such a deep panic state. Seizure was the first thing that came to her mind, ready to rush him to the hospital. The seizure turned out to be a violent reaction to a nightmare that drove John into absolute panic. Here is John's horrendous dream:

> As a good son, he took his mother shopping. After a calm spree at some stores, he took her for a drink at a bar. The hostess welcoming them was his wife, the waiter was one of his male lovers, and when he went to the bathroom, he bumped into two of his mistresses, who were chatting and giggling at the bar. All of the contexts of his life had coalesced into one.

John woke up in a cold sweat when, in his dream, he eventually stood frozen in the middle of the bar with all the eyes of the protagonists staring at him: mother, wife, mistresses, and male lover. Under the crossfire of these gazes, John, in his dream, felt that his embodied person was melting. This is when he woke up in a panic. The multiple contexts of his affective life were collapsing, and he was dying, his personhood vanishing.

One could argue that John's dream is driven by guilt, that it is just a dream about being unmasked, a situation where well-kept secrets are being brought to daylight, in this case, compartmentalized relations running into one another. There is certainly an element of truth, but this interpretation overlooks the fundamental question of John's experienced personal identity. In the dream, there is someone, that is, John, who presumably experiences strong emotions, whether guilt, embarrassment, jealousy, love, or ultimately the panic fear that wakes him. A first-person perspective is the prerequisite for the experience of guilt or any kind of emotion. So who is John in the end, as expressed in his dream?

John, in reality and in the dream, lives multiple lives that, apparently, are not incompatible. He managed to survive the juggling of relational involvements for years. In his case, there have been a few bumps and convoluted instances, but nothing out of the ordinary. One time, for example, he had unsafe sex with a man and worried that he could contaminate his female lovers. For a few weeks he had to make up stories to avoid sex with them until his HIV test result came back negative. This was a constant worry in John's adventurous and risky love life, but other than that, nothing out of the ordinary for John.

His life was fulfilling and he was obviously not hurting any of those involved with him. For the most part, he was a decent husband who enjoyed being with his wife, a caring father, and an intense lover in all his extramarital affairs. So what went wrong in his dream?

The life John manages is marked by tightly compartmentalized contexts that call for specific roles: the role of husband, the role of straight lover, gay lover, and father. All these roles are linked to different sets of values and emotions, a variety of intimate relations and relational domains or micro-cultures: the family culture, the culture of durable husband and wife relationship, the excitement of passing passions, and the lust of momentary sexual encounters. Each context requires John to play a different role, assume different values, and change the pace and the intensity of his exchanges with the particular protagonist(s) crossing his intimate lives. This juggling of roles is possible only if each relational context of John is well delimited and confined, allowing for a smooth switching from one to another, with no interference from any of them with another.

In the dream, the hermetic barrier separating each of John's contexts collapsed, and his sense of person literally vanished, as in death. John's reaction to his nightmare was the virtual death of his personhood, I would suggest. In relation to the discussion of what is the self and what might constitute identity, we are still evading the question of who is John, namely, who is the person dying in his nightmare, and what constitutes the notion of his personhood?

My take is that John, in his juggling of roles, is *none* of them in particular. Although for moral comfort we might be inclined to think that there is a primary role in John's life, the fact is that probably there is none. He is not first and foremost a husband and a father who is going astray from normal family life. No. I would argue that John is *all* the roles he created in his life driven by circumstances, encounters, and propensities he carried within him (his sexual appetite, for example). However, John, in the way he experiences his personal identity and how his person is experienced by others, is not just the sum or average of all his social roles.

The essence of what John is as a person, his subjective self-experience and what he might eventually come to conceptualize as "Me," is what emerges from the *process of transition from one role to another*. I would say that John's personhood is primarily based on what he experiences and eventually conceptualizes from invariant features of this maneuvering from context to context. It is through this maneuvering from role to role and context to context that he gains subjective and conceptual access to himself as a person. In other words, as for clouds, John as a person is primarily the process of his hat changing. It is in this process that he can acquire a sense of who he is and eventually conceptualize it for others and for self.

John needs all the social contexts and the roles associated with each of them to approximate who he is conceptually. What John perceives and represents of himself as a person rests on switching among all the social roles he plays. It is in the switching of roles that he gets some grasp of what he might be. John's identity is all the roles that compose his person, yet he is none, since what he is, is *in between* roles, revealed as he switches from one to another.

What caused John's horrendous nightmare is the coalescence of all the intimate protagonists of his life in one single context. In his dream, I would argue, John lost touch with what he was as a person because the whole process through which John could experience his personhood was suddenly suspended. He lost the opportunity to control and experience the transition from one context to another, all collapsing into one in the dream, no longer compartmentalized with him jumping from one to another at will: no more transition to be experienced, no more invariants specifying who he was as a person. The source of panic and terror is that in the dream John is vanishing, literally dying as he loses the means to reveal himself as a person in the *process* of transiting from role to role. Personhood is indeed a social process, not a static thing. There is no self in itself, as there is no cloud in itself: there is just something revealed in transition.

Once again, we feel our personhood as some invariant entity only as we transit from context to context and from social role to social role. John's nightmare illustrates that the fusion of contexts kills the possibility of transition. It kills access to the notion of identity and, in general, the sense of a unified self. Such loss is indeed the worst nightmare, a source of major suffering associated with self-disintegration, as reported, for example, in schizophrenia.[4]

As babies learn by four months that objects cannot be in two places at the same time, in his dream John cannot reconcile the impossibility of being in different contexts simultaneously, at different places in his life at the same time. By losing the possibility of transiting across contexts, John loses track of who he is and disintegrates in cold sweat. The case of John and his dream is paradigmatic of our lives, which consist of parallel existences. We all behave and invest ourselves in well-compartmentalized contexts, having different roles in life, whether professional, familial, or political: all the roles that suit us and we adopt to maintain intimacy and affiliation with others, by choice, by accident, or following social conventions, adapting to the power structure of our particular social circumstances.

[4] See Parnas, J., Møller, P., Kircher, T., Thalbitzer, J., Jansson, L., Handest, P., & Zahavi, D. (2005). EASE: Examination of Anomalous Self-Experience. *Psychopathology* 38(5): 1–23.

We all strive to wear multiple social hats. In this respect, the case of John, although extreme in many ways, is paradigmatic of the profoundly dynamic dimension of personhood.

In short, and following a long philosophical tradition, it is often wrongly assumed that when talking about "me," "I," or more generally the notion of "self," we are talking about one *thing*, some kind of a well-delimited whole or core entity. What I suggest instead is that the self amounts primarily to a collection of social roles co-constructed in relation to others, roles that depend on relational contexts. In the end, it is this compartmentalization that defines what we are: all the different roles *others* demand of us, whether this demand is real or imaginary.

If personhood exists, it is what emerges and is revealed as invariant in a process of constant social role switching. When immersed in a role, personhood is lost to the social exchange. It dilutes in it and becomes intertwined with the reflection of others onto the self. In other words, first-person perspective becomes mixed with the consideration of third-person perspective (experiencing oneself through the evaluative eyes of others). It reemerges in the transition to the next role before personal identity is lost again in the new social exchange with others in mind. If there is such a thing as a core self, or core subjectivity, a pure first-person perspective à la Descartes or Locke, it might only be what emerges and can be revealed in between roles, in the process of their transition. It would be only in this transition phase that we might be able to experience our own experience, the "core" person we are from a purely first-person perspective. This speculation, as arguable as it might sound, takes the dynamic nature of personal identity, an aspect that is fundamental and too often overlooked, seriously.

HUMAN DISSOCIATION

In our very human ability to immerse in role playing, we are quick to learn the rules of the social game. We wear ties in particular circumstances, chew food differently when alone watching sports or in the company of someone we are trying to charm. Deception, impersonation, self-presentation, seduction, and constant social monitoring are our trade as we try to gain and control proximity with others. This trade is the trait of our species, although some precursor signs exist in other animals, particularly our great ape relatives.

Humans have evolved deception, seduction, and Machiavellian intelligence to levels that are unique. No other species even comes close in the convolution and metalevels governing our social transactions (e.g., he thinks that I think that he thinks that we think, etc.).

A common feature of the complex and convoluted trade characterizing human social exchanges and control to gain social proximity is the process of *dissociation*. *Dissociation* in the sense used here is the act of separating oneself, literally of undoing oneself in the process of role changing and successive role adoption.

Switching roles, and leaving some individuals or groups of individuals for other individuals and other groups, entail constant dissociation, constant undoing of the current self-presentation for further repackaging. We might be fighting with someone, and in the midst of the fight the phone rings. After some heated argument as to who will pick it up, we finally answer the phone with a voice and attitude that are in total contrast with what we were just portraying of ourselves in the argument. Your host might be stressed out in the kitchen to get the dinner party ready when the first guest rings at the door. She throws her apron, fixing her hair as she runs to the door to welcome the guests with a large, warm grin that is a total front, in sharp contrast to the expression of stress she experienced seconds earlier preparing dinner. She tells the guests that they are right on time, when in fact, in the back of her mind, she thinks they have arrived much too early.

We live with fronts displayed to others. In humans, these social fronts are, more often than not, *metafronts*, like the front of the host with her guests. There are important psychological consequences to the process of dissociation that are the trademark of human social transactions.

As has been put forth in the fictive case of John, dissociation entails the necessity of compartmentalization. Roles must have no interference with each other to be credible fronts. When roles are not well compartmentalized, they can reveal hypocrisy, an undesirable trait in the human trade. Social fronts need to be tight in order to be effective. Tightness warrants sincerity and assurance that the person is no other than her present "impersonation," that this person does not raise doubts about who she pretends to be; that, for example, at the end of the evening when the guests finally leave the party, they do not see their host sighing in relief as she collapses with her back against the door she has just closed. Such a revelation would be a reason for major embarrassment: the exposure of the host's dubious front during the evening, the public exposure of her hypocrisy. It would be experienced as social betrayal from the guests' perspective.

PRIVILEGED SELF-EXPLORATION IN TRAVELING

In traveling to foreign lands, it is common knowledge that we are not just visiting new countries: we are visiting ourselves. We gauge what we are in separation from known territories and cultures. If not herding in a bus or a cruise liner, packing souvenir shops, or following a guide with familiar peers, we can enjoy anonymity and the surprise of new encounters. We get privileged glimpses at what we might be when confronted with new situations, when we challenge our basic fear of separation and abandonment.

But why is traveling often recognized as a privileged avenue of self-exploration? Following the idea of personal identity as a dynamic emergence, it is because it offers an abundance of "in-between" moments: moments that capture the transition from one situation to the next, from one role to another. These moments are rich moments of self-exploration because we are temporarily forced into new social roles, hence new in-between moments.

When traveling and meeting new people from all corners of the world, the first questions typically starting up conversations are all quests for identity: What is your name? Where do you come from? What is your profession? Are you married? These start-up questions are not random; their order is actually quite predictable anywhere. They reveal how we construct our representation of others, brick by brick, moving from label, to context, and into social status. This is the terrain for the co-construction of affinities and affiliation with others, familiar and unfamiliar alike.

Traveling is a privileged laboratory of what we are in relation to others. This digression emphasizes once more the importance of the process rather than the product corresponding to our personal identity.

In the song "Truth Serum" by the talented underground British-American singer and songwriter Smog, the refrain goes: "There is no truth in you, there is no truth in me . . . it is between." This refrain is the excerpt heading the chapter and goes on, "Love is an object, in an empty box. It is not in me, it is not in you. It is between." Smog, in his song, captures the essence of my argument about the self and how we construe who we are. The object of self-consciousness is not in us; nor is it in others. It is *in between*. We are fundamentally co-conscious of who we are, not just self-conscious. What we perceive and represent of ourselves is the result of our encountering others, and self-identity is a public rather than a private matter. It is the result of a social rather than an individual construction.

SOCIAL CONSTRUCTION OF SELF-IDENTITY

To conclude this chapter, I would like to return to one of the six propositions guiding this book, the proposition that self-consciousness is in essence triadic, emerging from a triangulation with others. As proposed by George Herbert Mead (1934), "It is impossible to conceive of a self outside of social experience." Self-consciousness, the representation of who we are, our identity, all is *co-constructed*, arising from reciprocal exchanges with others, not private meditation.

Self-consciousness and identity do not arise from private meditation, even in the most extreme solitary experience, when we feel that we are absolutely alone in what we experience and nothing can truly be shared: when, for example, *I* listen to *my* doctor revealing the diagnosis of an incurable disease, or when *I* listen to a judge reading *my* death sentence. Even in these most extreme instances, what we experience as an absolutely solitary experience of the self is rooted in social experience, as suggested by Mead. In both of these two extreme instances, the experience of the individual is unbearable. But why? It is because these instances are rooted in the pending absolute separation and rejection from others.

There is a plain logical argument in support of the assertion that self-consciousness is socially constructed rather than the product of internal or private experience or cogitation in the Cartesian tradition. The argument is simply that an absolute private conscious experience of the self can only be revealed in contradistinction to its opposite, a publicly shared conscious experience of the self. One cannot exist without the other.

By necessity, I would argue, the latter always precedes the former: social experience has precedence over the private conscious experience of the self, because it arises from it. Analogous to form perception, a figure can only reveal itself in contrast to a ground, but the ground always precedes the form, the latter arising from the former.

The experience of someone listening to his doctor's grim diagnosis or to his judge's death sentence is an absolutely solitary experience because the person knows the contrast of not being solitary. The person knows perfectly well what it means to be with and like others. To experience rejection, one needs to know what it means to be socially affiliated.

The point is, in my two grim examples, that the solitary, private experience of the self is constructed in the context of social experience, which forms its background and its cradle.

Solitary or nonsolitary experiences of the self do not exist each in itself, independently. They are codefined or mutually constructed as figure and ground are mutually constructed in the realm of perception. It follows that self-conscious experience is only possible in reference to and by triangulation with the consciousness of non-self entities (i.e., others).

However, the analogy with the mutual construction of figure and ground in the realm of perception has a serious limitation. Contrary to self and others, figure and ground are not engaged in a conversation; they are not engaged in a process of *negotiation*, as in social transactions. The relation between figure and ground in perception is fundamentally closed and typically static. It might be conflicting, leading to ambiguous perceptions, as in the case of some optical illusions, but this relation remains essentially static and closed. It is obligatory.

As I have insisted all along, this is clearly not the case in reciprocal social exchanges, in which the relation is typically open and dynamic. The self that is revealed in triangulation with others is mutual and operates both ways: I objectify myself in interaction with others as others objectify themselves in interaction with me.

The objectification of the self, hence self-consciousness and self-identity, arises from mutual triangulations. It is anything but a passive or static phenomenon. Rather, it is a fundamentally dynamic process, always active, always revised, always changing. Self-consciousness arises from constant negotiation between self and others, *co-constructed* in reciprocal exchanges with others.

Once again, the basic idea here is that self-consciousness is not within the individual, nor within others as a social mirror in which we contemplate and objectify ourselves to become eventually self-conscious. What we represent as ourselves is *in between*. We identify who we are on the basis of invariant features that are revealed in the midst of constant changes, constant switching of social roles and social fronts.

In conclusion, in this chapter I have tried to show that identity, that is, the conscious representation of who we are in relation to others, is a form that emerges from the systematic manipulation and negotiation of self-presentations in the context of reciprocal exchanges. In this context, identity is primarily a social construction, not a private elaboration internal to the individual. It is in the history of reciprocal exchanges that we cospecify ourselves and cospecify what we are for each other.

Arguably, without others, there is no self-consciousness, hence no explicit or *conceptual sense* of what we might be as an objectified entity. In short, there is no identity. The explicit sense of who we are is constructed in reciprocal exchanges and negotiations, both forming a cardinal trait of our species.

Conclusion: Moral Space and the Self

> To know who I am is a species of knowing where I stand.
> Charles Taylor, *Sources of the Self*[1]

I have organized this book along two axes – a blunt, commonsense evolutionary statement and a simple emotional matrix. The blunt statement is that without others, we are nothing. The simple matrix is that the bottom line of what we feel, we do, and we think is driven by the fear of rejection. Coping with the basic need to be with others and fearing rejection by them are constitutive of the context in which we, as a species, evolved self-consciousness. All we do, as a result, is with *others in mind*.

This schema is admittedly simple and leaves many questions unanswered. In particular, two questions are left out that I would like to address in this conclusion. These questions are, respectively, Why do we have this basic affiliation need? Why do we have this basic fear of being rejected?

My goal here is to address these questions beyond the utilitarian interpretation that we need to affiliate and fear being rejected because we are biologically designed to maximize our resources and our chances to survive as members of our species. We need to go beyond the idea that the constitutive needs to affiliate and fear of being rejected are the expression of evolutionary adaptations of our species, beyond the truism that they are just consequences of phylogeny. This kind of sociobiological account, even if illuminating on the scale of evolution, is profoundly unsatisfactory at a psychological level. It does not capture the complex, specifically human psychology behind such consequences.

---

[1] Taylor, C. (1989). *Sources of the Self*, p. 27. Cambridge, MA: Harvard University Press.

The human experience of rejection and the human need to affiliate deserve more than a sociobiological account. They deserve psychological and metapsychological treatment and interpretation. This is what I would like to present next in relation to the issue of self-consciousness.

If I put forth the idea that self-consciousness, ultimately the sense of identity, develops in relation to and in negotiation with others in the context of reciprocal exchanges, there is one aspect of the process I neglected. This aspect is the moral (i.e., normative) dimension always attached to self-consciousness and self-identity. If we develop an explicit sense of who we are in relation to others, we do not do so in a neutral, valueless way.

In fact, the negotiation of who we are, is a process that always entails values. In the social construction of our identity, we are immersed in a negotiation on the *value* of who we are, not just who we are as an individuated person. Self-worth is a crucial and meaningful aspect of self-consciousness that eludes any sociobiological interpretations. Self-worth is at the core of the psychology that surrounds the issue of identity.

In this concluding chapter and in the footsteps of the work of Charles Taylor, I would like to make the point that to know oneself, to be self-conscious, it is to know where one stands in relation to others. It is to situate the self in a moral space, – a *world of socially constructed values and norms* – not just a neutral, predetermined, and static world made of nonself entities.

SELF-CONSCIOUSNESS AND NORMS

There is an abundance of studies documenting from the perspective of development how children come to manifest value and standing in relation to others. Those documenting how children react to their own image in a mirror and the extent to which they show signs of self-conscious emotions are particularly telling of the inseparability between self-consciousness and social norms.

Again, it is by the middle of the second year that children typically pass the mark test, pointing to their own body and removing a mark surreptitiously put on their face as revealed by their own mirror reflection. This development is reported even in children growing up in an environment where clear mirrors are rare or nonexistent, in circumstances where there is presumably little to no opportunity for children to learn directly what their face looks like.[2]

---

[2] Priel, B., & de Schonen, S. (1986). Self-recognition: A study of a population without mirrors. *Journal of Experimental Child Psychology* 41(2): 237–250.

But this finding is not as robust as it might sound. We recently collected evidence suggesting that this developmental phenomenon is not as predictable as it has been typically reported, not as universal or transcultural.[3] We found marked differences in the manifestation of mirror self-recognition depending on the *social* and *cultural* circumstances of the child. Aside from expressing explicit self-consciousness, when, for example, the child says, "Look! It is me in the mirror!" or "Ooops, what is that on my face?" the passing of the mirror test in fact indicates much more than self-recognition per se. It tells about the representation of a normative self, the sense of how we *should be* compared to others. This normative sense of self accompanies mirror self-recognition from the outset and develops rapidly, as I will try to show.

One central question that tends to be curiously overlooked by researchers studying the emergence of a conceptual sense of self using the mirror test is, Why do children have the generalized propensity to touch and eventually remove the mark they notice on their face in the mirror? Why is the perception of the mark an apparent source of embarrassment and estrangement from others? In some instances, we observed children noticing the mark in the mirror (a yellow sticker that was surreptitiously placed on their forehead), quickly removing it, and then spontaneously *apologizing* to the experimenter for the anomaly. It is not uncommon for a child to say, "Ooops, I am sorry." This expression resembles the apologetic response of an adult who accidentally spits a piece of food into someone else's plate around the dinner table. The child's response is not unlike the apology and the embarrassment we, as adults, typically show when someone points out to us that we have a big chunk of spinach covering our front tooth.

These are all clearly self-conscious responses, but they are more than the expression of an ability to objectify oneself either in the mirror or in others. More importantly, they are also the expression of an objectification of the self in relation to a norm – the norm of how we are supposed to look like – the normative sense of who we are in relation to others. It is the expression of self-worth we represent, the values we stand and strive for. All these responses are at the core of human psychology. Once again, all are expressions of the basic need to affiliate, to maintain social proximity, and ultimately to avoid rejection from others.

In our cross-cultural study of mirror self-recognition, we observed over a hundred children living in small rural communities of Kenya in Africa,

[3] Broesch, T., Rochat, P., Callaghan, T., & Henrich, J. (under review). Cultural variations in children's mirror self-recognition. *Journal of Cross-Cultural Psychology.*

recording their reaction to the mirror after a yellow sticker was surreptitiously placed on their forehead.[4] These children were aged between two and seven years. To our great surprise, only 2 of the 104 children tested "passed" the mirror test by either just touching or removing the mark. This is in sharp contrast to the vast majority of two-year-old Western children, who are typically reported passing the mirror test by which they show an explicit sense of mirror self-recognition. There is no reason to think that the Kenyan children did not know that it was they in the mirror. Obviously they knew it and the results correspond to false negative responses, children freezing in front of the mirror, transfixed by their specular image as if paralyzed: a very different response from what we observe at this age with American children, for example.

So why? What prevents Kenyan children from touching and removing the anomalous sticker they perceive on their face in the mirror? Why do they freeze? The most probable explanation is that Kenyan children do express a normative sense of the self that they unquestionably recognize in the mirror. They recognize themselves with the sticker on them, but they do not know whether it would be a transgression to touch and remove it.

We think that these children, and contrary to North American children, question the anomaly in relation to a strong sense of the adult authority that surrounds them. In the context of the authoritarian culture of Kenyan children, when they notice the sticker on their face in the mirror, they question whether it has been placed there for reasons they do not know and whether it is appropriate for them to touch and remove it. Their culture contrasts to the more permissive and lenient culture promoted by the parents of Western middle-class children we typically test in the United States or Western Europe. More often than not, Western children are encouraged to take individual initiatives; Kenyan children are not, and this likely explains the sharp difference in responses between the two groups.

Kenyan and North American children in their opposite responses during the mirror test do express, de facto, the same level of self-consciousness. They both express an explicit sense of themselves in relation to a norm. One group is significantly more inclined to question the authority and take it upon themselves to modify their appearance in the mirror that they judge off-norm from how they should project to the public eye. The other cultural group is, on the contrary, significantly more submissive in relation to the authority that set them up in the mirror test. In fact, both express a normative sense of

[4] Ibid.

themselves, the sense of how they should be perceived by others, either physically or by behaving in an adult-compliant and obedient way.

These observations are simple, yet striking, because they show that children see in the mirror not only themselves, but themselves as they are recognized, evaluated, and tolerated by others. The specular image is what is seen by others from the outside and that the child is allowed via the mirror to see for herself. The specular image is thus construed by the child not just as a reflection of himself, but also as his public self, the self who can be perceived and evaluated by others. They see the self as a more or less good fit with what is normative from the point of view of others' evaluative eyes.

In short, children manifest an internalization of these norms, perceiving themselves with others in mind, not in an isolated, solipsistic, and contemplative manner à la Descartes. What they see and recognize is a public and normative self, not a neutral self.

Another study[5] we recently conducted confirms this point. We invited middle-class parents to take their two-year-olds to the lab for the mirror test. However, this time, everybody at the lab welcomed the child with a yellow sticker on his or her forehead as if it were a normal feature or part of a uniform. We even discreetly put a sticker on the mother's forehead as she entered the lab (they were warned of the procedure beforehand). We thus created a social norm surrounding the child in the visit to our laboratory, namely, that everybody in this environment has a yellow sticker on the forehead. We then tested the child in the mirror test.

We collected data showing that two- to three-year-olds, in this normative context, are more reluctant to remove the sticker from their forehead after discovering in the mirror that they too have one on their face. In many instances, if they touched and removed the sticker, it was immediately to put it back on, as if they figured that it was part of the lab uniform, part of the lab's normal environment. This is unambiguous evidence that children by two years do perceive themselves in relation to others. In particular, it shows that they recognize themselves in relation to surrounding social norms. They adjust their relative embarrassment or corrective behavior in relation to these perceived norms and as a function of their own evaluation of the social situation. Social conformity modulates their expression of self-consciousness.

Two-year-olds begin to *conform* to what they perceive as the rule. In the context of our research, they either tended to keep the sticker on their

---

[5] Rochat, P., & Broesch, T. (under review). Self-consciousness and social conformity in 2-year-olds.

forehead or quickly removed it to put it away for good, depending on their evaluation of the social norms within the new context of the laboratory. But why are they so inclined already at such a young age to conform?

The answer is straightforward. It is because children from this age on strive for social inclusion and affiliation. They strive to fuse with the group, hungry for social proximity and intimacy. Ultimately, children fight off the fear of being social outcasts, separated from others by sticking out, targets of rejection and social distance, *fearing to be disliked by being unlike*. Fusing with the group and conformity allay such fear of rejection.

If two- to three-year-olds in our mirror situation show conformity and prevention of rejection, adolescents in their opposition and "identity crisis" as described, for example, in the seminal work of Erik Erickson,[6] seem to show just the opposite. But in fact, they express as much conformity, even sometimes in a much more conspicuous fashion. Often, the identity crisis of adolescents manifests itself by blind adhesion and group affiliation outside family and school contexts, as in gangs or other close-knit groups of youngsters who share the same taste, speak the same words, and often wear clothes like uniforms. All these attributes are conspicuous social billboards. They advertise not only rebelliousness, but also and more importantly, the urgent need for social affiliation beyond biological family bonds.

IDEALIZED SELF AND THE FEAR OF REJECTION

One of the six propositions guiding this book is that we have a tendency to inflate qualitatively the view of our embodied self and devaluate the representation we have of others' perception and evaluation of us. Part of this proposition stems from the intuition that we generally tend to have higher regard for ourselves from within our body than in relation to what we see of our own person projected in a mirror, a photograph, or even an audio recording. I have proposed that there is an irreconcilable gap between these two views (private vs. public), a gap we are endlessly trying to fill via intersubjective negotiation and spending most of our time controlling the way we project ourselves to the outside world, systematically manipulating the public presentation of ourselves.

The rationale is that there is an authority of first-person perspective on the self. This authority rests on the permanent and simultaneous engagement of multiple sense modalities giving direct access to information on the own body and its emotional states. These modalities include proprioception, a

---

[6] Erikson, E. H. (1993). *Childhood and Society*. New York: W. W. Norton.

modality that informs us about our own bodily movements, the modality of the self "par excellence." However, this proposition does not explain why such privileged access to perceptual information specifying the self would be associated with an inflated or higher view of the self. Why such a qualitative gap between the private and the public views of the self? Why do we tend to idealize our embodied self and look down on what is publicly represented of us (e.g., mirror image, ourselves in photographs)?

To interpret this qualitative imbalance, it is necessary to return to norms and conformity, to the normative dimension of self-consciousness. The common experience of disappointment in the view of ourselves in the mirror, particularly as we age, results from the basic fact that what we see does not match what we expect others should see in order *to like us.*

Driven by the basic fear of rejection, we realize that what others are actually seeing of ourselves might repulse them. It might cause estrangement and rejection, a universal deep-seated fear in all of us, except sociopaths and others with pronounced narcissistic personalities and whose psychopathological symptoms revolve ultimately around social disconnection and delusion. This realization of being public is a realization of *truth* to the extent that mirrors, photographs, or audio recordings reveal a shared or public reality about the self. What I see of myself in the picture or the mirror is also what *they* see. And this is a source of terror demonstrated by the adult Biamis of Papua New Guinea when confronted for the first time with a clear view of themselves in mirrors or photographs.[7]

The fact that we tend to experience a *negative* match between what we project publicly and what we expect others should see in order to like us explains our surprise and typical disappointment, but it does not explain where this mismatch might originate and why we should have an idealized, positively inflated view of ourselves from within our own body. Somehow, we tend to show surprise and disappointment when we witness our public self, quick to show embarrassment and vulnerability. But why is that? Why do we idealize ourselves privately and tend to deflate when public? Furthermore, why such anxiety? The answer is, once again, the basic, powerful, and presumably universal fear of social rejection.

We could imagine that the discrepancy between the experience of the private and the public selves could be a source of either indifference or elation, but it is not. It is the source, more often than not, of a deflated affect: disappointment, sadness, even depression. We need to explain the

---

[7] Carpenter, E. (1975). The tribal terror of self-awareness. In P. Hikins, ed., *Principles of Visual Anthropology*, pp. 448–476. The Hague: Mouton.

negative quality of the experience, and I propose that it is inseparable from our basic fear of being rejected by others.

The basic need for proximity with others and its counterpart, the basic fear of rejection, lead us to construct a complex representational system (the "Ego ideal" in Freud's terms) of what others might like, but also might *dislike*, about us.

The origins and content of such a representational system are obviously complex, depending on the life history of the individual and her particular cultural circumstances. It reflects the representational and belief systems of the parents, the culture, and all the significant others surrounding the child, from teachers to siblings and peers. This is the context in which one develops a representation of how he is liked or disliked by others, what puts him closer to or farther from them. This is true whether we are young or old; famous, anonymous, or infamous; mundane or serious; modest or powerful. There is indeed a generalized drive to be socially recognized, to maintain proximity and get closer to others, particularly if they are significant.

At important junctures in our lives, this representational system is particularly engaged, when, for example, we choose a profession, decide to or not to marry a particular person. When the choice of profession exists or marriage is not prearranged, we choose and decide with *others in mind*, weighing whether the decision will make us closer to gaining us more recognition from people whose approval we seek. Inversely, we weigh whether it might generate disappointment and resentment, hence distance and rejection from those whose opinions about our person count. But the avoidance of disappointment and resentment from others typically outweighs the focus on getting closer to them. There are a precedence and general overtone of fear over the positive aspect of social closeness, although both tend toward the same ultimate goals: the maintenance, control, and reinforcement of social proximity and affiliation, the quest for social recognition.

The rationale for insisting on the negative affective valence of the representational system about the self rests on the robust fact that with the public self is typically associated the experience of fear and anxiety, the fear and anxiety of losing ascendance and control over social affiliation. Once again, we are driven toward others primarily out of the fear of losing proximity with them, not of gaining approval from them. In general, I would say that the fear of rejection tends to precede and override recognition as a drive to affiliate.

To use a simple metaphor, as do alcoholics in fear of running out of booze, we tend to focus more on the fact that the bottle is half-empty than half-full. We are socially addicted to the proximity of others, overwhelmed by the fear of repulsing them, hence looked down, put down, and ostracized. We are generally inclined to be socially nervous and jealous, rather than serene and fearless of others.

Rejection *is* the epitome of punishment, something that is universally recognized as the source of the worst psychological suffering. Across cultures, it is the prime choice of repayment for crimes toward others and toward society at large. We isolate and literally "put away" criminals, and we put them in solitary confinement when they keep misbehaving and committing crimes in prison. The death penalty is appropriately called "capital punishment" for its absolute severance and definitive rejection of the individual from society.

HUMAN STRUGGLE FOR RECOGNITION

The need for social proximity and intimacy makes us particularly astute at monitoring signs of separation. We are exquisitely sensitive to any minute changes in what we interpret as either avoidance or approach toward the self by others. We are like finely tuned gauges permanently recording every move others make in relation to us. Sometimes, the monitoring of others takes strange forms. We tend to create intersubjective crisis for the sole purpose of gauging and asserting our situation in a relationship.[8]

It is not uncommon to see young toddlers running away from their mother and ignoring her calls. In doing so, they appear to gauge their own existence in relation to their mother, excited by the tonality and persistence of the calls. Obviously, this phenomenon can be observed to some degree in other animals, particularly in the young progeny and mother of most mammalian species who are very engaged in monitoring and gauging their relative physical proximity, astute and highly driven to maintain close contact.

Numerous comparative studies demonstrate that attachment as a distinct phenomenon is evident in nonhuman species and that it cannot be simply explained by a primary drive reduction mechanism linked to food and feeding. Rather, it appears that attachment forms a distinct behavioral propensity linked to a basic need, a need for physical comfort and protection, warmth and proximity, as shown by the pioneer work of Harlow with rhesus monkeys. However, if we share with other animals the basic

---

[8] A similar idea that one endangers himself in relation to others to probe affiliation and assert reputation is proposed by Zahavi and Zahavi, who interpret such behaviors as a principle that cuts across animal species and is cardinal to human and nonhuman social acts; see Zahavi, A., & Zahavi, A. (1997). *The Handicap Principle: A Missing Piece of Darwin's Puzzle.* New York: Oxford University Press.

need for proximity and intimacy, what we have evolved as a species are new meanings regarding the comfort of proximity as well as a much richer grammar of the signs that specify rejection of the self by others.

From the time children recognize themselves in mirrors, begin to use possessives like *mine*, and manifest empathy via differentiation, projection, and *identification* with others, the meaning of social proximity and rejection changes. The sense of comfort of being with others is *redescribed* to accommodate this unique developmental progress, all arising in the context of reciprocal exchanges and the negotiation of values with others. With the developmental emergence of self-consciousness (i.e., knowledge of knowing and self-objectification), the meaning of social proximity and rejection changes. They are understood differently by the child while remaining central and basic in terms of need and fear.

But what are these meaning changes and what is the product of this representational redescription of social proximity and rejection associated with the developmental emergence of self-consciousness?

What changes are the levels of interpretation of others, the reading of intentions and mental states, and in particular the reading of *what is on the mind of others in relation to us*. This change is what is commonly labeled in the literature as the development of "theories of mind" or folk psychology. Prior to the emergence of self-consciousness, the monitoring of social proximity and rejection is based on surface characteristics of others' behaviors in relation to the self such as the form and timing of exchanges, the degree of contingency in face-to-face protoconversational exchanges, the degree of physical proximity and contact, what, for example, is discussed by Donald Winnicott as "holding," namely, the various qualitative ways infants feel that they are handled by others.

By at least the second year, children begin to read more than what is publicly expressed in the behaviors and responses of others in relation to the self. They begin to infer mental states and belief systems in others by *simulation*, now engaging in the active mental reenactment of others' behaviors, getting into their shoes to represent what they feel and what might be on their mind in relation to the self. Note that some researchers would say that children, as little scientists, begin to build and test theories about the mental states of others. But this hypothesis is controversial and too cold an intuition as it tends to overlook important emotional and affective dimensions.

The unambiguous emergence of self-consciousness by the second year is associated with a new reading of others, particularly a new reading of others in relation to the self. From then on, children infer mental states and construct complex representations of how people construe them, not only in terms of how close they are physically and emotionally, but also in terms of abstract conceptual *values*. These values correspond to what we label as esteem, trust, commitment, or respect. These values are complex and difficult to define, elusive at best. However, following the ideas put forth by the contemporary philosopher Axel Honneth,[9] who offers an interesting integration of Hegel's, George Herbert Mead's, and Winnicott's ideas on the social determinant of self-concept, these elusive values can be treated as spinoffs of the general human struggle for *recognition*. From a developmental standpoint, much of Honneth's theory rests on Winnicott's idea that children develop a capacity for attachment by being "oneself in another," the model for love in general.

In association with the emergence of self-objectification and the knowledge of knowing, children seek a different kind of comfort with others, and the need for social proximity takes on new meanings. Children by now seek a special place in the mind of others, a place that is exclusive and privileged. They seek more than just physical proximity and comfort from the physical presence of others. They seek mental comfort, expressing a new urge to be *recognized* by others.

The struggle for recognition is the struggle for existence itself. By the second year, this is an urge that has become more abstract and existential. It is as if the child could now exist only if the approving eyes of others were on them. From then on, they need the constant approval of others to feel good about themselves. The struggle for recognition is a cultural prerequisite that will accompany the child all through the life span. It is a curse, but it is also what makes children integral parts and contributing members of their culture, the human culture.

I have stated in a few places throughout the book that to be human is to care about reputation. The caring about reputation is just part of the human struggle for recognition. We care about what others think of us simply because we need their approval to exist. This is a major trait of the human psyche, the major psychological distinction of our species.

In ontogeny, this trait emerges with self-consciousness as children begin to triangulate and objectify themselves in reciprocal exchanges with others. It is from this point on that they begin to simulate and identify with others, mainly to figure out what is in their mind as well as in their heart in relation to them. They seek recognition to situate themselves in relation to others and to the world in general. They also seek social recognition to build esteem for themselves. From this point on, children appear to

---

[9] Honneth, A. (1995). *The Struggle for Recognition – the Moral Grammar of Social Conflicts.* Cambridge MA: MIT Press.

experience vital reassurance in the feeling that they exist in the eyes of others, that they capture their attention. They experience vital reassurance when they understand that they are not transparent to the world like *the invisible man* in the famous novel by Ralph Ellison.[10]

The painful observations of neglected children in crowded orphanages, unrooted people of war-torn countries surviving in refugee camps, or illegal immigrant families seeking work in hostile rich countries, all demonstrate that the lack of recognition and the loss of identity in the eyes of others have devastating psychological consequences.

To be ignored and rejected by others is indeed the worst punishment and the worst of all sufferings. It is psychological death.

SELF-CONSCIOUSNESS AND AUTHENTICITY

I would like to conclude with some final thoughts on the moral consequences of the deeply rooted human struggle for recognition and the fear of social rejection. I have mentioned in a few places that self-consciousness and the concern about reputation are not just geared toward what others represent about us. They are also about how we feel about ourselves, what in psychological jargon would correspond to *self-esteem*.

Self-esteem is a complex issue at the core of human psychology. It is associated with the self-conscious emotion of shame and all its derivatives such as pride or guilt. It is also associated with the complex representational system that underlies the normative and idealized sense of self discussed in a previous section. What I would like to suggest now is that the moral sense of what we feel and eventually construe as right or wrong – in the most generic sense – is linked to what we feel as *authentic* or *inauthentic*, what we feel has value and is real, and what has no value and is fake.

The basic dichotomy of experience between what is authentic and inauthentic probably arises from a transcendence of our basic affiliation need and its necessary counterpart, the basic fear of rejection. To illustrate this idea, I will use as paradigm what I understand to be the tragic life story of the abstract expressionist and action painter Jackson Pollock.[11] I will try to express my idea through him.

---

[10] See the interesting discussion of Ellison's *Invisible Man* in Honneth, A. (2001). Invisibility: On the epistemology of 'recognition'. Supplement to the *Proceedings of the Aristotelian Society* 75(1): 111–122.

[11] My interpretation of Pollock's "authenticity" complex is based primarily on the authoritative biography of the painter by Bernard Harper Friedman: Friedman, B. H. (1972/1995). *Jackson Pollock – Energy Made Visible.* New York: Da Capo Press.

As you certainly know, Pollock is an influential artist who is recognized as one of the major shapes on the mid-twentieth-century North American art scene. In the 1940s and 1950s he was at the origins of a new movement and a radically new style in painting by which he tried to leave on the canvas direct traces of inner feelings via gestures of pure vitality. Pollock died after producing a series of large paintings that he covered with energetic drops of paints, his most famous paintings or "drip paintings." Obviously, this new style was revolutionary and highly controversial, derided by most, but admired by a few clairvoyant, avant-garde connoisseurs.

Pollock was from the rural South of the United States. Improbably, he left his hometown, driven by his art to live in a very different community of artists and gallery owners in New York City, where things were hopping and happening. During his lifetime and unlike many other highly successful artists, Pollock became very famous and received much recognition in terms of money and public exposure, for better or worse. He had a serious drinking problem that got worse and eventually killed him at the pinnacle of success and recognition. *Life* magazine had a cover story on him and a film documented his art. His work was shown in major museums and galleries. He was highly regarded and supported by rich collectors and respected art critics. So what happened? I will submit that it is all about the issue of *authenticity*. With success come expectations and social pressures, the risk of disappointing others, and the feeling of possibly having reached a ceiling. This is what probably killed Pollock.

Despite the rare recognition he received from others, including much of the derision and criticism that are the normal side effect of success, Jackson Pollock doubted whether he was for real, or, on the contrary as some of his critics would suggest, a fake, a temporary fad in the art scene: whether or not he was an *impostor*. It seems that what killed Pollock was an impostor or authenticity complex. As his success grew, so did self-doubt, his sense of potentially being a fake, not able to live up to what was expected from him at the pinnacle of recognition. Potential shame and social rejection haunted Pollock and spiraled out of control by the last years of his life, as he drank to excess and eventually killed himself as well as others in a car wreck. In his book, Friedman describes Pollock's final year: "Now blocked, unproductive, un-alive, he had no present work to fall back on, no work immediately ahead of him, nothing but the empty canvas, waiting to receive him but receiving instead reflections of the world."[12] The world

---

[12] Friedman, B. H. (1972/1995), p. 213.

in his mind, the social world of elusive critics in particular, turned out to be debilitating and killed him.

Pollock's story points to something that I find crucial and that transcends the human struggle for recognition by others. It is the recognition for oneself, the feeling of our own worth, what Freud would label as our deeply rooted propensity toward *narcissism*.

We strive to get recognition from others, but ultimately it is to be confirmed in the value we ascribe to and aspire for ourselves. This is how we fulfill the sense that we exist and, that we are not psychologically dead, that we have a self that has coherence, meaning, and, more importantly, that has some *worth* in itself. It is the expression of a deep abstract and existential need, a transcendental and moral expression (in the sense of value system) of self-consciousness.

From this transcendental expression derive values, the values of what we see as authentic and what we see as fake – true recognition and false recognition from others, true respect and false respect from others, true reputation and false reputation.

In reciprocal exchanges and intersubjective negotiation, children from an early age develop a sense of what is right and what is wrong, in particular – *what is genuine and what is not*. Very early on, at least from two months, when infants begin to engage in reciprocal exchanges and proto-conversations with others, if they are accustomed to receiving from their mother a particular affective return from their own positive bid (e.g., a smile), they will notice a difference in a stranger who might respond differently, with a less warm smile for example, hence a lesser bid. In noticing this difference this infant begins to construct complex implicit systems of norms as to what return bid should be expected in face-to-face reciprocal exchanges.[13] These are probably the roots of a protomorality in the sense of a primary, implicit system of values.

Morality is indeed *felt* before it can be explicit and formalized into shared codes of rules and laws. It is felt by children who, outside face-to-face reciprocal exchanges, will begin by two to three years to feel for others via differenciation, projection, and identification, expressing empathic emotions and even beginning spontaneously to perform benevolent acts (e.g., helping, consoling).

---

[13] See the research by Bigelow, A. E., & Rochat, P. (2006). Two-month-old infants' sensitivity to social contingency in mother–infant and stranger–infant interaction. *Infancy* 9(3): 313–325. The research provides support for the very early development of canonical patterns of social reciprocation that are predicted by the mother's style of interaction.

In relation to self-worth and the trust we place in others, these values are probably based on a primitive sense of the "authentic" and the "fake." The sense of authenticity could be the cornerstone and the origins of our moral sense, the primitive sense of right and wrong in which all explicit value systems originate. The sense of authenticity is what guides us primarily in our moral decisions, the decisions we make in relation to others, but also in our value judgment regarding the moral decisions of others. As Charles Taylor proposes in *Sources of the Self*, we live in a moral space – a world of shared values. In human affairs, self-worth and reputation are determined by how we navigate and situate ourselves in the moral space that ties us all together (the *stand we take,* as Taylor would put it).

I have tried to show that the consciousness of who we are in relation to others is deeply rooted in our basic fear of social rejection, the necessary counterpart of our insatiable need to affiliate with others. If rudiments of self-consciousness develop early, the sense of identity and the consciousness of the value of who we are in relation to others develop all through the life span.

As good obituaries sometimes show, this is a delicate and lifelong enterprise. We tend to be remembered, judged, and eventually recognized by the shape of our own moral enterprise. We like it this way and this is also how we like to think about ourselves. We like to feel and be recognized as *authentic*, true to what we believe deep down, true to what we think we are. This is our ultimate refuge – the recognition we are all striving for and by which we exist.

POSTSCRIPT NOTE: POWER TO THE INDIVIDUAL AND ASSOCIATED PANIC

Self-consciousness as discussed in this book is a modern syndrome. It participates in major social and psychological changes since the postindustrial revolution. This revolution assigned moral responsibility to the individual, *away* from the moral authority of collective systems or traditions embodied in institutions such as the church or the state. Modern individuals might have beaten the fear of God or of the king but were quick to replace it by the modern panic of being responsible for failure and the constant fear of rejection by peers. They were quick to replace it with the unbearable fear of being left alone and feeling responsible for such separation. The pulse of this transformation is particularly palpable when looking at some rapid developments in recent art history.

Marcel Duchamp revolutionized the art world by introducing mundane objects into the sphere of galleries and museums. He spoofed the sanctity of aesthetic canons by adding moustaches to Da Vinci's *La Joconda* with a funny commentary indicating that she feels heat on her butt (an anagram made of a five-letter string below the altered reproduction, spelling *L.H.O.O.Q.*, which in French reads, "Elle a chaud au cul").

With this benign and humorous initiative, Marcel Duchamp raised utilitarian objects to works of art. Urinals and bottle racks were transformed into objects of contemplation by being hijacked from their mundane reality, deliberately placed by the artist in a new viewing context for pure inspection. Duchamp's act was revolutionary, as he intended to blur the distinction between reality and art, scrambling the distinction between the thing to be depicted and its actual depiction.

As an artist, Duchamp is recognized for having forced viewers, in somehow inescapable ways, to question the nature of art and its function in society. He forced art lovers to question what art is in the end. What is a masterpiece? Why is a moustache added to this epitome of beauty? What is so special about this box or this thing I usually urinate in? Duchamp's response in his gesture was, "Go figure! But figure it out *yourself!*"

Duchamp's message is loud and clear: there are no aesthetic canons out there; beauty is in the eyes of the beholder; and let's not forget; there is a political order that imposes what art is and what it is not. As a case in point, see Hitler's exhibit of "degenerative art" during the heyday of Nazism. Therefore the message is eminently political, meant to free viewers from the oppression of curators and art dealers, the power of the capitalist marketplace of collectibles that dictates what is art and what it is not, what is good taste and "worthwhile" art, and what art should or should not be.

The message was that the modern capitalist market was replacing what used to be the power of the church, of kings, or of rich art benefactors like the Medici or other cultivated elite groups of wealth and power. This message was expanded and exploited in the 1960s with "pop artists" like Andy Warhol who began producing merchandiselike paintings; repetitive, factory line looking chromo images; as well as long feature films made of a single frame of the Empire State Building while boosting self-advertising with claims of a universal craving to become public, to come out of dreadful anonymity to give meaning and worth to one's life via recognition, even for just fifteen minutes of fame.

Duchamp and his followers played with the fact that art was becoming a new modern commodity, increasingly the intrinsic part of an investment market offering great profit potential for collectors with an astute eye for what is hype or might become interesting in the close, self-referencing circle of modern art, a culture that is shaped essentially by art critics, collectors, gallery and museum curators, as well as an always growing crowd of "elite" urbanite art fans who have developed what appears to be an insatiable taste for edgy aesthetic statements and intellectual stimulation.

What I find interesting in all this is that Duchamp's instrumentation of a new approach to art participates in the larger movement toward modernity that finds its root in philosophers like Nietzsche, who, by announcing that God was dead, admonished individuals to rely on themselves for rediscovering their long lost freedom, to free themselves from imposed morality, and finally to find dignity and heroic courage in themselves, only in themselves, not in the gregarious alignment of their aspiration to the dictates of supernatural power.

Modern philosophy is a political manifesto for autonomous responsibility. The prerogative of no one but the individual is the main motto of the existentialist movement led by Sartre during and after World War II in France, still very influential today in different ideological disguises. It is a call for the redefinition of freedom as individual responsibility: whether you are free or not rests on no one else's but your shoulders. There is an admonition for modern individuals to carry the weight of their own freedom, therefore to recognize themselves in their free will.

In relation to Duchamp and his revolutionary gesture in the art world in the 1920s and 1930s, individuals are left with the responsibility of deciding the value of things, be they moral decisions, political ideologies, artistic worth, or aesthetics. Duchamp's own responsibility as an artist was to raise questions for viewers, to push them to find meaningful answers on their own. He defined a new conceptual mission for artists, the mission of delegating decisions regarding the value of things, the value of art, to the individual viewer's discretion, making those decisions his responsibility and his freedom to decide ultimately what is worth thinking about and looking at. In short, it participates in the modern attempts at liberating the individual from the oppression of large authoritative value systems.

The long line of modern philosophers since the eighteenth century of the Enlightment, and particularly since Nietzsche at the turn of the last century, formulated and had a strong premonition of the contemporary solitary tragedy of individuals in the industrial West.

Contemporary individuals are left with the responsibility to decide on their own, as the great value systems of our parents are losing power. They are collapsing, replaced by the direct expression of the law of supply and demand, the basic law of the marketplace. Like art, individuals are becoming increasingly commodities: commodities made of career trajectory, job offers, and a renewable workforce.

It is now trivial and common sense to state that the market is becoming God in our lives, the almighty power driven by the basic rules of getting by and getting rich if all goes well. Postindustrial or hypermodern individuals, as they are sometimes called, all the contemporary individuals who survive, procreate, and try to get by in the industrialized West are left to decide what is important in life, what makes a decent and good life.

But, in fact, the word *decision* is more an oxymoron than a true statement. For the most part, career moves and basic survival strategy for self-maximization seem to dictate what needs to be done next. It is the law of the market, the marketing of self that has taken over in contemporary life, at least in the rich Western world. But this law is spreading eastward like an economic tsunami, with the fast-growing urbanite classes of booming marketplaces in China and India, for example, in cities like Shanghai and New Delhi.

Modern freedom entails modern anxieties. There is pressure on individuals to define their own moral space, their own individual responsibilities, while struggling to maximize resources for self and promote themselves to others. Associated with this dynamic is a modern panic syndrome, the panic syndrome of failing. There is a generalized fear of failure, the fear of not earning enough, of not achieving goals we are compelled to assign to ourselves, not meeting self-imposed expectations on the basis of what is represented as others' views on the self and others' valuation of the self. This valuation of the self by the self to meet others' fantasized (represented) expectations is the core drama of individuals entangled in contemporary industrial life.

Experiencing the life of remote and isolated small traditional communities, as I have over the years in the South Pacific, in Samoa (Polynesia) and Vanuatu (Melanesia) in particular, allows you to measure how much the fear of failure is a very secular panic syndrome of the postindustrial global world, particularly for individuals who are moving upward socially as measured by wealth and education.

It is remarkably common to hear members of small rural communities expressing their deep appreciation for the sense of security and solidarity they experience in their simple village life, where everyone knows and checks on each other. They dread the life of modern cities, particularly what they see as the wild and anonymous competition for resources. It is very common to hear villagers acknowledging the simplicity and the sparseness of their life but to point to the fact that nobody will ever starve among them, even those who are lazy and are acknowledged freeloaders in the community. The freedom of choice of individuals to freeload, contribute equally, or work in excess for the community seems to be a major component of what they claim is their comfort in life. Good life is for these people primarily the sense of being accepted and taken care of by other members of the community, no matter what. Excessive work and gratuitous acts are obviously rewarded with higher prestige and political clout, but someone who does not have much ambition is not stigmatized. He is given food and a respectful place within the community, given tasks that are tailored to his ambition and relative ability to contribute. The group appears to accommodate all individuals, adjusting expectations according to the individual's profile, expectations not resting solely on the individual's shoulders but rather being a self-organizing collective matter. This is the impression one gets over and over talking to members of traditional villages in Polynesia and Melanesia, regardless of individuals' relative wealth and power within the group. Lower-class individuals express relief and higher-class individuals express satisfaction when they provide for others. Contrary to modern industrial group living, everyone seems to have a decent social place, no matter what, and although life is simple and there are few material resources to fight about, although some have wealth that others do not have, all recognize the great comfort of basic social insertion and integration, the basic provision for all of food, shelter, and, more importantly, *social attention and care*. No reason to panic about failure; everyone seemingly falls into some respected and useful social place.

I might be accused of simplistic idealism, reifying the myth of paucity by generalizing from impressions gathered from casual conversations with possibly unreliable informants. Nevertheless, let me end with a simple observation that keeps resonating in my mind, probably the source of a major insight that motivated this book.

Walking around in South Pacific island traditional villages, during the day or in the pitch dark of moonless nights, it is almost impossible to cross paths with someone, young or old, woman or man, familiar or absolute stranger, without some greeting, without some acknowledgment of your existence, either called by your name or being asked what you are doing and where you are going, even if the response is very obvious. For individuals like me who grew up in rich postindustrial regions of the world, who struggle for their career and place in society, constantly under the spell of a panic fear of failure, of having failed, or of being an impostor, such simple, yet constant social acknowledgment amounts to the experience of tremendous relief. Finally one experiences the peace of being effortlessly recognized by others, the absolute sense of being socially substantial, as opposed to socially transparent.

This kind of small village experience lifts the curse of social transparency. One rediscovers what might be a long-lost intimacy and bonding with others, something like the absolute trust and acknowledgment we might have experienced once in love or with our mother in the long-lost high-dependence state of infancy. Who knows? What I am convinced of, however, and have tried to convince the reader of this book is that this kind of intimacy and bonding with others that is the wealth of small traditional society is what we all strive for, regardless of where we live and where we grew up. It is the force that leads us toward self-consciousness, probably more forcefully if we grow up in an industrial region of the world. If there is such a thing as a universal criterion for "the good life," a comfort we would all aspire to, then it must be the sense of social proximity. It must be the sense of being acknowledged and recognized, of being included and intimate with others, no matter what. It is being *safe*, the ultimate prize and the ultimate refuge.

REFERENCES

Abbott, J. H. (1981). *In the Belly of the Beast: Letters from Prison.* New York: Random House.

Aslin, R. N., Saffran, J. R., & Newport, E. Probability statistics by human infants. *Psychological Science* 9: 321–324.

Austin, A. K. (1982). Sharing a cake. *Mathematical Gazette* 66: 212–213.

Bahrick, L. E., Moss, L., & Fadil, C. (1996). Development of visual self-recognition in infancy. *Ecological Psychology* 8(3): 189–208.

Barr, G., Paredes, W., Erikson, K. L., & Zukin, S. R. (1986). Opioid receptor–mediated analgesia in the developing rat. *Developmental Brain Research* 29: 145–152.

Barsalou, L. (1999). Perceptual symbol systems. *Behavioral and Brain Sciences* 22: 257–660.

Bates, E. (1990). Language about me and you: Pronominal references and the emerging concept of self. In D. Cicchetti & M. Beeghly, eds., *The Self in Transition: Infancy to Childhood*, 165–182. Chicago: University of Chicago Press.

Bigelow, A. E., & Rochat, P. (2006). Two-month-old infants' sensitivity to social contingency in mother–infant and stranger–infant interaction. *Infancy* 9(3): 313–325.

Binet, A. (1887). "Le Fétichisme dans l'amour." *Revue philosophique* 24: 143–167: 252–277.

Blass, E. M., Fillion, T. J., Hoffmeyer, L. B., Metzger, M. A., & Rochat, P. (1989). Sensorimotor and motivational determinants of hand-mouth coordination in 1–3-day-old human infants. *Developmental Psychology* 25(6): 963–975.

Bowlby, J. (1969/1982). *Attachment and Loss.* New York: Basic Books.

Brentano, F. C. (1874) *Psychologie vom empirishen standpunkte (Psychology from a empirical standpoint).* Leipzig: Duncker & Humbolt.

Broesch, T., Rochat, P., Callaghan, T., & Henrich, J. (under review). Cultural variations in chidren's mirror self-recognition. *Journal of Cross-Cultural Psychology.*

Bruner, J. *Acts of Meaning.* Cambridge, MA: Harvard University Press.

Bruner, J. (1972). Nature and uses of immaturity. *American Psychologist* 27(8): 687–708.

Bruner, J. S. (1983). *Child's Talk.* New York: Norton.

236   References

Byrne, R. W., & Whitten, A., eds. (1988). *Machiavellian Intelligence: Social Expertise and the Evolution of Intellect in Monkeys, Apes, and Humans.* New York: Clarendon Press/Oxford University Press. See also the sequel on the same topic by the same editors:

Byrne, R. W., & Whiten, A., eds. (1997). *Machiavellian Intelligence. II: Extensions and Evaluations.* New York: Cambridge University Press.

Callaghan, T., & Rochat, P. (2003). Traces of the artist: Sensitivity to the role of the artist in children's pictorial reasoning. *British Journal of Developmental Psychology* 21: 415–445.

Callaghan, T., & Rochat, P. (2008). Children's theories of the relations between artist and picture. In C. Milbrath & H. M. Trautner, eds., *Children's Understanding and Production of Pictures, Drawing, and Art: Theoretical and Empirical Approaches*, 187–207. Cambridge, MA: Hogrefe & Huber.

Callaghan, T., Rochat, P., Lillard, A., Claux, M. L., Odden, H., Itakura, S., Tapanya, S., & Singh, S. (2005). Synchrony in the onset of mental-state reasoning: Evidence from five cultures. *Psychological Science* 16(5): 378–384.

Camus, A. (1955). *The Myth of Sisyphus, and Other Essays.* New York: Vintage Books.

Carpenter, E. (1975). The tribal terror of self-awarness. In P. Hikins, ed., *Principles of Visual Anthropology*, pp. 56–78. The Hague: Mouton.

Darwin, C. (1872/1965). *The Expressions of the Emotions in Man and Animals.* Chicago: University of Chicago Press.

Decety, J., & Jackson, P. L. (2006). A social-neuroscience perspective on empathy. *Current Directions in Psychological Science* 15(2): 54–58.

DeLoache, J. S. (1991). Symbolic functioning in very young children: Understanding of pictures and models. *Child Development* 62(4): 736–752.

Diamond, A. (2002). On normal development of prefrontal cortex from birth to young adulthood: Cognitive function, anatomy, and biochemistry, In Stuss, D. T., & Knight, R. T., eds., *Principles of Frontal Lobe Function*, 466–503. New York: Oxford University Press.

Eisenberg, N., ed. *Social, Emotional, and Personality Development*, pp. 710–778. New York: Wiley.

Eisenberg, N., & Fabes, R. (1998). Prosocial development. In W. Damon, ed., *Handbook of Child Psychology*, 5th ed., vol. 3.

Erickson, E. H. (1993). *Childhood and Society.* New York: W. W. Norton.

Field, T. M., et al. (1982). Discrimination and imitation of facial expressions by neonates. *Science* 218(4568): 179–181.

Friedman, B. H. (1972/1995). *Jackson Pollock – Energy Made Visible.* New York: Da Capo Press.

Frith, C. D., & Frith, U. (1999). Interacting minds – a biological basis. *Science* 286: 1692–1695.

Furmark, T. (2002). Social phobia: Overview of community surveys. *Acta Psychiatrica Scandinavica* 105(2): 84–93.

Gallup, G. G. (1982). Self-awareness and the emergence of mind in primates. *American Journal of Primatology* 2: 237–248.

Gergely, G., Bekkering, H., & Király, I. (2002). Rational imitation in preverbal infants. *Nature* 415: 755.

Gibson, J. J. (1979). *The Ecological Approach to Visual Perception*. Boston: Houghton Mifflin.

Godbout, J. (1998). *The World of the Gift*. Montreal: McGill-Queen's University Press.

Goffman, E. (1959). *The Presentation of Self in Everyday Life*. New York: Doubleday.

Gould, S. J. (1977). *Ontogeny and Phylogeny*. Cambridge, MA: Harvard University Press.

Haith, M. M., Wass, T. S., & Adler, S. A. (1997). Infant visual expectations: Advances and issues. *Monograph of the Society for Research in Child Development* 62(2): 150–160.

Harlow, H. F. (1958). The nature of love. *American Psychologist* 13: 673–685.

Harris, P. (1991). The work of the imagination. In A. Whiten, ed., *Natural Theories of Mind*, 283–304. Oxford: Blackwell.

Honneth, A. (1995). *The Struggle for Recognition: The Moral Grammar of Social Conflicts*. Cambridge, MA: MIT Press.

Honneth, A. (2001). Invisibility: On the epistemology of "recognition." Supplement to the *Proceedings of the Aristotelian Society* 75(1): 111–122.

Hume, D. (1928). *A Treatise of Human Nature*. Oxford: Clarendon Press.

Jacob, P. (2004). *L'intentionalité, problèmes de philosophie de l'esprit*. Paris: Odile Jacob.

Kagan, J. (1984). *The Nature of the Child*. New York: Basic Books.

Kahneman, D., & Tversky, A., eds. (2000). *Choices, Values, and Frames*. Cambridge: Cambridge University Press.

Kant, I. (1798/2004). *Anthropology from a Pragmatic Point of View*. New York: Cambridge University Press.

Karmiloff-Smith, A. (1992). *Beyond Modularity: A Developmental Perspective on Cognitive Science*. Cambridge, MA: MIT Press.

Lacan, J. (1953). Some reflections on the Ego. *International Journal of Psychoanalysis* 34: 11–17.

Lacan, J. (1966). *Ecrits*. Paris: Seuil.

Lévi-Strauss, C. (1987). *Introduction to the Work of Marcel Mauss*. London: Routledge & Kegan Paul.

Lévinas, E. (2003). *On escape* (De l'évasion). Stanford, CA: Stanford University Press.

Lewis, M. (1992). *Shame: The Exposed Self*. New York: Free Press.

Lewis, M., & Brooks-Gunn, J. (1979). *Social Cognition and the Acquisition of Self*. New York: Plenum Press.

Lipovetsky, G. (1983). *The Era of Emptiness*. Paris: Gallimard.

Lowry, S. T. (1987). *The Archeology of Economic Ideas: The Classical Greek Tradition*. Durham, NC: Duke University Press.

Malinowski, B. (1932). *Argonauts of the Western Pacific: An Account of Native Enterprise and Adventure in the Archipelagoes of Melanesian New Guinea*. London: Routledge & Sons.

Mauss, M. (1952/1967). *The Gift: Forms and Functions of Exchange in Archaic Societies*. New York: Norton.

Mead, G. H. (1934). *Mind, Self, and Society*. Chicago: University of Chicago Press.

Meltzoff, A. (1995). Understanding the intentions of others: Re-enactment of intended acts by eighteen-month-old children. *Development Psychology* 31(5): 838–850.

Meltzoff, A. N., & Moore, M. K. (1977). Imitation of facial and manual gestures. *Science* 198(4312): 75–78.

Meltzoff, A. N., & Moore, M. K. (1992). Early imitation within a functional framework: The importance of person identity, movement, and development. *Infant Behavior and Development* 15: 479–505.

Merleau-Ponty, M. (1945). *Phénoménologie de la perception*. Paris: Editions Gallimard.

Metzinger, T. (2003). *Being No One*. Cambridge, MA: MIT Press.

Moessinger, P. (2000a). *The Paradox of Social Order: Linking Psychology and Sociology*. New York: Aldine de Gruyter.

Moessinger, P. (2000b). *Le jeu de l'identité*. Paris: Presses Universitaires de France.

Montagu, A. (1961). Neonatal and infant immaturity in man. *Journal of the American Medical Association* 178(23): 56–57.

Montagu, P. R., et al. (2002). Hyperscanning: Simultaneous fMRI during linked social interactions. *Neuroimage* 16: 1159–1164.

Montgomery, M. R. (1989). *Saying Goodbye: A Memoir for Two Fathers*. New York: Random House.

Odden, H., & Rochat, P. (2004). Observational learning and education. *Educational and Child Development* 21(2): 39–50.

Olson, D., & Campbell, R. (1993). Constructing representations. In C. Pratt & A. F. Garton, eds., *Systems of Representation in Children: Development and Use*, 11–26. New York: Wiley & Sons.

Parker, S. T., Mitchell, R. W., & Boccia, M. L. (1994). *Self-Awareness in Animals and Humans*. Cambridge: Cambridge University Press.

Parnas, J., Møller, P., Kircher, T., Thalbitzer, J., Janson, L., Handest, P., & Zahavi, D. (2005). EASE: Examination of Anomalous Self-Experience. *Psychopathology* 38(5): 1–23.

Perner, J. (1991). *Understanding the Representational Mind*. Cambridge, MA: MIT Press.

Perry, J. (1975). *Personal Identity*. Berkeley: University of California Press.

Piaget, J. (1936/1952). *The Origins of Intelligence in Children*. New York: International Universities Press.

Piaget, J. (1962). *Play, Dreams and Imitation in Childhood*. New York: Norton.

Piaget, J. (1965/1995). *Sociological Studies*. London: Routledge.

Picq, P. (2003). *Au commencement était l'homme: De Toumaï à Cro-Magnon*. Paris: Odile Jacob.

Pinker, S. (1994). *The Language Instinct*. New York: HarperCollins.

Pinker, S. (2002). *The Blank State: The Modern Denial of Human Nature*. London: Allen Lane.

Plotnik, J., & de Waal, F. B. M. (2006). Self-recognition in an Asian elephant. *Proceedings of the National Academy of Science of the United States of America* 103(45): 17053–17057.

Polanyi, K. (1957). *The Great Transformation*. Boston: Beacon Press.

Povinelli, D. J. (2001). The self: Elevated in consciousness and extended in time. In C. Moore & K. Lemmon, eds., *The Self in Time: Development Perspectives*, 75–95. Mahwah, NJ: Lawrence Erlbaum Associates.

Preston, S. D., & deWaal, F. B. M. (2002). Empathy: Its ultimate and proximate bases. *Behavioral and Brain Science* 25: 1–72.

Priel, B., & de Schonen, S. (1986). Self-recognition: A study of a population without mirrors. *Journal of Experimental Child Psychology* 41(2): 237–250.

Proust, J. (2006). Rationalitly and metacognition in non-human animals. In Hurley, S., & Nudds, M. (eds.), *Rational Animals?* 247–274. New York: Oxford University Press.

Proust, J. (2007). Metacognition and metarepresentation: Is a self-directed theory of mind a precondition for metacognition? *Synthese* 159: 271–295.

Pylyshyn, Z. W. (1984). *Computation and Cognition*. Cambridge, MA: MIT Press.

Reiss, D., & Marino, L. (1998). Mirror self-recognition in the bottlenose dolphin: A case of cognitive convergence. *Proceedings of the National Academy of Sciences of the United States of America* 98(10): 5937–5942.

Rizzolatti, G., & Craighero, L. (2004). The mirror-neuron system. *Annual Review of Neuroscience* 27: 169–192.

Rochat, P. (1987). Mouthing and grasping in neonates: Evidence for the early detection of what hard or soft substances afford for action. *Infant Behavior and Development* 10: 435–449.

Rochat, P. (1989). Object manipulation and exploration in 2- to 5-month old infants. *Developmental Psychology* 25: 871–884.

Rochat, P. (1995). *The Self in Infancy: Theory and Research*. Amsterdam: North-Holland/Elsevier.

Rochat, P. (2001a). *The Infant's World*. Cambridge, MA: Harvard University Press.

Rochat, P. (2001b). The dialogical nature of cognition. *Monograph of the Society for Research in Child Development*, Vol. 66, 2(265): 133–144.

Rochat, P. (2003). Five levels of self-awareness as they unfold early in life. *Consciousness and Cognition* 12(4): 717–731.

Rochat, P. (2005). Humans evolved to become *Homo Negotiatus* ... the rest followed. *Behavioral and Brain Sciences* 28(5): 714–715.

Rochat, P. (2006). What does it mean to be human? *Journal of Anthropological Psychology* 17: 100–107.

Rochat, P. (2007). International action arises from early reciprocal exchanges. *Acta Psychologica* 124(1): 8–25.

Rochat, P., Blass, E. M., & Hoffmeyer, L. B. (1988). Oropharyngeal control of hand-mouth coordination in newborn infants. *Developmental Psychology* 24(4): 459–463.

Rochat, P., & Broesch, T. (under review). Self-consciousness and social conformity in 2-year-olds.

Rochat, P., & Callaghan, T. (2005). What drives symbolic development? The case of pictorial comprehension and production. In L. Namy (ed.), *Symbol Use and Symbolic Representation: Developmental and Comparative Perspectives*, 25–46. Mahwah, NJ: Lawrence Erlbaum Associates.

Rochat, P., Dias, M. D. G., Guo, L., MacGillivray, T., Passos-Ferreira, C., Winning, A., & Berg, B. (in press). Fairness in distributive justice by 3- and 5-year-olds across 7 cultures. *Journal of Cross-Cultural Psychology*.

Rochat, P. Goubet, N., & Senders, S. J. (1999). To reach or not to reach? Perception of body effectivities by young infants. *Infant and Child Development* 8(3): 129–148.

Rochat, P., & Hespos, S. J. (1997). Differential rooting response by neonates: Evidence of an early sense of self. *Early Development and Parenting* 6(3–4): 105–112.

Rochat. P., & Senders, S. J. (1991). Active touch in infancy: Action systems in development. In M. J. Weiss & P. R. Zelazo, eds., *Infant Attention: Biological Constraints and the Influence of Experience*, 412–442. Norwood, NJ: Ablex.

Rochat, P., & Striano, T. (1999a). Emerging self-exploration by two-month-old infants. *Developmental Science* 2: 206–218.

Rochat, P., & Striano, T. (1999b). Social cognitive development in the first year. In P. Rochat, ed., *Early Social Cognition*, 3–34. Mahwah, NJ: Lawrence Erlbaum Associates.

Rochat, P., & Striano T. (2002). Who is in the mirror: Self-other discrimination in specular images by 4- and 9-month-old infants. *Child Development* 73: 35–46.

Sagi, A., & Hoffman, M. L. (1976). Empathic distress in the newborn. *Developmental Psychology* 12: 175–176.

Sartre, J. P. (1947). *Baudelaire*. Paris: Gallimard.

Savage-Rumbaugh, E. S. (1994). *Kanzi: The Ape at the Brink of the Human Mind*. New York: Wiley.

Simha, A. (2004). *La Conscience – du corps au sujet* (Consciousness – from the body to the subject). Paris: Armand Colin.

Simmer, M. L. (1971). Newborn's response to the cry of another infant. *Developmental Psychology* 5: 136–150.

Smith, D., Shields, W. E., & Washburn, D. A. (2003). The comparative psychology of uncertainty monitoring and metacognition. *Behavioral and Brain Sciences* 26: 317–373.

Sokolowski, R. (2000). *Introduction to Phenomenology*. Cambridge: Cambridge University Press.

Sptiz, R. A. (1965). *The First Year of Life: A Psychoanalytic Study of Normal and Deviant Development of Object Relations*. New York: Basic Books.

Steinhaus, H. (1948). The problem of fair division. *Econometrica* 16: 101–104.

Striano, T., & Rochat, P. (1999). Developmental link between dyadic and triadic social competence in infancy. *British Journal of Developmental Psychology* 17(4): 551–562.

Striano, T., & Rochat, P. (2000). Emergence of selective social referencing. *Infancy* 1(2): 253–264.

Taylor, C. (1989a). *The Malaise of Modernity*. Canadian Broadcasting Corporation, 1991; Paris: Les Editions du Cerf, 2005.

Taylor, C. (1989b). *Sources of the Self: The Making of Modern Identity*. Cambridge, MA: Harvard University Press.

Thompson, E. (2007). *Mind in Life: Biology, Phenomenology and the Sciences of Mind*. Cambridge, MA: Harvard University Press.

Tomasello, M. (1995). Joint attention as social cognition. In C. J. Moore & P. Dunham, eds., *Joint Attention: Its Origins and Role in Development*, 103–130. Hillsdale, NJ: Lawrence Erlbaum Associates.

Tomasello, M. (1998). One child early talk about possession. In J. Newman. ed., *The Linguistics of Giving*, pp. 349–373. Amsterdam: John Benjamins.

Tomasello, M. (1999). *Cultural Origins of Human Cognition.* Cambridge, MA: Harvard University Press.

Tomasello, M., Striano, T., & Rochat, P. (1999). Do young children use objects as symbols? *British Journal of Developmental Psychology* 17(4): 563–584.

Trevarthen, C. (1980). The foundations of intersubjectivity: Developments of interpersonal and cooperative understanding in infants. In D. R. Olson, ed., *The Social Foundations of Language and Thought: Essays in Honor of Jerome S. Bruner*, pp. 316–342. New York: W. W. Norton.

Trevarthen, C., and Hubley, P. (1978). Secondary intersubjectivity: Confidence, confiding and acts of meaning in the first year. In A. Lock, ed., *Action, Gesture and Symbol*, 183–239. New York: Academic Press.

Triandis, H. C. (1989). The self and social behavior in differing cultural contexts. *Psychological Review* 96(3): 506–520.

Vygostky, L. (1978). *Mind in Society: The Development of Higher Psychological Processes.* Cambridge, MA: Harvard University Press.

Weir, A. A. S., Chappell, J., & Kacelnik, A. (2002). Shaping of hooks in New Caledonian crow. *Science* 297: 981.

Wertsh, J. (1991). *Voices of the Mind: A Sociocultural Approach to Mediated Action.* Cambridge, MA: Harvard University Press.

Williams, B. A. O. (1993). *Shame and Necessity.* Berkeley: University of California Press.

Wimmer, H., & Perner, J. (1983). Beliefs about beliefs: Representation and constraining function of wrong beliefs in young children's understanding of deception. *Cognition* 13(1): 103–128.

Winnicott, D. W. (1982). *Playing and Reality.* London and New York: Tavistock.

Winnicott, D. W. (1989). *Psycho-Analytic Explorations.* Cambridge, MA: Harvard University Press.

Woolf, P. H. (1987). *The Development of Behavioral States and the Expression of Emotions in Early Infancy.* Chicago: University of Chicago Press.

Woolf, V. (1925). *Mrs. Dalloway.* New York: Harcourt, Brace and Company.

Zahavi, A., & Zahavi, A. (1997). *The Handicap Principle: A Missing Piece of Darwin's Puzzle.* New York: Oxford University Press.

Zahavi, D. (2006). *Subjectivity and Selfhood–Investigating the First-Person Perspective.* Cambridge, MA: MIT Press.

Zahn-waxler, C., Radke-Yarrow, M., Wagner, E., & Chapman, M. (1992). Development of concern for others. *Developmental Psychology* 28: 126–136.

INDEX

acknowledgement of, 233–234
children's plea for, 87–88
co-consciousness, 80
death, 19–20
empathy/sympathy, 170
gifts, 134
"the good life," ix–x
group ideals, 29
neuroses, 123–124
of others, 158
parallel, 207
recognition, 223
of self, 5
suicide, 19–20
existential angst, 19–20
"exterogestation," 62

fairness, 151–154
feelings, 111–112. *See also* affect/affective
    experiences
fetishism, 167–169
first-third-person perspective
    in affective marketplace, 150
    authority of, 36–37, 38, 40–41, 218–219
    awareness, 47–48
    construal of self, 193
    development theory, 42
    dissonance between, 41
    emotion matching, 173, 174
    empathy, 114–115, 174–175
    expectation gap, 108
    Jekyll/Hyde transformation, 196–197
    narcissism, 28–29
    performance fears, 108
    personhood, 208
    phenomenological approach, 6, 7–8
    reconciliation of, 26–27, 35
    self-consciousness, 92, 128–129
    self-contemplation, 26
    self-identity, 203
    self-recognition, 29–31
    selfhood, origins of, 13–14
    in social transactions, 10–11
    value inflation/deflation, 41–42
"folk/people" psychology, 185–186
freedom
    art, 230, 231

of choice, 232
locomotion, 159
in modern times/philosophy, 230–231, 232
postural, 78, 96
in self-awareness, 102
Freud, Sigmund
    attachment needs, 77
    oral activity, newborns, 160–162
    repression, 123–124
    on unconsciousness, 45–46
funeral rituals, 20–21

gambling, 151
gestation, human, 62
Gibson, James J., 10
giving/sharing. *See also* ownership/
    sharing
    debt, social value of, 138–139
    exchanges, accounting for, 130
    fairness/perfect sharing, 151–154
    gift giving/receiving, 133–135
    money, archaic, 135–138
    negotiation, 149–151
    as self-conscious species, 130
    trust/promise, 139–141
Godbout, J., 135, 138
Goffman, E., 37, 41–42, 194–195
Greeks, ancient, 4, 145
guilt
    in development, 118
    human imagination, 17
    self-perspective, 26
    vs. shame, 123–128
    social rejection, 3
    suicide, 19–20

Harlow, Harry, 23, 77, 157
Hegel, Georg Wilhelm Friedrich, 223
Heidegger, Martin, 6, 8
Heriodes, 145
Hitler, Adolf, 196, 230
holistic (ecological) theory, 10
Homo negotiatus, 149–151. *See also*
    negotiation
Honneth, Axel, 223
hubris. *See also* shame

Breinigsville, PA USA
06 January 2010
230113BV00001B/3/P